TO HELL
AND BACK

D0817788

TO HELL
AND BACK

*Personal experiences of trauma
and how we recover
and move on*

JOHN MARZILLIER

ROBINSON

ROBINSON

First published in Great Britain in 2012 by Robinson,
an imprint of Constable & Robinson Ltd.

This edition first published in Great Britain in 2016 by Robinson

3 5 7 9 10 8 6 4 2

Copyright © John Marzillier, 2012

The moral right the author has been asserted

All rights reserved.

No part of this publication may be reproduced, stored in a retrieval system, or transmitted, in
any form, or by any means, without the prior permission in writing of the publisher, nor be
otherwise circulated in any form of binding or cover other than that in which it is published
and without a similar condition including this condition being imposed on the subsequent
purchaser.

Journalists Under Fire: The Psychological Hazards of Covering War by
Anthony Feinstein © 2003 reprinted by permission Johns Hopkins University Press.

Stress and Trauma by Patricia Resick © 2000 reprinted by permission Psychology Press.

Red One: A Bomb Disposal Expert on the Front Line by Capt Kevin Ivison, GM
© 2010 reprinted by permission Weidenfeld & Nicholson.

The Trauma Treatment Handbook: Protocols across the Spectrum by
Robin Shapiro © 2010 reprinted by permission Norton.

Out of the Tunnel by Rachel North © 2007 reprinted by permission The Friday Project.

In an Unspoken Voice: How the Body Releases Trauma and Restores Goodness by
Peter Levine © 2010 reprinted by permission North Atlantic Books.

Aftermath: Violence and the Remaking of a Self by Susan Brison © 2002 reprinted by
permission Princeton University Press.

EMDR (updated edition) by Francine Shapiro & Margot Silk Forrest © 2004
reprinted by permission Basic Books.

The Triune Brain in Evolution by John MacLean © reprinted by permission
The Plenum Press.

One Morning in July by Aaron Debnam © 2007 reprinted by permission John Blake.

Transforming Trauma by Laurel Parnell © 1997 reprinted by permission Norton.

A copy of the British Library Cataloguing in
Publication Data is available from the British Library

ISBN: 978-1-4721-3753-1

Printed and bound in Great Britain by CPI Group (UK), Croydon CRO 4YY

Papers used by Robinson are from well-managed forests
and other responsible sources.

Robinson
An imprint of
Little, Brown Book Group
Carmelite House
50 Victoria Embankment
London EC4Y 0DZ

An Hachette UK Company
www.hachette.co.uk

www.littlebrown.co.uk

For Mary, Kate and Sarah, with love

Contents

Part 4: Aftershocks

Acknowledgements

I am particularly grateful to all the people who volunteered to be interviewed for this book. Talking about a traumatic event is not easy, even if that event occurred years in the past. My heartfelt thanks to Annie, Raj Babbra, Andy Barefield, Richard Blakemore, Steve Burchett, Graeme Cairns, Tim Coulson, Janine di Giovanni, Matthew Engel, Georgie, Susanna Graham-Jones, Mark Henderson, Esther Hyman, Chris Keeble, Tim Knatchbull, Kathryn Little, Janine Luck, Jo Macleod, Tom Nabarro, Jacqui Putnam, George Roskilly, Keith Upton, Susan Verghese, Anna Walker, Elaine Young.

I would also like to thank Rob Scott for allowing me to describe his accident, and my daughter, Sarah, for sharing her interest in spiritual matters and in energy psychology.

I was fortunate to talk to several experts on trauma therapy. Although they bear no responsibility for what I have written, their insights helped shape my thinking. My thanks to Sue Clohessy, Nick Grey, Ann Hackmann, Simon Harper and Nikki Scheiner. Three psychologist friends, Anne Cullington, Janice Hiller and Martina Mueller, were kind enough to find people for me to interview and to allow me to make reference to their therapeutic work in the book. Without their contribution, the book would have been all the poorer.

My thanks to Professor Chris Brewin and Professor Simon Wessely who sent me articles and reports on their research work.

I am grateful to my friend, Richard Greenhall, for the forensic eye he cast over my grammatical constructions and use of language, to Sue Brewer who did a sterling job in transcribing the interviews, and to Mary, Kate and Sarah who commented on each chapter as it appeared.

Part 1
When lightning strikes

Chapter 1: When lightning strikes

Friday, 23 February 2007, the end of a long and busy week for Richard Blakemore. He was in London, looking forward to a break he had planned in Scotland, staying with old friends, doing some walking and a bit of climbing. He had thought of flying to Glasgow but meetings took up the whole day and all the cheap flights had gone. So the train it was and, although that took longer, it was a chance to unwind, to read a book and recover from the exertions of the day. At Euston Richard got a seat on the Glasgow Express and settled down for the long journey north. The ride was smooth and uneventful up to Preston, the last stop before Glasgow. But, as they sped through Cumbria, things suddenly changed. The train began to vibrate violently. Richard knew instantly there was something wrong. Here is how he described what happened next when I interviewed him two and a half years later, in November 2009.

> '. . . all of a sudden the train started vibrating violently, up and down, side-to-side, and I immediately realized that something was very seriously wrong here. We'd been derailed and . . .'
>
> 'You knew that right away?'
>
> 'Yes. There was no feeling of impact, so I knew we hadn't hit anything. But I knew that the train was no longer running on the rails . . .'

Richard felt the train pitch onto its side. The lights went out. He was being thrown around the carriage, and things, objects, people, were hitting him.

I was bouncing off the seats inside the carriage. I think the carriage rolled over at least once. It also rotated through 180 degrees so that when it came to rest, the front of the train was pointing back in the direction it had come from. I think there were two things that immediately struck me. Firstly, how quiet it was after the violence of the impact. I couldn't hear any sound from the carriage to begin with. But I was aware that there was a huge weight on top of me.

Richard was trapped under two other people. All he could move was his left arm.

The thought of Hillsborough went through my mind then, and it just seemed it would be stupid to survive a crash and then be crushed to death because you couldn't free yourself ... I was just determined to get free and, still reaching around in the darkness trying to find something to hold onto, I finally found what a rock climber of my era would call the 'thank God hold' that appears when you really need it, and strength comes to you in moments like that. I managed to pull myself free ... I stood up and initially I just felt absolutely fine. Nothing seemed to be broken. I was clearly alive. I thought, 'Well, this is amazing. I've survived!' I thought, 'Phew, I got away with that one.'

The event Richard was involved in was the train crash that took place in Grayrigg, Cumbria on 23 February 2007. A Virgin Pendolino tilting train travelling at 95 mph came off the rails and rolled down a 50-foot embankment. One person died and twenty were injured. A subsequent inquiry revealed that the crash was caused by a faulty set of points that had not been detected by the maintenance workers. Richard was not, as he first thought, uninjured. He had broken four ribs and, when he began to move, he suffered a horrendous searing pain that turned out to be a punctured lung. But it was the later psychological damage that affected him most. Richard regularly commuted to his work in Swindon and London by train. After he had recovered from his physical injuries, he found it increasingly difficult to travel anywhere by train. A heightened awareness that the train he was on might be derailed and crash was always with him. Memories of the accident would come into his mind. He lost his normal equable composure and became tense, irritable and depressed. Although he had survived a horrific train crash, Richard, like many others who have been through major trauma, experienced significant psychological problems that affected him deeply.

20 August 2005. A young WPC, Janine Luck, has arrived for work at Milton Keynes police station. Upstairs in a second floor office she and three PCs are getting ready for the briefing that starts their shift. Unlike the other officers she is not yet kitted up when suddenly gun shots are heard, followed by urgent shouting coming from somewhere outside the station. This is how she took up the story when I interviewed her in February 2010, four-and-a-half years after the incident.

> . . . all I could hear was gun shots and shouting and I can remember the windows were open but the blinds were down and my colleagues flung the blinds over their heads and were peering down towards where this poor man was shouting. And I was stood there in the middle of the room asking the question, 'What can you see? What's going on?' They just completely ignored me.

The three police officers took off in different directions without Janine being any the wiser. She heard someone shouting 'Help me, help me'. She grabbed her radio and took off down the stairs.

> 'I was just desperate to get to this guy and give him first aid. I got to this big black gate that separates the police station from the rest of the world. I couldn't see anything, but

I could still hear him shouting. So I opened the gate and I saw this poor man standing there. He was covered in blood. I will never forget the image of him putting his hands out to me, in the kind of way that a child would to be picked up or cradled, with his palms facing upwards, and he was just repeating over and over again, "I've been shot, I've been shot". Blood was running down his face so I could tell he'd been shot in the head. He was also staggering on his feet in the way someone would if they were drunk, and he looked confused. I tried to tell him to get down on the ground and he wouldn't and so I literally had to get hold of his wrist and just kind of put all my body weight to get him to his knees.'

'You pulled him down?'

'I pulled him down but, as I was doing that, he collapsed on top of me and he was quite heavy, a big, big chap. I had one arm trapped underneath him just because of the way he fell. It was bizarrely intimate, you know. This guy, all his body fluids were pouring out of his head and pouring onto me, and even though he was confused, I could tell he was petrified. He even said to me, "Am I going to die? Am I going to die?" and I was saying to him, "No, you're not going to die, everything is going to be fine." I didn't know if it was going to be fine or not but that seemed to be the best choice to make. I did manage to get on my radio and call for an ambulance, but it took a long time coming.'

Janine was unable to move anything but her right arm. The ARV (Armed Response Vehicle) officers arrived, but instead of freeing her immediately, they carefully searched the man for possible weapons, something that upset and angered her, for the man was going in and out of consciousness and might have died. In fact, although very seriously injured, the man survived. Then the paramedics attended to him, and all the while Janine was trapped beneath him, holding him up. She was finally freed after about twenty-five minutes. I asked her how she felt at that moment.

> I think I was in shock. I was free and, initially, I felt relief because I thought, 'Thank God for that'. It wasn't until I asked my colleague to use the radio to keep the control room updated and he said to me something like, 'Wow, you handled that really well', that I just broke down and cried.

This highly charged incident, unusual even for police officers, as shootings in this country are rare, had a marked effect on Janine's wellbeing. I was the Force psychologist at the time, and a few days later she was referred to me for psychological help. In the aftermath of the incident, Janine suffered from an acute stress reaction with high levels of anxiety and distress. She was unable to sleep and memories of the incident were constantly replayed in her mind. She was exhausted and had been signed off work. She was also angry at being let down by her colleagues. The extreme emotions that Janine felt were the result of having been through a major trauma. Heightened emotion is a common and expected reaction to such a dramatic and life-threatening situation. Janine went on to make a full recovery but only after she and I had met for many months.

I am a clinical psychologist by profession. This book is about the psychological consequences of major trauma. It is about what happens to people, what they feel and think, both at the time of trauma and later on; how they are affected by the experience, what impact it has on their sense of themselves and on their family and friends, and how they cope – or sometimes fail to cope – with a sudden, unexpected, life-transforming, and often terrifying event. Both Richard and Janine experienced trauma first hand, one a train crash and the other the aftermath of a shooting. In the course of this book I will present more of their stories and the stories of others who have been through major traumas.

When I worked as a clinical psychologist I assessed and treated people who had been through various traumas. One part of my work was to be an expert assessor for the courts in compensation claims made by those who had been through road accidents, train crashes, accidents at work, assaults and similar traumatic events. My job was to assess people's psychological state, paying particular attention to whether their traumatic experience had left an unwanted legacy, a change that could be directly attributed to the trauma. If it had, they could be entitled to compensation. This was rarely a straightforward task, as it meant unravelling the effect of earlier experiences, ones that predated the so-called index trauma, from that of the trauma itself. This often involved arguments with other experts about whether a person's current anxiety, depression, alcohol problems, stress or whatever it was, reflected a *pre-existing* illness or personality problem, rather than being caused by the trauma. After some years of working in this way I began to think more deeply about trauma and its effects, in particular how varied people's experiences were, and the fact that the diagnoses the courts insisted on failed to do justice to the complex and interesting stories that the claimants told me. People's voices, their personal accounts of their experiences, their feelings and thoughts about what was happening to them, got lost in the medico-legal framework of symptoms, diagnosis and compensation. In this book I want to give people a voice, to allow trauma sufferers to tell their stories largely in their own words.

Although I work now as a writer I am still a psychologist. The psychological puzzle of trauma continues to interest me. What happens when, suddenly and unexpectedly, we are thrust into the midst of a major trauma? How do we react and why? Does it matter how we respond at the time or what sort of person we are? What happens afterwards? Why do trauma memories continue to haunt people weeks, months, years or even, in a few cases, decades later? I remember listening to a Second World War veteran, a man in his seventies, tell me that it was only after he retired from working as a fishmonger that horrifying memories of the war resurfaced. For forty years he had been free from such memories and now they had reappeared. Why, he asked? I did not know and said something banal about memory being a strange thing. But it is a good question. Why do trauma memories persist? I will try to give a better answer in this book.

One matter about trauma strikes me as particularly poignant, and that is the element of chance. *Wrong place, wrong time*, people say. The phrase does not do justice to the extraordinary effect chance can play in people's lives. The unforeseen disruption to one's normal life is what makes trauma difficult for many people to come to terms with. We do not expect anything untoward to happen; in fact, we expect normal life to continue as it always has. On a day in July 1998, Jo was driving back home from work when a white van came hurtling round the bend on the wrong side of the road and crashed into her head-on, leaving her severely injured and facing many years of arduous medical treatment. On 7 July 2005, George took the tube to work, his mind on what he had to do that day. He was aware of how crowded the train was, how he was pressed up against other people. But he had no inkling of any danger, that a bomb might go off, and that he would see horrific sights of death and destruction. On a hot summer's day in 2006, Steve was driving his car home from work from Oxford to Banbury when he heard a loud noise overhead. Through his sun roof he saw a Harrier Jump Jet flying extremely low directly over his car. His car's windscreen smashed, the car spun out of control, turned 360 degrees, and ended up in a ditch as the plane crashed onto the road ahead. These are unforeseen events: dramatic, often life-threatening and devastating in their effect. There is no warning. People like Jo, George and Steve were unprepared, in a state of innocence, one might say, until one moment when everything changed.

Life can change in an instant. Even as a result of something as ordinary as a casual game of cricket played in a garden on a balmy day in the summer of 1976. In my mind I can still see the trajectory of the ball as it flew off the bat towards the pram in which my daughter, Kate, was innocently sleeping. The horror as I imagined the impact of that hard missile on my daughter's developing, still delicate, brain, and the relief as the ball shot past and landed with a soft thud in the lawn. Chance governed where that ball landed on that day. Had the outcome been slightly different, a matter of angles and velocity, my life and my family's would have changed totally.

The meaning of trauma

The word *trauma* has become increasingly familiar in recent times. A couple of years ago I heard a radio report of a crash. A coach carrying schoolchildren had veered off the motorway and down an embankment, leaving some injured and others badly shaken, but fortunately none dead. At the end of the report it was announced that counsellors had been called in to help the children cope with the trauma. Leaving aside the value of bringing counsellors in so soon after a major traumatic event (and there are serious doubts about doing this), it showed that trauma had become a recognizable phenomenon and that those unlucky enough to be caught up in such events might be expected to suffer emotionally as a consequence and need professional help. This is a relatively new notion. Those of my parents' generation, who lived through two World Wars, would have been astounded at the idea of trauma counselling. But theirs was an era when people were not geared up to talk about emotional problems to any degree. *Stiff upper lip* was the phrase, as though it would not do to confess to feelings of anxiety and fear. You simply got on with life. Times have changed. Expression of emotion is more common, and I would say, generally a good thing, with the exception of the artificial stimulation of emotion in reality TV shows! As a psychotherapist I encountered many people who were unable to express how they really felt when they were children, and suffered for it. One of the questions I will be covering in this book is whether expressing one's feelings after a major trauma is a good thing. Like many such questions there is no definitive answer, but there are some guidelines and, through the stories of the people themselves, we can learn what others have experienced and what they discovered.

The Cambridge Dictionary of Psychology defines the word *trauma* as 'any event which inflicts physical damage to the body or severe shock to the mind or both'. *Trauma* can refer to life-threatening or serious physical injuries such as those seen every day in A&E departments. It can also be used to describe those experiences or events that lead to serious psychological damage, even where there is no obvious physical injury. In this book I am concerned with psychological traumas rather than physical ones. However, the distinction between the physical and the psychological is not as clear-cut as it first appears. Being assaulted or being in a car or train crash is very much a physical as well as a psychological experience. The sense of shock that is produced by any traumatic event, the sudden rush of adrenaline through the body, is experienced physically. In Chapter 3 I consider, in some detail, what happens to the body and, in particular, the brain when people experience acute stress during trauma. Emotions such as fear, anxiety, guilt, shame and anger all have physical correlates; they are experienced bodily as well as mentally. The distinction between the psychological and the physical can sometimes be unhelpful – the phrase, 'Oh, it's only psychological', when refer-ring to someone's complaint of ill health, for instance. The impli-cation is that the complaint is not real. Psychological experiences are undoubtedly real, and it is quite wrong to dismiss them in this way. In the course of writing this book I met trauma sufferers who, at first, found it hard to credit that their psychological experiences merited professional help, because they were 'all in the mind'. Their problems were not immediately visible, like a broken leg or a fractured skull. Seeking help seemed wrong. Some felt embar-rassed to do so, thinking that they would be wasting a doctor's time; others worried that they might end up being diagnosed as mad and admitted to a psychiatric hospital. I will discuss this important issue in more depth later. Suffice it to say that almost all people who have been through major trauma will commonly show some psychological disturbance during and immediately afterwards. In a few individuals the problems persist, and it is here that professional help can be beneficial. But it is worth emphasizing that, even in the more severe cases, the experience is not the same as serious mental illness, and it is extremely rare for anyone to be admitted to a psychiatric hospital, the few exceptions usually being those with pre-existing mental-health problems. Put simply, if you are caught up in a major trauma, it will affect you psychologically; the effect is real, mostly it is short-lived and, in the cases where it is not, help can be provided.

Type I and Type II traumas

Psychologists have made a distinction between single-incident traumas (Type I), that are experienced by a person going about their ordinary business, and complex traumas (Type II), ones that occur repeatedly over a period of time. Examples of the latter include a brutalizing childhood, being trapped in an abusive relationship, imprisonment and torture, and exposure to cataclysmic and violent events, as in war. Complex traumas, unsurprisingly, have more severe effects and these effects are more difficult to treat. It is not just that the traumas are multiple and take place over a long period, though that is important. People who have been traumatized over a long time, especially if this has included their childhood, will have been significantly changed by that experience. They will have learned not to trust other people and come to experience the world as fundamentally an unsafe place. Many will have problems with self-worth, finding it hard to value themselves because others have treated them as having little value. The people you will meet in this book fall into the category of those who have been through a single-incident trauma (Type I). This is because I wanted the focus to be on the sudden disruption of normal life by a single, unforeseen event like a rail or road accident. In complex traumas there are multiple factors that contribute to an individual's state of mind and this would make for a more complicated picture. Like all categorical distinctions, there are some fuzzy areas. One of these is that, in some people, a single-incident trauma can trigger the memory of a forgotten earlier trauma. Consider this example.

Outside a supermarket, a middle-aged man saw a group of youths badgering a woman. He remonstrated with the youths and was badly beaten up for his pains. Later, after making a full physical recovery, he was plagued by feelings of intense anxiety, including very disturbing nightmares. This is not unexpected; it is common for a traumatic incident to be replayed in the mind in the form of memories and nightmares weeks, months or occasionally years later. But the psychiatrist whom the man consulted noted that the nightmares were not specifically about the assault. He took a history and discovered that, when he was a child, the man had been brutally assaulted by his father, who had also regularly assaulted his mother. The terror and the nightmares were related to those earlier experiences as much as – perhaps even more than – the trauma of the later assault. Only when therapy was focused on the man's childhood experiences did he begin to show significant improvement.

The commonest Type I traumas

Table 1.1 lists the commonest single-incident traumas in order. The first two are more common in women, numbers three to six more common in men, the rest equally common between the sexes. This list is largely compiled from North American surveys; it will reflect, to a degree, something of that particular culture. The impression most of us have is that these events are rare; we would be unlucky to experience them. This is certainly true of some traumas. In the course of this book I interviewed several survivors of the London bombings of 2005. While they were lucky to survive – especially those in the same tube train carriage as one of the bombers – they were also simply unfortunate to be there at all. Given that more than two million tube journeys are taken in London every day, the chances of any individual being caught up in a rare event such as this are very low. But if we take *all* the categories of trauma, the chances of us experiencing one of these in our lifetime is actually high. In a Canadian survey, three-quarters of women and over 80 per cent of men reported having experienced at least one such trauma. To experience two or more traumas in a lifetime is also fairly common. Surveys suggest that experiencing trauma more than once happens to 46 per cent of women and 55 per cent of men; that is, around half of us. In other words, contrary to what most people may think, experiencing a single-incident trauma is not rare, but is quite likely to happen to most of us at some point in our lives.

Table 1.1. LIST OF TYPE I TRAUMAS	ORDER
Rape	1
Sexual molestation before age 18	2
Combat	3
Witnessing severe injury or death	4
Being threatened with a weapon	5
Serious motor-vehicle accident	6
Robbery or hold-up	7
Physical attack	8
Violent death of friend or family member	9
Fire	10
Natural disaster	11
Other	12

What this book is about

This book is a journey through trauma and how it affects those caught up in it. In my research for the book I interviewed over thirty people, from those who had been in extreme events like the London bombings of 2005, to those whose trauma was more common yet still devastating, like a major road accident. I recorded the interviews on a digital voice recorder and had the recordings transcribed. I did not structure the interviews, other than asking the person to tell me about the trauma, what they felt and did at the time, and what happened to them afterwards. It was soon clear to me that, once someone got going, I needed to do very little. The stories told themselves. The extracts that can be found throughout the book come directly from the interviews as they were transcribed.

When I asked people to describe the traumatic event they had gone through, to tell me what it was like, I quickly realized that the question 'What was it like?' is not one that trauma sufferers find easy to answer. This is partly because recalling traumatic events risks rekindling the associated emotions, casting the person back into the horrors, and causing them to relive them. But there is another aspect. The experience recalled is different from that experienced at the time. Giving something a name, a description in words, changes the experience, and so there can never be a definitive answer to the question 'What was it like?' You had to be there, as people say about all such unique and dramatic events. Yet words are our lifeblood, our means of making sense of the world, a way of bridging the gap between one human being and another. Putting traumatic experiences into words is what this book is about. As I became more immersed in my research I became aware that this is not a simple matter. For those who had been through the horrors of a major trauma, describing the experience in words was a mixed blessing. Words could heal, helping to make sense of what happened at the time and, later, soothing the rawness of the experience, transforming it into something else. But words could also inflame the wound. For a 7/7 survivor, for instance, an account of another terrorist attack, perhaps overheard on the radio or read in the newspaper, could trigger memories of the trauma, casting the person back into the horrors. Many avoided such reports, not wanting to be reminded of what had happened to them. Recovery from trauma is, in the end, about conquering it through words. How that is best done is a major theme of this book.

When I first began planning the book, I remember thinking I had not been through a major trauma, at least not one that came upon me dramatically and unexpectedly, one that turned my life upside down. I had worked with traumatized people in my professional work, but I knew that direct experience of trauma was of a different order. I certainly did not wish a trauma on myself, but a couple of times I vaguely wondered what it would be like. I did not for a moment think I would find out.

It is the Thursday before Easter 2009, Maundy Thursday. The phone rings. We are in bed, my wife and I, reading. It is late at night. I answer and hear my daughter Sarah's worried voice. *It's Rob,* she says. *He has had an accident. He's hit his head. There's some blood. We've called an ambulance. It's just arrived. Have to go.* We find out later that Rob, her partner, had taken his skateboard onto the road one evening and must have fallen off it and hit his head on the road. Despite all my professional knowledge, I react as though this is a minor accident, a bit of concussion, perhaps, and he'll be all right. It is exactly the sort of wishful thinking people report during trauma, failing to see the seriousness of the event because, at some level, the mind does not want to. My wife and I tell Sarah to keep us informed and we will come down in the morning, if need be. My main concern is a selfish one, that my weekend plans will be disrupted. Later, I feel embarrassed about having reacted so ignobly. At the specialist hospital the next day we have assimilated that this is more serious than concussion, but even then I seek to reassure Sarah that everything will almost certainly be fine. Again it is what I want to believe. We are in the waiting room along with Rob's parents, waiting for what seems an eternity for a doctor to tell us the news. Here is what happened as I experienced it at the time.

The doctor comes into the waiting room, followed closely by the nurse we had met earlier. They close the door behind them. I know he's a doctor by an aura of authority about him, even though he looks impossibly young. He's wearing royal-blue scrubs, an incongruously jaunty dash of colour in the drab environment of the hospital. He sits on a hard-backed chair by the door.

'What do you know about Rob's situation?'

What do we know? The question surprises us. We are expecting to be told, not asked. We know that Rob came off a skateboard last night and hit his head on the road. We know that he was briefly unconscious, that there was bleeding from the skull and that he was taken to A&E, from where he was later transferred here, a specialist head-injury unit. We know he has been sedated and tests are being done. That is all we know. The doctor continues. He speaks in a measured, serious tone.

'Rob has a significant head injury. His brain has been bruised on the right-hand side and there are severe contusions. A pressure monitor has been inserted and we are keeping him fully sedated. It's a serious and potentially life-threatening injury.'

The shock pulses through me like a surge of electricity. I look at Sarah, whose face is convulsed with tears. This cannot be true, I think, while knowing that it is. I am close to tears myself. Rob's mother is crying. His father's face is unreadable. My wife, Mary, is hugging Sarah, trying to console her as best she can. Again I think this cannot be true. Not Rob. Not carefree, easy-going, happy-go-lucky Rob.

Rob suffered a serious head injury which, for him and for those of us around him, was, by any definition, a major trauma. I mention it here because I responded like anyone else, like the people I interviewed for the book. I realized, from that personal experience, how difficult it is to take the trauma in at the time, partly because the experience of trauma changes with time, but not just that. A part of my mind did not want to accept that it was happening – a defence mechanism that operated without any volition on my part. I also felt, in a very physical way, the shock when the doctor broke the news. This is the surge of adrenaline that people report. I noted at the time that it felt like an electrical current surging through me. I learned many other things about trauma, too, particularly the huge disruption it causes to normal life. I fervently wish it had not happened. But it did and as a result I understood, in a way that I might not otherwise have done, just how powerful trauma can be.

Chapter 2: 7 July 2005

8.30 a.m., 7 July 2005. CCTV footage shows four young men with backpacks arriving at London's King's Cross station to take the underground. An apparently innocuous picture, except that, as the world now knows, these four men would go on to kill themselves and fifty-two other people, injuring more than 700, in what came to be known as the 7/7 bombings. The event is one of those iconic moments that give rise to a flashbulb memory. Many know exactly what they were doing when they heard the news; the event has such intensity that the memory is burned into the mind. The 9/11 terrorist attack on America, the death of Diana, Princess of Wales, and, for those with longer memories, the assassination of John Fitzgerald Kennedy are similar iconic events. Mary and I were on the East Coast of North America in a beautiful place called the Acadia National Park, in the state of Maine. We had been walking and were returning to our car. In the queue for the toilets an American woman turned to Mary and said: 'You're British, aren't you? We're so sorry to hear what happened in London.' Gradually, we came to understand that, some hours before, there had been bomb explosions in London. We had only hazy details of what had happened, except that there had been a terrorist attack on the transport system in the morning rush hour. At that time both of our daughters might have been travelling to work in London. In the rational part of my mind I knew the odds were overwhelmingly in our favour that they were fine. But I could not help thinking that, somewhere, a similarly concerned parent, husband, wife, partner or friend was thinking the very same thought, only to find that their worst fears had been realized. Fortunately for us, neither of our daughters had been using public transport in London on that day.

Others were not so fortunate. The facts of the London bomb-ings are well documented. At 8.50 a.m. on 7 July 2005, three sui-cide bombers set off their lethal explosions on three separate tube trains packed with commuters. Just under an hour later another bomber blew himself up on the top floor of a bus in Tavistock Square. These events occurred the day after London had been awarded the 2012 Olympic Games. What had been a mood of jubilation and celebration in the city turned into one of horror and incomprehension. The bombers struck at the capital's transport system, on which people of all nationalities, religions, ethnicities and political affiliations travelled, killing and maiming innocent people who were simply going about their ordinary business. It was an act of indiscriminate terror. Those unfortunate enough to be caught up in it, the survivors and the families and friends of those who had died or been injured, were thrust into the heart of a major trauma. For many it changed their lives.

I had not planned to interview people who had been involved in the events of the 2005 London bombings. It just turned out that way. In early March 2009 I sent a letter to those of my colleagues in the Oxford Cognitive Therapy Centre (OCTC) who worked with trauma cases, asking if they might know of people who would be prepared to be interviewed for this book. One of the first people who volunteered was Elaine. She had been on the underground on 7 July 2005, when a bomb exploded in the tube train alongside her. She had heard and felt the explosion and had seen something of its awful effects. I will be telling Elaine's story throughout this book. At the end of our first interview, which took place on 20 March 2009, Elaine suggested I put a request for more volunteers on the closed website for 7/7 survivors and their families. This led to me interviewing six more people, four who had been directly caught up in the bombings and two who had lost a loved one, a sister in one case and a girlfriend in another. I began to read the stories of survivors and those involved in the rescue. Here was a major trauma on my doorstep, so to speak. It became a significant part of my journey to understand what happens when disaster strikes.

Confusion and uncertainty

At the time of the first explosions on the underground no one knew exactly what was happening. The first explanation was a power surge on the tube. Then there was a report of a man being under a train, a possible suicide, but that turned out to be a person who had been ejected by one of the explosions. Another report said that a train had derailed. In retrospect, the events are much clearer than they were to those involved at the time. A striking feature of events like bombings, earthquakes and tsunamis is of a constantly evolving scenario that people are desperately seeking to understand. Even if they understand in broad terms what has happened, confusion as to what to do or what else might happen adds to people's fear and sense of helplessness. This uncertainty is vividly conveyed by Aaron Debnam, a British Transport Police officer who responded to the call for help to go to Russell Square tube station. 'I cannot explain properly the way I was feeling at the time,' he wrote in his book, *One Morning in July*.

It seemed like the whole world had gone mad and that we were running round in circles chasing our tails. Calls were going out all over the place and confusion was rife. My adrenaline was up, I had driven from one end of London to another and then back again on the blues and twos (the flashing lights and siren on police cars) and now I was heading into the unknown.

Aaron was to play a key role in evacuating survivors of the Piccadilly-line train that was bombed between King's Cross and Russell Square stations. He too was to suffer psychologically as a consequence.

Those caught up directly in the bombings did not necessarily know what had happened. Elaine, who was on the east-bound Circle-line train that was brought to a juddering halt alongside the bombed west-bound train travelling from Edgware Road to

Paddington, thought her train had crashed and that the debris thrown up by the bomb was smoke from a fire. She was terrified that another train would crash into the train she was on, or that she would burn to death underground. It was not until hours later that she discovered that this had been a terrorist attack. A bomb exploding is something beyond most people's experience; it is not surprising that people seek to make sense of what is happening by relating it to something slightly more familiar, like a train crash.

Even in retrospect and with the benefit of hindsight, there remain uncertainties and confusions. As I gathered more inform-ation about that momentous day, the picture became more diffuse, more like an impressionist painting than a faithful reproduction. This is because the event is seen from different points of view and the act of recall is partial, subject to selectivity and distortion, as all recollection is. Yet there are commonalities, and it is on these that I wish to concentrate in this chapter.

Trauma is physical

We exist in time and space. The first knowledge we have of some-thing seriously wrong is physical. A person is on a crowded tube train, sitting on a seat or standing in a crush of people. The train is moving in that screeching, shuddering way of underground trains. The glare of artificial light illuminates the carriage. Minds may be elsewhere, replaying an argument, planning a dinner with friends, worrying about the day's work or in that state of vague reverie that often comes over people when travelling. Then it happens. Jacqui was on a Circle-line train from King's Cross to Paddington on her way to work. She had just got a seat near the door at Baker Street when a bomb went off in a neighbouring carriage. Here is how she described the events to me when I interviewed her in July 2009.

'The doors closed, the train pulled off, we pulled into the tunnel and then there was, in the space of a second, a noise like a firework, like a banger. There was a flash, the air was full of broken glass, tiny shards of glass. I was finding them for weeks in my house. But it wasn't just like glass breaking, they were like bullets coming through the air and the pressure, it felt like somebody pushed me forward in my seat. I was sitting up and suddenly I was going forward.'

'Did you have any idea what was happening?'

'No. It was an explosion, I knew that. As I went down, I could feel the force of what I now know was a bomb blast. It pushed me forward in my seat; it also went under the train and pushed up the panels, engineering panels – there was one in front of me – and it just disappeared. I never saw it again. The train had lost power but it kept rolling; you could feel the engines weren't working. The force of that pressure was over in a flash and all the crud that had been on the walls, the soot, whatever it was, was suddenly in the air, and we were breathing it in. It felt like it was gritty and slimy and grimy and I couldn't breathe, and I couldn't see anything. I got my jacket and I picked it up to put it over my mouth and it was worse because it was all over my jacket and had an acrid taste to it, and a horrible smell. And I thought, 'This is worse. I'm breathing all this stuff in.' I covered my face with my hands. And then there were screams. You know when you watch movies and they have somebody screaming, and sometimes you think that's a very scary scream. It isn't. These screams were – nobody should hear screams like that.'

Tim Coulson was on the east-bound Circle-line train in the same carriage as Elaine. A lecturer at a further education college in Basingstoke, he was in London for a meeting to launch a new qualification in teacher training for adults. This is how he experienced the first moments of the explosion.

The train proceeded into the first and then the second tunnel and within a very short space of time ... there was an enormous explosion and a great deal of both change of colour and change of sound, as far as I was concerned. First of all, everything went incredibly black. Now I am already partially sighted and for me to suddenly be plunged into complete blackness was perhaps more worrying than for somebody who had 20–20 normal sight.

Robbed of sight, Tim told me that the sounds were incredible; firstly, the sheer volume of the explosion itself, 'a sound louder than I ever hope to hear again', and then the sound of glass shattering, which 'was almost like the sound of a torrential rain storm'. Worst of all was the sound of people screaming in agony, which was like nothing he had heard before. The sound of those screams remained with him for a long time afterwards.

For those in the actual carriage with the bomber, the experience was exponentially more powerful. Twenty-six people died in the carriage on the south-bound Piccadilly-line train that was running from King's Cross to Russell Square; many more were injured, some very severely. One of those who survived was Rachel North. She wrote about her experiences in her book, *Out of the Tunnel,* and it is a tribute to her skill as a writer how well she conveys those awful first moments. The impact of the explosion threw her onto the floor and into utter darkness. Here is how it felt to her.

Night diving, without a regulator. Breathing in liquid, drowning. The taste of blood. Sharp grit in my mouth. Choking, lung-filling dust. It was no longer air that I breathed but tiny shards of glass, and thick, heavy dust and smoke. Like changing a vacuum-cleaner bag and pushing your face into the open dust bag and taking deep breaths. It made my tongue swell and crack and dry out like leather. I never covered my mouth. I had nothing to cover it with, and there didn't seem any point. There

was a metallic taste in my mouth, like vaporizing cop-
per particles. It tasted like sucking a coin. That was the
blood. It sprayed us, our clothes, our faces, our hair. My
lips were wet with it. The walls dripped with it. It was
black blood, viscous like oil, because it was mixed with
smoke.

It got hotter and an acrid smell filled her nostrils, a mixture of
chemicals, burning rubber and burning hair. She had been deaf-
ened by the explosion which 'punched my eardrums so violently
that my cheekbones and sinuses and teeth rang with it and ached
with it'. Then she heard awful screams. Caught at the heart of the
explosion, lying trapped under bodies, Rachel tried to make sense
of what had happened, to stay calm and to help others stay calm.

These accounts convey the physicality of trauma, the way the
brain and body are assailed by unforgettable sensory experiences:
sights, sounds, smells, tastes and touch; all of the senses are
involved. The physicality is crucial to a full understanding of the
psychological legacy of trauma. This assault on the senses lays
down memory traces that provoke the experience to return later
in the form of nightmares, flashbacks and unwanted memories
(see Chapter 3).

Anxiety and the fear of death

In extreme traumas – wars, disasters such as earthquakes, bombings, major accidents and murderous assaults – the imminence of
death is a profound factor: 'the jarring awareness of the fact of
death', as Robert Lifton put it in his account of the survivors of
Hiroshima. We are forced to face our essential vulnerability and,
for some, to come face to face with death. This was the experience
of Elaine who, as we have heard, was travelling to work on the
east-bound Circle-line train when the bomb went off in the west-
bound train. This is what went through her mind as she tried to
make sense of what was happening.

'I thought I was dead, nothing was there. I just couldn't hear anything, I couldn't see anything. It was just this time of nothing.'

'So the thought came into your mind that you were dead?'

'Yes, it was just black, so everything was black. It took some time to realize I was all right. I'm still here.'

But her realization that she was not dead was replaced by the fear that she now was going to die.

I knew the train had crashed. It had hit another train . . . Out of the window, although it was dark, I could kind of see another train alongside, you know, when you get two that go side by side. So it was very, very close . . .

The train she could dimly see in the darkness was the one in which a bomb had exploded. In her carriage Elaine could hear various sounds, though they were muffled, as her hearing had been affected by the explosion: glass breaking, debris falling, some banging and crashing, people screaming and others moving around. This reinforced her belief that the two trains had crashed. She thought that the best thing to do was not to move, to minimize the risk of further damage or injury, and wait for the emergency services to arrive, as they would know what to do. She retreated into herself, even returning to a game that she had been playing on her mobile phone. Then the darkness lifted a little.

And I started to see what was going on. But I thought, 'Hang on a minute, there is nobody here and I know that those trains go about every two or three minutes, so we've hit another train and another will come in a minute . . .' And at that point I'm thinking I didn't die but I'm going to because I can't get out . . . something else is going to

hit us and I can't get away . . . I think I wished I'd died
really because I don't want to die now. If something happens and you die that would be that, wouldn't it? But I
found the anticipation of 'there is more to come yet' was
far worse.

Elaine's account of her thinking, even years after the event, conveys the way her mind was restlessly trying to make sense of what
was happening around her, the strange sensations and the unforeseen events. It was a train crash. She was alive. But there will
be another train. So she will die after all. Eventually, Elaine was
rescued along with the other passengers in the carriage, but she
waited for what seemed an eternity to her, all the time in a state of
anxiety, worried about dying either in a fire or from another train
ploughing into them.

Ronnie Janoff-Bulman, one of the most influential writers on
trauma, wrote that 'the essence of trauma is the abrupt disintegration of one's inner world', the shattering of core assumptions
that we all have. The imminence of death dispels the illusion that
death is something that happens to others. Although rationally we
know that we must die at some point, we happily live out our lives
believing we shall go on forever, or if not forever, for the foreseeable future. For those in the London bombings, the foreseeable
future was greatly foreshortened; death was all around in harsh
and horribly vivid technicolor. The prospect of dying in the next
few minutes was very real.

George was on the south-bound Piccadilly-line train travelling
between King's Cross and Russell Square in the same carriage
as Rachel North. He was standing quite close to the bomber,
Germaine Lindsay. This is how he described his reactions when I
interviewed him in London on 27 July 2009.

You try and make sense of what has actually happened.
In my view we had hit a train. After that there was the
screaming. A West Indian woman started praying, reciting

the Lord's Prayer. Other people were moaning. And then it
went quite quiet.

Some people in the carriage switched on their mobile-phone lights
and waved them around. George could now see a little.

> I hadn't moved. I still hadn't moved. I just knew there was
> nobody around me alive ... The people around me and,
> obviously, near him [Germaine Lindsay] were either dead
> or seriously injured.

Fortunately, the darkness prevented George from seeing the extent
of the carnage around him. Lindsay's bomb had killed twenty-six
people. Many more were seriously injured. Just opposite George,
although he could not see her, was Gill Hicks, who lost both her
legs in the blast. She was very close to dying but, amazingly, with
the help of the emergency services, survived to tell her courageous
story. George continued his account.

> I thought to myself, if this situation gets any worse, and I
> thought it was bad enough as it was, we aren't going to get
> out of this. George, this is where it all ends. I remember
> thinking to myself what a stupid way to go. You know the
> silly thing that goes through your mind, the paper will say
> 'Property inspector blown up on tube'. I thought if this
> turns to fire, then you're gone, that's it, finished.

The almighty bang of the explosion. Being plunged into darkness.
Fear of death. The presence of people dead and dying, the screams,
the sights, the smells. Senses assailed as never before. The abrupt
change from an everyday scenario to something nightmarish,
something out of hell. The mind whirring, restless, seeking to
understand. Confusion and uncertainty: what else might happen?
Will I die? Is this it? All this in the first few moments that seem to
go on forever. Then what?

What happened next

For Elaine and Tim, who were in the same carriage, their very different actions had consequences that neither foresaw. Elaine had remained where she was, fearful and anxious about the possibility of burning to death or another train crashing into hers. As time passed she began to think that she might just be able to get out alive. For some time she had resisted looking across into the train close by. But then the noise made her look.

> There was a man and I thought he had fallen through a hole in the floor as he was quite low in the carriage. He'd got his arm up and he was reaching out and he looked at me, and I really wanted to get him out. I was leaning out the window and I thought if I got hold of his hand, I'd be able to pull him out. He looked really scared, but he was also calm. I was trying to lean out, but he was too far away. I couldn't get him out.

What Elaine did not know was that the man was fatally injured and that there was no way she could have helped him. But at the time she felt bad about not being able to do anything for him.

> I ended up putting my coat over my head, and I thought I don't want to look any more. Also the air was horrible. I kept breathing in all this dirt. When I came up from under the coat again, he'd gone. I don't know where he went. He'd vanished.

Elaine then had a profoundly disturbing experience. She looked over into the carriage of the bombed train and saw, or thought she saw, a person she knew. This was a young relative of hers who, some years before, had died in an incident involving a train. When he had died, the family had wanted to see him in the Chapel of Rest but his body was in such a state they were persuaded not to, making it hard for them to believe he had actually died. Now Elaine saw him in the carriage opposite, a visual hallucination that seemed entirely real to her. She was so shocked that she looked away. When she looked back, he was no longer there. At that point she decided she did not want to look at anything any more.

Tim's first reaction after the explosion and the darkness was to ensure he was physically intact.

> What I can only be honest about is my own anxiety for whether I'd lived or died at that particular point . . . I did what I think every human mind makes you do. You check whether you've got arms and legs and if you can feel them, you think, 'Well that's OK.'

Tim's initial reaction was completely understandable. But later he was plagued by guilt, feeling that he had been selfish to focus on himself first of all, when many others had died or were severely injured. I think, as I imagine many others will think, that he is being unnecessarily hard on himself. After all, it is eminently sensible to ensure that one is not injured. But Tim's guilt was not a product of a rational appraisal of what he should or should not have done, but an intense irrational feeling.

Tim then set off down the carriage. Two others followed him. They tried to open the doors at the end but found they could not.

> We managed to find a cupboard in which there was an iron bar with a scraper on the end of it. So P and I smashed at the glass of the door. We couldn't actually get those doors open so I climbed out of the broken window. It might sound foolhardy to do that, with no thought for your own safety in terms of the electricity that runs between the two trains, no thought about cuts from glass, or any other secondary explosions, any of that stuff. I still think to this day that I didn't have a choice. That was the purpose I took on with

complete disregard for my own security of tenure on this planet. That just never occurred to me. My instinct said you can do something to help these people.

Tim's decision to help others and his subsequent actions were to place him, reluctantly, in the media spotlight, leading to his being described in the newspapers as a 'hero' or 'angel'. A Channel 4 film was made about him.

On arrival in that carriage . . . that was probably where the greatest challenge to my own psychological balance came from, of seeing to my right a charred corpse. I'd not seen one before. I now know that was the bomber, and [there were] other people in varying states of both clothing and not clothing, and agony, and some not moving.

This vision of the carriage and the carnage therein was so powerful that it continued to haunt Tim for months afterwards. It was, he said, 'like a negative that you can't get rid of; it keeps coming back'. Two other people had come with him and, as the three of them surveyed the scene, they realized that they had to concentrate their efforts on those who were most in need. Tim saw a man whose leg was badly damaged, whom he later came to know as David.

I tied a tourniquet around David's top thigh. That did result in a loss of a leg in the end, the damage was so severe . . . I placed a paperback book under somebody's head and then I became aware of a chap who was lying across the carriage . . . What I chose to do was to go over and see the man I now know as Stan. He'd got no clothes on his upper torso at all and I couldn't see the lower part of his body as that was beneath the train floor. He was alive.

This was the man who Elaine had seen reaching out to her. Tim took Stan's pulse, which was feeble and very slow. He managed to get hold of a bottle of water and poured it into Stan's mouth. There was no gag reflex, suggesting that he was near to death. And indeed, a few moments later, Stan died. For Tim this was a hugely painful experience.

> I had experienced death before. My father had died when I was only sixteen. But we had preparation for that. We had chosen to be there. A whole range of other facilities come into place to enable you to manage it in a controlled way. This was a stranger. It was not chosen. And for me to have Stan die in my arms, as he then did within a minute or two, it's very painful.

Tim felt angry that he had not been able to keep Stan alive. What he did not know at the time was that Stan's body had been severed in two. There was no way he could have survived.

> When people die, they die in various ways. I was fortunate to be able to be strong enough to hold Stan as his muscles relaxed and lower him to the floor. I did also choose to close his eyes because, I think, again – I thought about that many times since – I did it because I sincerely believe and accepted that he had finished with this world. He was now dead, and for me it felt wrong that he was staring at the world that he'd just left without being able to see it. So, as a mark of respect I did it . . . I also said a prayer for him to wish him well in whatever he believed in and whatever he perceived was the next stage, if in fact there was one.

Tim went on to help other people in the carriage, including a young woman whom he stayed with throughout the rescue.

What these personal accounts show is how profoundly shocking a major trauma can be. From living out the normal concerns of a normal day, Elaine, Tim, Jacqui, George and Rachel were thrust into a nightmarish world of intense, horrifying sensations and strange happenings. Although they all knew that something was seriously wrong and that there had been some sort of explosion, they did not know what had caused it or if this was the beginning of something worse: a conflagration, as George and Elaine thought; or another bomb exploding, or a train crash. The vivid immediacy of the events, however, could not be ignored. Yet it was hard to take it all in. Elaine's account illustrates that very clearly. She struggled to retain her composure, fearful of further danger, unsure what best to do. She withdrew into herself, shutting herself off from those around her, covering her head with her coat. But she also saw Stan in the other train and tried to help him, even though she was unable to do so. In the extremity of her emotional state, her mind played tricks on her. When she looked into the other carriage she saw a young relative who had died some years before, something that could not be real but seemed real to her at that moment. I have no better explanation for this vision than that her intense anxiety and the sudden strangeness of the world about her caused her to conflate the two events: the one she was experiencing, and the earlier one in which her relative had died. It must have been a frightening sight, and it is no surprise that Elaine withdrew into herself further as a result. I will return to Elaine's story in subsequent chapters. The pattern of avoidance that had begun on the train continued for a long time afterwards, and was to cause her serious psychological problems.

In Tim's account we see a different state of mind. Along with two other passengers he made his way into the bombed carriage and helped the people there as best he could. He said he could not have done otherwise and that it was an instinctive response on his part. In the next chapter I describe how, to a large extent, an individual's initial reaction to trauma arises from long-established, innate reactions of the brain and body to threat. In taking action, Tim had a definite purpose, to help others, if he could. Some theorists have argued that being able to do something positive in trauma can be beneficial to us, since it means that the energy built up in the intense bodily reactions we undergo can be discharged. But it is not that simple. Tim's actions brought him face to face with severe injury and death. The care he took during Stan's death is moving and commendable. But this led to traumatic memories that haunted him later. He saw sights up-close that were horrific. Like Elaine, Tim went on to suffer serious psychological problems as a result.

What happened in London on 7 July 2005 was unprecedented. It affected many people, not just those unlucky enough to be directly in the path of, or close to, the explosions. It affected families, friends, emergency-service workers and all those who treated and cared for the survivors. Everyone's experience is unique. Yet for those caught up in the middle of a major trauma the immediate impact is experienced in an essentially similar way. First, the abrupt interruption of normal life. Then the sheer physicality of the impact – in this case the sound of the explosion, the shattering of glass, the darkness, the strange smells and sounds, the awful screaming. The awareness of death and the fear of dying. The confusion and the uncertainty. The difficulty of knowing what is the right thing to do. The shock, above all, is felt deep in the body and the brain, for the event triggers elemental survival reactions that are innate, and shared with other animals. It is these reactions I will turn to next, for they provide a key to the problems that many trauma survivors go on to experience.

Chapter 3: The nature of fear

Karen didn't see the man until he materialized in front of her. Later, she worked out that he must have been waiting in the doorway of the old apartment block across the way. There was space enough there for him to hide, and no light. Her first reaction was shock; she was startled by the unexpected appearance of the man: her heart hammered in her chest and her body went rigid. He was short, no taller than her, wearing dark, baggy clothes and a hood that was pulled down, shielding his face. There was no doubting the menace in his posture. She had stopped dead when he had appeared. Now she felt unable to move, frozen in fear, her heart continuing its rapid, frantic beating, her breathing shallow, her mouth dry and her mind racing, a jumble of scary thoughts, mainly that she was about to be raped or robbed or both. Or killed. That last thought sent a shockwave through her body. I don't want to die, she thought. I'm too young. This shouldn't be happening.

'Don't fuck with me, lady. I have a knife *and* a gun. So fucking do as you're fucking told, bitch.'

The voice was young and there was a note of desperation to it. She had heard kids talk like this all the time at the school she taught at. The bluff and bravado. Playground talk. She could not see a gun or a knife because his hands were buried deep in his sweatshirt pockets. Did he have one? Would he have both?

'What do you want? What are you doing?'

The words came out quickly and there was anger in them that she had not known was there. Her heart lurched at her presumption, but she took a step forward, her eyes fixed intently on him.

'Fucking do as you're told, bitch, I said.'

'You haven't told me to do anything, you idiot. Get out of here! I'm not afraid of you.'

She took a second step forward and a surge of feeling ran through her body, emboldening her.

'I'm warning you, lady.'

But he was backing away as he spoke. She took another step and the feeling strengthened, a feeling of power, elation almost.

'You're *warning* me. Just how old are you? Piss off, before I call the police.'

A moment's hesitation and then he was off, running like a deer, leaping over some cardboard boxes on the pavement, so that she saw the flash of his white trainers just before he turned the corner and disappeared.

For a moment Karen stood still, looking at where the youth had fled. She took a deep breath. Bloody hell, she thought. What was I doing? She swallowed, her mouth still dry. Her heart was thumping away, but less fast. The whole sequence of events must have been over in a minute, less, but it had seemed a lifetime. Time slowed down, she thought. It's what people say and it did. She was trembling now, as though she was cold, the after-effect of all those jumbled emotions, the excitement, the fear and anger. *Suppose . . .* she thought, but she did not let herself follow the thought through. Instead, she turned, walked to the door of her block of flats and let herself in.

I doubt if anyone will be surprised at Karen's encounter; we know that there are people who try to rob others or to harm them. We hope it does not happen to us or to people we are close to. But it might. Fear. That is what Karen experienced as she was confronted by the youth. She was instantly afraid and her fear drove her to confront him and drive him off. Fear is a common thread in the experiences of those caught up in a sudden-onset trauma. Jacqui experienced it when a bomb exploded in the carriage next to her and she was pitched forward in her seat. Janine felt it as she lay trapped under the bleeding, wounded man outside Milton Keynes police station. Richard felt it as the speeding Pendolino train began to vibrate and he was pitched out of his seat with objects crashing all around him. In this chapter I will consider the nature of fear, what the bodily signs are, how our instant reactions are related to fundamental mechanisms in the brain, and why this is important. I will examine the way people respond when they are afraid and how that can affect how they feel later on. I will clarify the differences between fear and fear-related states like anxiety and stress (these terms are scattered throughout trauma literature). Finally, I will discuss the part played in the experience of trauma by people's personalities and their personal histories – something that we will be considering at several points throughout this book.

The biology of fear

Fear is a vital, adaptive emotion; without fear no animal would survive for long. This is true of human beings, too, although we have protected ourselves from experiencing fear in its raw form, constructing an elaborate, sophisticated world where direct threat to life is rare. When I walk down the street in my neighbourhood, I am not frantically checking every nook and cranny for a predator who may be out to kill me. Unless, that is, I live in Iraq, Afghanistan or other parts of the world where violent, lethal assaults are to be expected, or I am a soldier in a war zone. Most of us are unused to sudden threat. When it happens, we are shocked, as Karen was when the youth stepped out in front of her. That jolt, the adrenaline rush, as it has come to be known, is a sign of fear. Karen's reaction was instantaneous and automatic. She did not consciously say to herself, 'Here's a guy who is threatening me', and then instruct her body to react with fear. Her body reacted first and the feeling followed. In that sense we are no different from any other animal under threat. We react instinctively.

The biology of any organism is fundamentally about survival. To survive entails the active monitoring of potential threats. Thus the body and the brain are biologically programmed to register what is going on at all times. The process is both *external*, in terms of the world around with all its dangers and attractions, and *internal*, in terms of what is happening inside our bodies – the regulation of body temperature, for instance, or the management of appropriate digestion. Emotion is what describes that process. It is a way of motivating the organism to take actions intended to prolong survival. Basic emotions, not just fear, are therefore at heart innate, biologically determined processes, the products of a long evolutionary history that make themselves known to us as feelings. Thus, Karen's instant appraisal and reaction were determined by innate processes in her brain and body. Understanding how the brain does this provides us with an important clue as to why traumatic reactions persist long after the trauma itself has passed.

Imagine that, through the wonders of modern technology, we are able to get inside Karen's brain as she sees her attacker and directly observe its internal processes as they occur. What would we see? Activity occurring at incredible speed. The brain consists of billions of neurons (nerve cells) that are constantly sending and receiving signals, registering and giving information about both the external world and the internal environment. The brain is a complex organ, one that has evolved over millions of years. Physically, it can be divided into three interacting, overlapping structures, sometimes known as the *triune* brain (see Fig. 3.1).

The oldest part of the brain in evolutionary terms is the 'reptilian' brain, which is located in the cerebellum and the brainstem, the deepest parts of the brain. Its function is to meet the organism's basic needs of reproduction, feeding, survival and maintaining a steady internal environment ('homeostasis'). Surrounding the reptilian brain is the 'paleo-' or 'old mammalian' brain, which most mammals share. It includes the limbic system, a part of the brain that is located between the brainstem and the cerebral cortex, and one that plays a key role in arousal. This part of the brain is involved in regulating our emotions, and determines whether something gives us pleasure or pain. It also plays a role in memory and learning. The last part of the brain to evolve is the neocortex, comprising almost the whole of the two cerebral hemispheres and the bridge between them, the corpus callosum. This is where the higher cognitive functions of rational thought, self-awareness and decision making take place. These functions are often seen as defining what constitutes being human, though many primates also have a neocortex, albeit simplified.

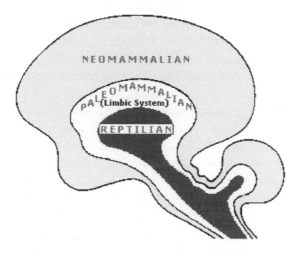

Fig. 3.1. Diagram of the triune brain. (From John MacLean, *The Triune Brain in Evolution: Role in Paleocerebral Functions* (New York: The Plenum Press, 1990). Reprinted with permission of the publisher.)

Each of the three structures of the triune brain interacts with the environment in a particular way that corresponds broadly to different levels of processing information. The reptilian brain is involved in the processing of basic sensory information – sight, smell, touch, sound, taste – and movement. The paleo-mammalian brain, and the limbic system in particular, is involved in processing emotions, while the neocortex is central to cognitive processing, that is, thoughts, interpretations, ideas and beliefs. This separation of functions is a simplification: some functions are regulated at more than one level, and the three levels of the brain interact closely with each other; at any one time, integrated activity is usually occurring between all parts of the brain. A useful metaphor is that of an orchestra: each part or instrument has a specific function, but to create an action or produce a melody, it interacts with other parts.

On certain occasions, however, one part of the brain predominates. This is what happens as Karen registers the threat posed by the sudden appearance of the youth. What occurs inside Karen's brain is a dramatic firing-up of the limbic system, resulting in an instantaneous increase in general arousal as her body is prepared for fight or flight. The limbic system evaluates the situation and sends off signals to the autonomic nervous system (ANS) whose function is to increase or decrease arousal. The ANS has two complementary branches, the sympathetic nervous system, which activates arousal, and the parasympathetic nervous system, which is responsible for reducing arousal. Homeostasis (the balanced regulation of the body's arousal systems) is accomplished by the constant interaction of the sympathetic and parasympathetic nervous systems. Under conditions of stress, however, the sympathetic nervous system is strongly activated and the parasympathetic is suppressed. Within the limbic system, a small, almond-shaped structure, the amygdala, becomes highly active. When activated the amygdala is, in effect, like a supersensitive alarm that has been set off, the equivalent of flashing lights and a blaring siren, signalling danger. Karen's heart rate increasing, her breathing speeding up and her body tensing are adaptive reactions to threat. Through these actions, blood is rapidly pumped into the major muscle groups, increasing their energy supply by mobilizing glucose, while at the same time the blood vessels at the periphery are constricted to limit possible blood loss in case of injury. The chemical basis for this arousal reaction is through the release of hormones, in particular adrenaline (also known as epinephrine), from the adrenal glands. Inessential bodily activity, such as salivation, is suspended or suppressed, which is why Karen's mouth feels dry. The jolt or startle reaction that Karen feels is the result of all this action. Its function is to make her body vigilant to the perceived threat, so that she is prepared to meet it. All this activity occurs in order to maximize her chances of survival.

What is important, in relation to traumatic reactions, is the fact that these actions of the brain and the body happen automatically and in microseconds; Karen is not consciously doing anything. We are used to feeling in control of our actions, making decisions, choosing what to do or not to. But when our very survival is on the line, our conscious mind is bypassed. Control is given over to our brain and body. Reactions become automatic, at least at first. Thus, sudden-onset traumas not only come at us without warning, but the body also responds without our willing it to do so. There are good reasons for this, as I have shown. But it can lead to the feeling of not being in control of one's body. As Tim said in the last chapter, describing the actions that led him into the bombed carriage of the train next to his: 'I still think to this day that I didn't have a choice'. This is a theme that I will return to later, as some traumatic memories, flashbacks in particular, also have the quality of feeling as though they are outside of the person's control. Some trauma survivors organize their lives in an effort to achieve far greater control than before, in the hope of preventing such an experience happening again, measures that can be counterproductive and often make matters worse.

The automatic activation of the brain's alarm system, the limbic system and within that, the amygdala, is what makes the traumatic experience so intense. Sensory details stand out. The focus of the mind's attention is narrowed in order to be better prepared, while peripheral details are excluded. The experience of time slowing down, known as tachypsychia, is due to the speeding up of the brain and body so that the outside world seems slow by comparison. Later in this book, when we discuss flashbacks and traumatic memories, we will find an explanation for these strange and upsetting experiences in those very structures of the brain. In essence, the alarm system continues to be activated long after the trauma has gone, re-creating the feelings of danger and threat when they are no longer appropriate.

To summarize, the immediate fear Karen experienced when the hooded youth appeared suddenly in front of her was an innate, bio-logically programmed reaction of her body to threat. Her physical reactions – her heart rate speeding up, her breathing becoming fast and shallow, her muscles tensing – occurred without conscious thought, activated automatically by specific control centres in the brain. The feeling followed from these physical changes; it is how Karen knew she was afraid. What happened next, however, involved more than the innate fear reaction.

The psychology of fear

Karen's initial shock is potentiated by her immediate appraisal that she is at risk of attack, a confirmation that here is a potentially serious threat. A hooded young man deliberately stepping out in front of her has a meaning that arises out of what she knows about twenty-first-century urban life. The words 'There was no doubting the menace in his posture' convey something of this appraisal. Her fear increases. This is what is known as 'primary appraisal'. The mind is taking in what the threat consists of and seeking to act accordingly. Even though Karen's bodily reactions are instinctive and she is not consciously willing them, she is very much aware of what is happening: thoughts flit through her mind that she might be raped, robbed or killed. In other words, almost immediately the innate, biologically driven emotion takes on meaning. Other cen-tres in the brain are involved, in particular those that draw upon memory and learning. Fear has taken on a human dimension. To clarify this process, suppose we imagine a different scenario, in which Karen is startled by the unexpected appearance of someone in front of her, but it turns out to be a friend whom she had failed to notice. She would have the same initial startle reaction but, once she saw who it was, her heart rate would rapidly return to normal and the temporary increase in arousal would dissipate. She would not describe herself as having been afraid, although she might have said to her friend, 'You gave me quite a fright'. That phrase captures the fact that the initial biological reaction is the same but the outcome different.

Primary appraisal is not a considered, rational process. It is as instantaneous as the fear reaction. It is also continually changing, as new information is taken in by the brain. The fear reaction has put Karen on full alert, prepared for action. Acute observation of the youth – his manner, his way of talking – suggests to her that he is young and acting out a bluff. She challenges him and her heightened emotion impels her forward. She knows about young men from her job as a teacher and, in effect, she treats him like one of her charges, forcing him onto the back foot. Her observations are confirmed by his responses and she continues to press him until she forces him into an ignominious retreat. Once the youth has run off, the threat is no longer there, but the fear response remains, albeit beginning to lessen. Her heart is still racing, her mouth dry, she is trembling from the emotion. Now her mind takes in what has just happened and a further appraisal occurs. *Bloody hell . . . What was I doing?* The words reveal how her behaviour seemed to Karen to be automatic, not based upon a conscious, rational consideration of options. She might have said afterwards to a friend, 'I just got carried away', indicating that she was not thinking about what was the 'right' thing to do. Karen's actions reflect her personality and personal history, as the incoming signals to her brain are integrated with her memory (kids in the school playground) and her sense of self (a teacher used to handling aggressive youths) to produce a response. Someone with a different personality and history might have acted quite differently.

In reflecting on the event, Karen realized that her counterattack put herself at risk, that the youth might not have been bluffing, might not have been a youth at all, but a full grown adult, might well have had a knife or a gun. She might have become an item in the next day's news, someone casually murdered on the street by a stranger. This is what is known as 'secondary appraisal', in which the incident is put into context and evaluated. Those who have been through trauma know this process well. It can lead to feelings of guilt, anger and shame as people castigate themselves for not behaving differently. We will discuss these important emotions in Chapter 8.

To summarize, fear has three components: the innate fear reaction; the primary appraisal of the threat; and the secondary appraisal of what happened and what might have happened. While the first two occur only during the actual event, the third can happen any time afterwards, from a few seconds to months or years later. When a trauma involves a threat to life, as many do, fear is inevitable. We saw how it affected those caught up in the London bombings. But while fear is the basic emotion, it is not the only one. Moreover, because everyone comes to an event with a particular history and personality, how people react when frightened varies. Someone who had been attacked by a youth before and badly hurt would react in a very different way from Karen. How people feel and behave once they are out of danger and the traumatic event is over is a product of the intensity of the experience itself, the nature of the person and the context – that is, what their life is *after the event*. The fear reaction, which is so powerful in the heat of the trauma, is transformed into something else.

What happens next?

Unpleasant, horrifying and frightening as an assault can be, it is often what happens next that causes people most upset. Why does fear continue long after the traumatic event is over, long after the person has recovered from any physical injuries and is presumed to be better? This is a question that we will address time and again in this book. One answer lies in the nature of fear itself. When I first trained as a clinical psychologist in the late 1960s, I was introduced to a psychological model of fear based upon the now familiar story of Pavlov's salivating dogs. Pavlov showed that dogs could be made to salivate at the sound of a buzzer, simply because they had learned to associate the buzzer with the onset of food, a process known as classical conditioning. In the 1960s it was assumed that this model explained why some people developed phobias and, using methods of treatment called behaviour therapy, we applied a de-conditioning treatment known as systematic desensitization to help people overcome their phobias. In my memoir, *The Gossamer Thread,* I describe how successful this can be in the case of 'Jackie', whom I helped overcome her fear of dogs in one powerful treatment session. Even then I realized that classical conditioning could not be the whole explanation of the genesis of fears and phobias. Many phobias arise without any clear traumatic incident. We also know that some types of fears are more common in humans than others, suggesting we are more prepared to be frightened of, say, snakes than butterflies, or to be afraid of enclosed spaces rather than when lying on a beach. Yet conditioning is important in explaining why fears persist.

The essential trigger of fear in the conditioning model is precisely the sort of event that Karen experienced, what is known as an unconditioned stimulus (UCS), an event that automatically provokes an unconditioned response (UCR), the innate fear reaction. Psychologists re-created the UCS in the laboratory by using electric shocks and other aversive stimuli on animals like rats, cats and dogs. These were the days when experimenters could do very much as they liked, and did. These poor animals were studied to see how easily they could be conditioned to a variety of different stimuli and how persistent the conditioned responses (CR) were. It is very easy to produce a conditioned response if the UCS is strong enough to provoke high levels of fear. Using the Pavlovian paradigm, any number of neutral stimuli, such as tones or lights, were shown to be capable of provoking fear simply by association. Where the animals could avoid an electric shock by escaping to another part of the cage, for example, avoidance was rapidly learned. If we think about major traumas, we have, in effect, a situation similar to the experimental paradigm that psychologists created in the laboratory. We have a supreme aversive stimulus (UCS) such as an explosion or a train crash, a powerful innate fear reaction that occurs automatically (UCR), and a context in which any number of stimuli could evoke the fear response simply by association i.e. by classical conditioning. When trauma survivors experience fear long after the trauma is over, could it not be that certain stimuli have become conditioned to produce the fear response and do so even without the conscious knowledge of the person?

For a long time after the London bombings, Elaine experienced sudden bursts of intense fear for no obvious reason, and at times when she was doing ordinary things. Often she was transported back, in her mind, to the carriage of the tube train. These flashbacks were generally short-lived, lasting a few seconds only, but they were very distressing to her for two reasons. Firstly, because she felt the return of fear physically in her body, vividly reminding her of what she had been through. Secondly, because the flashbacks seemed to happen without warning, meaning that she had no control over them. For Elaine, being out of control was something she particularly hated. This is how she described one of the flashbacks to me.

'There is another one where the man was holding his hand out and I'm trying to reach him and I can't. And I can't hear anything and it's all black and white. All the flashbacks are black and white, not colour. But this man is just stretching out and I'm trying to get him and then I can't. That is really vivid.'

'And presumably quite upsetting?'

'It's real. It's almost as if I'm [there]. It wasn't a memory of something that happened. It was happening there and then.'

Elaine's traumatic flashback was of Stan, who had held out his hand to her. For no reason that she understood, she experienced this image at times when she was at home. Years later, when Elaine was in therapy, she told Martina, her therapist, about it.

One of the things that Martina did was about the man with his hand out. She said, 'What do you think triggers it off?' I said, 'I don't know, it just happens at home a lot.' And she said, 'OK, where were you at the time?'

Elaine described where she had been located in the train, and where Stan had been. In the office Martina stood where Stan had been in relation to Elaine.

So she stood there and I stood here. And she said, 'If he stood there and you stood there, what could you see?' I said, 'I'd just see him.' She said, 'Was he at the same level as you?' I said, 'He was a bit lower than me.' So she went down on her knees and she said, 'Was he at this level?' 'No, lower than that.' So she just went down a tiny little bit and put her hand out and, all of a sudden, it got me straight away. And that was really horrible. But I realized that it was Martina putting her hand out that had triggered it. And it didn't last very long. And it just put it in my head that if something similar occurs, it can do that.

Martina had evoked a conditioned fear response to the trigger stimulus of a hand held out at a certain level. Elaine also experienced flashbacks triggered by her grandchildren running into the room to see her. This distressed her so much that she avoided seeing them.

'I don't go downstairs when they're there much now . . . and I do feel bad about that.' Martina said, 'Do you think they ever run to you?' And I said, 'Yeah, they do.' I was thinking about a couple of times where I would have flashbacks when one of the little ones would run in to see me, saying, 'Nanny'. It would trigger it off.

As a result of her therapist's creativity Elaine learned that her inexplicable bursts of fear were triggered by specific stimuli, including her grandchildren, who were at the same level as Stan had been in the train. They were classically conditioned fear reactions. In later chapters I will take this notion further. But it illustrates how the experience of intense fear can condition certain stimuli or triggers and that these go on to evoke the fear later, often without the person knowing what those triggers are.

Arousal, fear, anxiety and stress

Anyone reading the psychological literature on traumatic reactions will come across terms such as anxiety, high arousal and post-traumatic stress. It is important to clarify what these terms mean and how they relate to fear. The term *arousal* is the most straightforward to define. It refers to a non-specific increase in activity in the body as, for example, arousal from sleep to wakefulness. Any number of specific emotions can be aroused: anger, fear, joy, guilt, shame, for example. Sexual feelings, too, of course, and so common has this usage become, that *arousal* is sometimes used purely to mean sexual arousal. But it actually means a general state of alertness, an activation of the body.

Fear is best defined as the emotional state caused by the presence of impending danger or threat. Fear has an object; we are always frightened of *something*. This is true even if we cannot identify exactly what it is. In the middle of the night we might hear an odd sound in the house that makes our hair stand on end. Although we may not know what caused the sound, we are frightened of what it might mean – a burglar, perhaps.

Anxiety is defined as a generalized emotional state rather than a specific response. Thus Karen's immediate reaction to the hooded youth is fear. Later, however, when the incident is over, she may become anxious about walking home at night, worrying about the possibility of another attack. After trauma, people often report that they are generally more jumpy, easily startled, restless and have difficulty concentrating, all of which are characteristics of anxiety. In fact, anxiety is what disturbs trauma sufferers most, for it affects all aspects of their life. Being anxious means that the body is in a state of generalized heightened arousal. This affects everything: relationships with loved ones, friendships, ability to do work, sleep, decision making, general wellbeing. A person suffering from anxiety is unable to relax properly and so comes to feel worn out most of the time. Mentally, it takes the form of extensive worrying, churning over and over what might go wrong or what dangers might lie ahead. Often people are anxious about being anxious, aware that they are not themselves any more and worried about what that might mean.

Stress, confusingly, is used in two different ways. It can describe the pressure placed upon a person or object. In designing a bridge, for example, the engineers need to use materials that can withstand stress. In psychology, stress can be used this way too. How good are students at coping with the stress of student life, for example? But stress is also used to describe the person's *reaction* to pressure. We can say, for example, that a student felt stressed by the academic demands of university life and sought help. Here stress describes a reaction, a feeling. One way of clarifying the usage is to call the stress that acts upon a person a *stressor,* and the person's reaction *stress*. I will employ this usage throughout this book. In the literature on trauma, the terms 'acute stress disorder' and 'post-traumatic stress disorder' (PTSD) encapsulate the idea that trauma is a major stressor, placing demands upon the person that lead to the experience of being stressed. In the next chapter I examine what PTSD is and what it can mean to be diagnosed with it.

Chapter 4: Post-traumatic stress disorder (PTSD)

'I had these tapes playing in my head. I couldn't communicate properly and probably didn't know what day of the week it was. So to all intents and purposes I was pretty insane. I know it's not a very nice word, and I know people sometimes flinch when I say it, but that's how it felt.'

'And at some point you got some help from the doctors, didn't you?'

'I came across a GP who had an interest in post-traumatic stress disorder. It was by pure luck and he was brilliant. I think he'd worked with the Forces. He was telling me about this officer who had PTSD. He hadn't actually seen action, but he had ordered people to go to war and they had died, and it had given him PTSD. It was something that he was interested in and something that he was very sympathetic about. He was the one who sorted out my sleep and gave me some drugs.'

'And when did you realize that you had something called post-traumatic stress disorder? I remember you came to see me shortly after the event and we talked about it then.'

'You gave me a little blue book . . .'

'I did.'

'. . . which I read, and we did talk about post-traumatic stress disorder. You said to me that, if it carries on, then it becomes PTSD.'

'Yes, that's right. There's an acute stress reaction initially, which many people have, but if after a month or longer, you are still experiencing symptoms, it's given the diagnosis of PTSD. It has the constellation of high levels of arousal, often avoidance of situations, repeated ruminations and memories of the trauma which you were having. Sometimes the experience of being slightly dissociated, being out of yourself and out of the world, being . . .'

'Detached.'

'Detached. Yes.'

'Like a television that isn't tuned in.'

'OK.'

'It's like living your life like a fuzzy television. It was pretty bad.'

'Did it help to have a diagnosis or not?'

'Yes. I'm 100 per cent sure, because I did think I was going insane. I did think that it was me. I was wondering if it wasn't just me throwing my toys out of my pram at the Thames Valley Police. But then you come along all learned with the letters after your name and stuff and, you know, having a diagnosis does help. I think once you've been diagnosed, you have this initial reaction that it's the end of the world. But then when you've actually got this diagnosis, you know where you can go. It gives you a foundation point and then you can set your direction off it. Whereas without it, you're kind of . . .'

'. . . all over the place?'

'Yeah. You don't have any kind of anchor.'

This is an extract from my interview with Janine Luck, the WPC who had been caught up in a shooting outside Milton Keynes police station (see Chapter 1). I'd got to know Janine well, as I had been her therapist from August 2005 to November 2006. Her experience is valuable for, as we shall see, it shows both the strengths and the limitations of the diagnosis of post-traumatic stress disorder. As is obvious from the extract, having the diagnosis helped Janine make sense of the experiences she had been going through, and counteracted her considerable anxiety that she was going mad. At its height, her anxiety was so strong that she hid herself in her house, refusing to open the door in case someone came round to section her. Seeing her symptoms in terms of a recognized syndrome gave her, as she put it, 'a foundation point and then you can set your direction off it'. A diagnosis is not only an explanation; it also points the way forward. It suggests that some help in the form of therapy may be available.

In this chapter I will examine the psychiatric diagnosis of post-traumatic stress disorder. I will describe what the definition of PTSD currently consists of and the changes that are in the pipeline. I will discuss whether it is a form of mental illness and what that term means. I will consider how PTSD came to be predominant in explaining people's reactions to trauma, what its strengths and limitations are, and whether it is as helpful as many professionals and sufferers think it is. Finally, I will give my personal view about the diagnosis of PTSD from my experience of working with people like Janine.

What is PTSD?

The term 'post-traumatic stress disorder' first appeared in 1980 in the third revision of the *Diagnostic and Statistical Manual for Mental Disorders* (DSM-III), the US bible of psychiatric illnesses. Its origins are unusual. Two military psychiatrists who had been through the Vietnam War lobbied hard to create a psychiatric diagnosis that took into account the fact that many returning soldiers were psychologically traumatized. Recognition of a formal illness could help counteract the negative perceptions of veterans that swirled around an unpopular and unsuccessful war. Atrocities committed by the American forces, like the My Lai massacre, might have been due not so much to moral failings but to something medical, such as an illness, something that overwhelmed the individual and thereby explained, if not excused, his conduct. Many Vietnam vets had problems reintegrating into American society after the war, difficulties that included high levels of aggression, drug and alcohol abuse, feelings of alienation, the breakdown of marriages or relationships, the inability to hold down a job, and a sense of grievance against a society that, in their eyes, had exploited and then abandoned them. If the cause of these problems was an illness, then not only did it excuse the sufferers from personal blame, including self-blame, but it also opened the possibility of treatment.

Psychological trauma after combat had been recognized well before the arrival of PTSD. As early as the American Civil War, the psychological effects of war were identified using the term 'soldier's heart' or 'irritable heart'. After the First World War, the traumatization of soldiers in the trenches was given the term 'shell shock'. In both cases the initial presumption was that there was an underlying physical explanation. In the case of shell shock, the vibration caused by shells exploding near soldiers was thought to have had a damaging effect on their brains. But there was no evidence for this and soldiers who had not been exposed to shells exploding nearby also developed shell shock. It is not surprising to us these days that those who go through the hell of war are affected psychologically afterwards. We have become more knowledgeable and more accepting of both psychology and psychological trauma (see Chapter 1). PTSD is the most recent term for something that had long been recognized, even if its nature and its exact causes have been, and still are, debated. The introduction of the term into the American Classification of Psychiatric Disorders, followed shortly by its inclusion in the World Health Organisation's International Classification of Disorders (ICD), meant that post-traumatic stress disorder was acknowledged as a psychiatric illness.

The psychiatric diagnosis of PTSD

In the current American psychiatric classification, DSM-IV-TR, post-traumatic stress disorder (code: 309.81) is listed as a diagnosis under Axis 1, which includes the main clinical syndromes such as depression and anxiety. Table 4.1 shows the diagnosis and the criteria used for arriving at it. The diagnosis of PTSD is made by working through a list of defining symptoms. If a minimum number of symptoms under each symptom category (Criteria B–D) fits the patient's experiences and the other defining criteria are met (A, E, F) the diagnosis is made.

Table 4.1. The DSM-IV-TR diagnosis of PTSD, 309.81
A. The person has been exposed to a traumatic event in which both of the following were present:
The person has experienced, witnessed, or was confronted with an event or events that involved actual or threatened death or serious injury, or a threat to the physical integrity of self or others
The person's response involved intense fear, helplessness, or horror
B. The traumatic event is persistently re-experienced in one (or more) of the following ways:
Recurrent and intrusive distressing recollections of the event, including images, thoughts, or perceptions
Recurrent distressing dreams of the event
Acting or feeling as if the traumatic event were recurring (includes a sense of reliving the experience, illusions, hallucinations, and dissociative flashback episodes, including those that occur on awakening or when intoxicated)
Intense psychological distress at exposure to internal or external cues that symbolize or resemble an aspect of the traumatic event
Physiological reactivity on exposure to internal or external cues that symbolize or resemble an aspect of the traumatic event
C. Persistent avoidance of stimuli associated with the trauma and numbing of general responsiveness (not present before the trauma) as indicated by three (or more) of the following:
Efforts to avoid thoughts, feelings, or conversations associated with the trauma
Efforts to avoid activities, places, or people that arouse recollections of the trauma
Inability to recall an important aspect of the trauma

| Markedly diminished interest or participation in significant activities |
| Feeling of detachment or estrangement from others |
| Restricted range of affect (e.g. unable to have loving feelings) |
| Sense of foreshortened future (e.g. does not expect to have a career, marriage, children, or a normal life span) |
| **D. Persistent symptoms of increased arousal (not present before the trauma), as indicated by two (or more) of the following:** |
| Difficulty falling or staying asleep |
| Irritability or outbursts of anger |
| Difficulty concentrating |
| Hyper-vigilance |
| Exaggerated startle response |
| **E. Duration of the disturbance (symptoms in Criteria B, C, and D) is more than 1 month** |
| **F. The disturbance causes clinically significant distress or impairment in social, occupational, or other important areas of functioning** |

In essence, *four* features define the diagnosis of PTSD:

   (i)   the individual has experienced or witnessed a major trauma

  (ii)   the individual experiences key defining symptoms that fall into three categories:

      a.   re-experiencing the trauma

      b.   avoidance/feelings of numbness

      c.   a high degree of arousal

 (iii) a month has elapsed since the trauma

 (iv) the symptoms are markedly interfering with the person's work or social life

Classifications of psychiatric disorders change over time, reflecting new knowledge as well as changes in theory and practice.

A provisional revision of the PTSD diagnosis, to be known as DSM-V, is underway and will be available officially in 2013. From the information currently on the DSM-V website, the diagnosis will not change radically; where the changes are important, I will explain what difference they will make.

What constitutes 'trauma' in the PTSD diagnosis?

People tend to associate PTSD with major traumatic events like natural disasters (earthquakes, floods, tsunamis), terrorist attacks (9/11, the 2005 London bombings), man-made catastrophes (the Bradford stadium fire, the Hillsborough disaster) and bloody insurrections and wars. This was clearly in the minds of those who created the diagnosis in 1980. Thirty years later, however, PTSD has become much more widely used. For example, it is possible to be diagnosed as having PTSD as a result of a minor car accident or a non-life-threatening injury at work. In fact, carefully following DSM-IV-TR's criteria, I have reached the diagnosis in exactly those circumstances. How can this be? The answer lies in the liberal way that experiencing trauma is defined in Criterion A: 'The person has experienced, witnessed, or was confronted with an event or events that involved actual or threatened death or serious injury, or a threat to the physical integrity of self or others'. Firstly, this allows an event to be *witnessed* not just experienced. This is sensible as it will include those who have to clear up after awful disasters (police officers and others) as well as people like Elaine and Tim in the London bombings who, while not directly bombed, witnessed the horrors and the carnage. (The proposed revision, DSM-V, however, allows only those events witnessed *in person*, thereby excluding the diagnosis for those who, say, saw 9/11 on television.)

Secondly, '*threatened* death or serious injury' might be constituted by something as apparently minor as a lump of masonry falling off a roof and landing a few feet from someone. Equally, a minor traffic accident that might have caused serious injury had not one or both drivers taken evasive action would fit the description. In these cases the sufferer must also show the minimum number of re-experiencing, avoidance/numbing and increased-arousal symptoms for the diagnosis to be made. That some people do, even when the trauma is minor, indicates something important – namely, that the individual's personality and personal history play a part in how they respond, something I will return to later.

Finally, 'a threat to the physical integrity of self or others' is open to various interpretations, although the phrase is to be dropped from DSM-V. The experience of 'intense fear, helplessness, or horror' also disappears, since these feelings are a *result* rather than a cause of trauma, and more appropriately placed elsewhere.

The defining symptoms

The three categories, B, C and D in Table 4.1 describe what people experience, their 'symptoms', to use the medical terminology. In the first of these categories the person feels he or she is re-living the trauma over and over again through intrusive and distressing reminders, sometimes called flashbacks. At the beginning of this chapter Janine said that the trauma was like a tape in her head being constantly replayed; later in the interview with me she used a striking analogy. It was, she said, 'like a VHS cassette, and my brain is the telly and someone has put this cassette inside me and it is literally playing everything from beginning to end, and you can't stop it, you can't forward-wind it, it just plays out and you just have to let it play out'. The trauma seems to be happening again, and moreover does so without volition or control. Most sufferers find this, understandably, very distressing. It made Janine feel she was going mad.

The second category (C in Table 4.1) describes two distinct types of symptom, those to do with avoiding anything connected to the trauma, and those to do with feeling numb or detached from oneself or the world. Janine shut herself in her house and refused to see anyone connected to the police force. She did not want to talk about the trauma and initially it was only with great reluctance that she did so in therapy. Even when she returned to work, she did not want to put on her uniform because of its traumatic associations. It is understandable why people avoid reminders, as they are often highly distressing or may trigger unwanted memories or flashbacks. But as we shall see in Chapter 7, the short-term gain of avoidance is offset by longer-term problems. The feeling of detachment and emotional numbness commonly occurs at the time of the trauma as a reaction to the shock, but it is its persistence later that is important for the diagnosis of PTSD. Janine said she felt detached and distant, 'like a fuzzy television', as she put it. Individuals can experience a sense of feeling unreal and difficulty in reacting in ways that are emotionally appropriate; for example, not feeling happy when a friend tells you they have become engaged or been promoted at work.

The third category, D, describes being in a general state of high arousal – not just when recalling the trauma. Janine told me she spent many nights not sleeping, and that both her memory and her concentration were shot to pieces. Typically, a loud noise can trigger a massive startle-reaction. Anyone reading about Vietnam veterans will come across anecdotes of vets diving under a table or searching for their gun when a plate is dropped or some similar innocuous event occurs. Also common is a state of hyper-alertness or hyper-vigilance to possible threats, which can occasionally turn into an almost paranoid state. Janine told me she was convinced, at one point, that police officers coming to her home were sent to section her (i.e. to get her forcibly admitted to a psychiatric hospital).

Criterion E indicates that a month must have elapsed since the trauma before a formal diagnosis can be made. The reason for the month's grace is that many people's initial reactions to trauma – high arousal, disturbing traumatic memories, dissociative experiences – decline over time. Put simply, almost everyone will show some immediate emotional reaction to a major trauma, but in most people those symptoms reduce markedly or disappear altogether by the time a month has elapsed. If the symptoms are particularly severe during that month, as they were for Janine, a diagnosis of acute stress disorder can be made. Finally, criterion F indicates that the symptoms must be adversely affecting the person's social and work life, which in my experience is always the case if the major symptoms are present. In truth, it is hard to imagine how it could be otherwise.

Is PTSD a mental illness?

Are people diagnosed with PTSD mentally ill and, if they are, what does that mean? Earlier, Janine related how useful it was to have the diagnosis, how it helped her make sense of what was happening to her, the turmoil of emotions she was going through. Before the diagnosis, she feared she might be going mad. Paradoxically, being diagnosed was a relief, as though having a specific psychiatric illness meant she was not mad! This is not as irrational as it sounds. To many, madness is synonymous with the peculiar and disturbing behaviour of those unfortunates who were locked away in lunatic asylums in the eighteenth and nineteenth centuries and the first half of the twentieth. The fear of going mad, which troubled Janine so much, is at heart a fear of suffering from a terrifying, lifelong and incurable condition. When I was in my teens and before I had even the notion of studying psychology, I read R. L. Stevenson's novella, *Dr Jekyll and Mr Hyde*. The way the good Dr Jekyll was transformed into the murderous Hyde seemed to me a classic description of the horrors of madness. I thought how awful it would be to go mad and be subjected to forces over which I had absolutely no control. Many people still see mental illness in those terms.

Yet in the twenty-first century, mental illness is very different from 'lunacy' or 'madness'. In the UK in the course of a year, one in four people will experience some form of mental illness, or *mental-health problem*, to use the preferred term. The commonest such experiences are anxiety and depression. Very few people will be admitted to hospital and in most cases the experience is short-lived. Most recover completely, sometimes with the help of treatment (medication, counselling, psychotherapy) and sometimes without. Even the more serious mental illnesses, such as schizophrenia and the bipolar disorders (known generically as *psychotic disorders*), are far less debilitating or intractable than they used to be. Moreover, the stigma associated with being mentally ill is changing, as many people in the public eye have admitted that they have suffered from anorexia, bipolar disorder, anxiety, depression and other conditions. The greater awareness of the diagnosis of PTSD can be seen as part of the normalization of mental illness, the recognition that it is commonplace for people to suffer from psychological problems, and equally commonplace for people to be prescribed medication or to have a course of psychological therapy.

This was brought home to me when I was on the radio publicizing my memoir, *The Gossamer Thread*. Almost everyone I met (interviewers and other guests) told me, without any prompting on my part, that they were having or had had some form of psychotherapy. It made me wonder whether it was now abnormal *not* to experience mental-health problems.

The proliferation of mental illnesses is captured in the changes over five decades to DSM, the American classification system for psychiatric disorders. In 1952, when DSM first appeared, just over sixty illnesses were described. At the last revision in 1994 there were nearly four hundred. Critics have questioned whether these are illnesses at all or simply categorizations of essentially normal experiences. There are vested interests involved in finding new psychiatric disorders. Not only does this provide work for professionals like myself, but it is highly profitable for the drug companies who market new drugs to meet the new diagnoses. Psychiatry has become something of a boom industry.

I do not intend in this book to go into the debate over the validity of calling states of mind like depression, anxiety and PTSD 'illnesses'. The psychologist Richard Bentall has written an excellent and readable book, *Doctoring the Mind*, on this topic. My personal view is that many psychological problems are not specific illnesses but part of a spectrum of normal experience that stretches from the everyday to the more severe. I include PTSD in that category. Professor Gordon Turnbull, one of the pioneers of the psychiatric treatment of PTSD in the military, realized early on in his career that the people he saw were not mentally ill but showing an essentially normal reaction to an abnormal event. Called in after the 1988 Lockerbie disaster to help the mountain rescuers who had the unenviable task of scouring the area around the wreckage of the bombed plane for possible survivors, he realized that these were amongst the most resilient and tough individuals he had known, and yet they were showing signs of psychological breakdown. This was not, he felt, due to a particular psychopathology in them, but a result of what they had been through in the wake of the disaster. As he put it, PTSD was 'a survival reaction in people who are normal and resilient, who were having a difficult time challenging this particular assault, this intrusion into their lives'. But to the person suffering from PTSD, whether it is an illness or not is not as important as the *recognition* that the diagnosis provides. The value of the formal diagnosis of PTSD is that it gives strange and worrying personal experiences 'a local habitation and a name'. The relief Janine and others have felt is that there are experts who recognize these experiences and can fit them into a template (diagnosis) and offer specialist help (therapy). Diagnosis recognizes that there are others who have been though similar experiences and releases the individual from self-blame (in other words, their experiences do not represent a personal failing). Research evidence can be drawn upon and statistics about prevalence and likely outcome cited. In the maelstrom of anxiety and other emotions that affect a person after trauma, this is a lifeline. Therefore, in this book I will continue to use the DSM diagnosis of PTSD as a heuristic device that brings a certain clarity and order to the experiences people may have after trauma. But it is also important to be aware of the limitations of the diagnosis and that there are other psychological problems that follow major trauma – for example, excessive alcohol or drug use, depression, anger, relationship problems and persistent feelings of alienation from the world. Not every problem after trauma is best described as PTSD.

Janine's story: PTSD and something more

I've described the experience of Janine Luck, who courageously went to the help of a man who had been shot in a gun battle outside Milton Keynes police station. As Staff Psychologist with the Thames Valley Police Authority, I formally assessed her using a DSM-IV-TR structured interview schedule, and found that she undoubtedly met the criteria for the diagnosis. For several months she was seriously distressed and for a while it seemed that she might not be able to return to her work as a police officer. However, with treatment from me, and her determination, Janine managed to return to work. I interviewed her again in February 2009, nearly four years after the event. By this time she had left the police and was pursuing a long-cherished aim of studying History at Oxford University. When I asked her to tell me what happened to her after the trauma, this is what she said.

> I don't know if you remember, but the incident kept playing and playing in my head, over and over and over and over. And I often wonder why that happened, and I think it was because it fuelled the anger. It kept the anger going. I often wonder why did I hold onto it so much and I think it's because, as a person, I have quite a strong sense of what's right and wrong.

What Janine focused on years later was her anger. It was hard not to be aware of it, for it had come up time and again in her therapy.

There had been an incident previous to the trauma, in which she was badly let down by the police force of which she was a member. Here is what she said when I followed up on her comment about her belief in fairness, in right and wrong.

'So that's what you brought to it. You're a person who is very clear about what is right and wrong . . .'

'Yes . . .'

'And that felt wrong to you, the whole thing, the way you were treated. You felt very angry about that?'

'Yes.'

'Did it also tie in with other previous experiences in the police?'

'I think so, yes. I had an injury before. I was left on a traffic point and my feet ended up getting too hot on this tarmac. In the end I had to go to the doctors and they had to stick needles in my toenails to release the infection. I didn't get any apology or anything. All they were worried about was me suing them. It was almost like I was made to feel that I was making it up.'

'So already there was an existing . . .'

'. . . foundation. It was a foundation for the trauma to build on. It was like something that it could latch onto.'

What Janine described was a sense of being let down by her employers, the police. She was off work for four weeks, which mystified the occupational-health doctor. She got little sympathy or understanding, certainly not an apology. This had rankled with her and this was the cause of the anger she refers to. When the shooting broke out, the three police officers with her ran off without bothering to tell her what they had seen. When she was trapped under the man, the first armed response officer to get to her searched the gunman for weapons, rather than helping either him or Janine. None of the senior officers checked on her welfare in the immediate aftermath, and she went home in blood-soaked clothing. To top it all, she got into trouble for not observing proper procedure, which is not to intervene when there is any risk of harm to oneself. Later on, in therapy, her anger became a focus of our work together as I tried to get Janine to let go of it.

Janine's example illustrates how any individual's response to a major trauma interacts with that person's personality and previous experience. She undoubtedly experienced PTSD, but her anger and her sense of fairness, of right and wrong, was just as important in understanding how she reacted to what was a life-threatening trauma. This is how she talked about it years later.

> And every time it [the flashback] played, it just reminded me. And anger built on anger and I got to a phase which is what I refer to now to my close friends as *my mental phase*, because it got so intense that I couldn't string a sentence together. I didn't want to leave the house. I didn't want to talk to anyone.

The re-experiencing symptoms tapped into her existing anger and exacerbated it hugely, to the extent that it got quite out of proportion. It is a tribute to Janine's resolve that she did not allow the anger to rule her life. With my help she returned to work as a police officer. When she eventually left, it was not because she was driven to do so by her symptoms, but because she decided that she wanted to pursue a different career.

Janine's experience shows that PTSD should not be seen in isolation from the individual and his or her history. We are not blank slates and how we are affected by a major trauma is in part due to who we are. The differing experiences of Tim and Elaine in the London bombings is one example of this (see Chapter 2). Nevertheless, PTSD has become the default diagnosis for those who have been affected by trauma. The psychological problems of combat veterans, for example, are now almost exclusively seen in terms of PTSD, even though other psychosocial problems, such as alcohol abuse, aggression, difficulties in employment or relationship breakdown may be more significant. It is a mistake to sweep all post-trauma psychological reactions into one simple category, or to assume that if someone shows PTSD symptoms then nothing more needs to be done but treat the person's PTSD. The usefulness of the diagnosis lies in the response that Janine had: that it helped her make sense of what was happening to her and provided her with a way of moving on. But we must not forget both the person and the context. The many stories in this book illustrate the uniqueness of the individual response, and in the next chapter we will spend some time with Richard, whom we met briefly in Chapter 1, as he recovers from his awful experiences in the 2007 Grayrigg rail crash.

Chapter 5: Richard's story

Richard Blakemore was on the Virgin Pendolino train that was derailed at Grayrigg, Cumbria on 23 February 2007. I gave a brief account of the event at the beginning of this book. In this chapter I will describe in greater detail what happened and how Richard was affected by the experience. His story illustrates how a sudden-onset trauma can disrupt someone's life, however strong or resolute they may be. Every story is unique, yet in all traumatic experiences there are common factors:

- The explosive impact of the experience on the senses.

- The individual's helplessness, their being at the mercy of events outside their control.

- The way the body responds automatically, activating innate survival reactions.

- Fear, in particular the awareness of death.

- An initial appraisal of what is thought to be happening.

- The way personality and personal history affect a person's response.

- Secondary appraisal, leading to feelings like anger, guilt.

These are all factors that I have introduced and discussed in the previous chapters. They come together, some of them at least, in Richard's story. What happens in the maelstrom of trauma and in the moments that follow lays down a legacy for future experience. For some, this includes significant psychological problems. A better understanding of what happens at the time can help prevent those problems becoming entrenched and pervasive. We will see how, in Richard's case, a diagnosis of post-traumatic stress disorder (PTSD) proved helpful in terms of his understanding his problems and setting him on a path to recovery. As with Janine in the previous chapter, Richard's personality and personal history also played a significant part.

I first met Richard in November 2009 at my home in North Oxford. He was coming to the end of a course of psychological therapy with a psychologist friend of mine and, having been informed what this book was about, agreed to meet me. Richard looked younger than his fifty-six years, with a fit, lean figure that may have had something to do with his hobby of mountaineering and rock climbing. When describing the accident, I noticed that he chose his words with care, determined to give as accurate an account as possible. Like many other people I have seen who have undergone similar experiences, Richard played down any sense of his having acted bravely or heroically. 'This is just what I did,' he seemed to say. 'No more, no less.'

At the time of the accident Richard had started working as an economist with the Natural Environment Research Council. He was in London attending various meetings and had arranged some time away with friends in Scotland, a weekend walking and climbing in the hills. He caught the fast train from Euston to Glasgow. He took a seat in the middle of the front carriage, the carriage that was to be derailed. Interestingly, the possibility of an accident was on his mind before he boarded the train.

'I remember thinking as I was walking down the platform, if there was a derailment which carriage would be best to be in and for some reason I thought the front carriage would probably be; it would plough through and it would be the ones behind that would start swinging from side to side.'

'So you actually had that thought?'

'I had thought about railway crashes and derailments for some time. I used to commute in and out of London. I was about two trains behind the 125 that was involved in the head-on collision just outside Paddington. I also remember reading an article by Nina Bawden, who was involved in the Potters Bar crash where her husband died. She was describing how she was sitting with her back to the engine and Austen, her husband, was facing the engine at the time of the crash. At impact, he went flying over her head. He died and she lived.'

Richard made a point of taking a seat that faced away from the direction of travel. I mention this as it shows that, at some level, he was aware of the possibility of a train crash. However, this was not the keyed-up state of mind that Rachel North was in when the bomb exploded in the tube (see Chapter 2). It was more a matter of limiting unnecessary risks. As a mountaineer, he said, 'you do get into a habit of doing things that maximize your chances of survival if you are ever in a tricky situation'. The derailment took him by surprise, however, and it is doubtful that his choice of seat had any effect on his wellbeing in this instance.

In Chapter 1 I described how Richard registered the changing vibration of the train and how he knew that it was no longer running on the rails. He felt around the seat for something to hold onto but very soon he was being thrown around like the other passengers, bouncing off the seats and being hit by flying objects. The train went completely dark. He realized that it had derailed (an accurate primary appraisal) and that he could do nothing until it came to a halt (a sense of helplessness). When the train finally was still, Richard was trapped under two people. This was the point that he thought of Hillsborough, the 1989 disaster in which many football fans were crushed to death during a Liverpool–Nottingham Forest FA Cup semi-final. Determined not to die from suffocation, Richard extricated himself, with some difficulty, from under the two people. His immediate feeling was huge relief at being alive. Richard then asked if he could help the people whom he had been under. But a man nearby, who turned out to be a relative of one of the people, thought it was best to wait until the emergency services arrived. Richard then heard a woman crying out, further down the carriage, and went to see if he could help her. This is how he described the event to me.

> The carriage is on its side, luggage is strewn all over the place. I managed to clamber over seats and debris to reach the lady who was calling out. She was on the floor and the main reason for her distress was that her husband, who was a large man, was lying on top of her and he was in turn wedged in position by a rack that had come loose. I remember kneeling down alongside her holding her hand and talking to her, and trying to calm her and telling her she would be OK. And, as I was doing that, I was looking at her husband's position. The remains of the luggage rack was trapping him. I thought that I might be able to shift that and then he'd be able to move and then his wife would be very much more comfortable.

Having something to do in the midst of a trauma is considered, by some, to protect against later problems. It is seen as a beneficial way of discharging the pent-up energy in the body that the trauma has evoked. For many people, however, action is simply impossible and they are left with a residue of 'undischarged energy' that, some theorists believe, remains in the body and the brain to trouble them later. I think this idea may have some value, although 'undischarged energy' is a vague term. Undoubtedly, Richard's first actions counteracted his initial sense of helplessness and, psychologically, that must have been beneficial. But then the pain struck.

> All of a sudden this huge pain hit me on the left side of my chest, like nothing that I have ever experienced before, and (I thought) well, this is truly stupid to have survived the rail crash, freed myself from the position where I've been trapped, try to help someone and then have a heart attack. This is not how it's supposed to go.

The pain was so severe that Richard thought he was having a heart attack. Later, he found out that one of the ribs that had been broken in the crash had punctured his lung and the lung had collapsed. Now he was no longer able to move around and help others. He had simply to wait for help himself. Moreover, the relief at surviving had been transformed into the fear of possibly dying. Helplessness and fear had returned. Richard lay in the dark in pain, trying to stay calm. Everyone in the carriage remained quiet, he told me. There was no panic or screaming. Eventually, he heard voices outside the carriage. A strong torch beam appeared and a voice said, 'Hello in there', or words to that effect. It was a great relief to Richard to realize that rescue was on hand. The rescuers went methodically through the carriage, assessing how bad the injuries were.

> [Then began] the slow process of getting people off the carriage, and when it came to my turn, I remember the rescuer asking me if I thought I could get out on my own. I explained to him that I had this chest pain and we had a discussion about whether I had any history of heart disease. And so, being an 'all right' sort of chap, I said I can do this on my own.

Despite severe pain, Richard clambered along the carriage and got to the end. There he saw that the carriage had completely detached from all the other carriages.

> . . . you get to the communicating door between the carriages and you are actually about six feet in the air at this point. I remember a group of men standing with their arms up ready to catch people. It was so nice to see these people and just to experience their touch.

Richard was carried out of the train to a barn that was being used as a field hospital. Fortunately, a doctor accurately diagnosed his problem. He had suffered a serious and life-threatening condition known as a tension pneumothorax. Whenever he breathed in, air leaked into the pleural cavity and could not return to the lung. Without speedy treatment there was a risk of the other lung collapsing and/or heart failure. He was given a massive shot of morphine. The doctor put a pipe through his chest and released the pressure that had built up in the lung. From there he was taken by helicopter to Preston Royal Hospital to begin the long process of physical and psychological recovery.

In our interview I asked Richard if he could tell me what the worst moments were up to the point of being rescued. I was interested in discovering what might have affected him most about the experience and how that might relate to what happened later. He described three particularly bad moments.

> Firstly, the realization that the train had left the rails and that something serious was happening. [I was] being thrown around the carriage, and [felt] the impact on various parts of my body. Just knowing there was nothing you could do about it. You're helpless. The second was . . . feeling completely trapped under what seemed to me like a huge weight, and thoughts of Hillsborough going through my mind. I remember thinking of my wife and daughter, and thinking, 'I'm not going to let this happen. I'm going to get out of this.' The third moment was when my lung collapsed. I didn't know what was going on and thought I was having a heart attack. There was that uncertainty.

These worst moments capture Richard's very real fear of dying, his feelings of complete helplessness, and his uncertainty about what the outcome would be. They confirm that the trauma would meet the defining criteria for the diagnosis of PTSD, although that diagnosis would not be made until months later. What else does Richard's experience tell us? The crash itself was an extraordinary event, powerful and frightening, assailing all the senses.

The physicality of it comes out in his account. We get glimpses of the part played by Richard's personality too. Strikingly, he had been aware of the possibility of a crash before he got on the train. He had chosen his seat with that in mind, although in the end this made no difference to what happened. But he was, in a sense, generally prepared for something to go wrong. He explained this in terms of his mountaineering background, how he was used to estimating risk. This preparation also points to a person who likes being in control, something Richard confirmed later in the interview. However, in the end he had no means of controlling the event or how it impacted on him, at least at first.

I went on to ask Richard about his recovery. He spent ten days in a hospital in Preston, during which time his whole body stiffened up and spectacular bruising developed all along one side of his body. He had a chest-drain inserted. He had difficulty walking even a few yards to the bathroom but, despite the pain and the problems, he maintained a positive attitude that helped him to cope. He attributed this to his family background.

> 'I'm alive and that's what matters. I come from a family where the tradition has always been you just get on with things. My grandfather, for example, was interned in Hong Kong by the Japanese in the Second World War . . . He lost a huge amount of weight but he survived. And he got on with his life.'
>
> 'So this was the philosophy which you inherited?'
>
> 'That is the philosophy, the attitudes that I have grown up with . . . It's the attitude of people who enjoy getting into the mountains, certainly rock climbing. You tend to have a fairly dry, sometimes rather black, sense of humour about adversity. Understatement is always preferred to overstatement. So yes, I felt I had survived this and I wanted to make a full recovery. I didn't want to let the fact that I happened to be involved in this crash mess up the rest of my life.'

Richard's physical recovery continued after he was discharged. But at home he developed intense pains in his shoulders and arms, particularly at night. These worsened and eventually he was diagnosed with Acute Brachial Neuritis, an autoimmune condition that may sometimes be triggered by trauma. Antibodies attack the body's nervous system, causing damage to the nerves. Although this condition almost always improves over time, in the acute stage it is extremely painful and debilitating. In Richard's case, he required regular physiotherapy and it took almost a year for the nerves to recover. By the time of our interview, two-and-a-half years later, he told me he was about 95 per cent physically recovered. This illustrates how one major trauma can lead to others, especially if there are physical problems that require treatment. Jo, a young woman I assessed in my practice, had survived a horrific car accident in which all her limbs were badly fractured. She endured six years of often painful and not always successful operations, as well as uncertainty about whether she might be handicapped for life. Fortunately, through her determination and the doctors' skill, she made a very good recovery. For her, the accident was not the trauma of the crash itself, as she was unconscious and had no memory of it, but the consequences of the crash. Like Richard, she had a positive attitude, focusing firmly on getting better, which undoubtedly helped her (see Chapter 18).

I asked Richard about the psychological problems he had had after the crash, how they had affected him, and what help he had received.

I remember seeing my GP shortly after I came home after the crash. I was having the dressings changed on a wound and we discussed PTSD. At the time, I remember saying that I don't want to see psychologists at the moment . . . I just wanted to focus on physical rehabilitation at first. There is only so much that you can cope with. Then if it turns out that there are psychological issues, we'll address those at a later date.

GPs are more aware than they used to be of psychological problems arising out of trauma. Specialist help may be needed. But there is the question of timing. I think Richard was absolutely right to concentrate on his physical recovery, especially as only three weeks had elapsed since the accident when he visited his GP. The need in that situation is to let the body recover; attempting to work on psychological problems adds an unnecessary strain. It is also the case that many people will improve psychologically with the passage of time, which is why a diagnosis of PTSD cannot be made until at least a month has elapsed after the trauma. Some six or seven weeks after the crash, Richard felt well enough to return to work.

> My place of work was the centre of Swindon, which was right next to the railway station. The only sensible way of travelling from where I lived was by train . . . I went to Didcot and changed [trains]. Unfortunately it was also the stretch of line where the 125s tend to go at maximum speed. Brunel built that bit absolutely dead straight apart from a couple of little wiggles in the middle which always make the train kind of shake and shudder. You are hurtling along at about 125 miles per hour in a train that does not feel quite as solid as a Pendolino. I went back to work just after Easter and I was increasingly aware that I was just not enjoying the experience of travelling by train.

The last sentence is characteristically understated. Richard found travelling by train extremely hard to do. But he was strongly motivated to get back to work and to normality. I asked him how he had first got back on a train.

> 'I remember standing on the platform when the train came in, thinking "Am I really going to do this?"'
> 'Sort of apprehension?'
> 'Yes. And then my feet started to take me towards the

door of the carriage, even though the mind was still kind of hovering a few yards away down the platform.'

Richard got on the train and completed the journey, although he felt very uncomfortable throughout. That journey, and subsequent train journeys, brought back memories of the train crash. I asked him what it felt like when he was on the train.

'[I was] just looking at other people on the train and thinking, "My God, how can you be so relaxed sitting on this train? You just have no idea of what could happen."'

'Was it particularly bad when the train speeded up?'

'I would say at about 60 miles per hour I would just start tensing up. And then there are a couple of sections on the line between Didcot and Swindon where the train will vibrate quite markedly and every time it went though those sections you were going back to that night.'

'Going back in what way?'

'This could happen again.'

'A thought? Or was it actually an image, a visual memory or . . .?'

'I think there are a number of memories. It's the darkness, the bodies lying on top of me, and also the kind of sensual memory, the feeling of being in the darkness, flying though a carriage and just being hit violently. And just a fear that it would happen again.'

What Richard experienced on the train was a hyper-aroused state caused by the trauma of the accident and by the fact that he was continually exposed to reminders of it on his daily journey to work. Memories came back to him, often vividly, in the form of images or flashbacks. Nevertheless, he persisted, and for some three months he travelled to and from work by train. He hoped that his anxiety would lessen as time passed. But it did not. Many people believe – or, like Richard, *hope* – that by forcing themselves repeatedly into a situation that provokes fear and anxiety, they will overcome their fears. In fact, some therapies for PTSD are based on that premise, which is sometimes called exposure treatment (see Chapter 13). But it is not exposure, per se, that is important; it is the way exposure occurs and how the experience is registered in the mind that is crucial to recovery. Repeatedly going through awful anxiety twice a day can in fact reinforce fears, constituting a *re*-traumatization, which is probably what happened in Richard's case. This can lead to feelings of shame, guilt or anger, as the failure to recover is seen as a personal failing (secondary appraisal). When Richard returned to his GP about three months after the first appointment, he was in a bad state.

> When we started talking about travelling by train, I just started crying in the surgery. We both realized that a lot of psychological stuff had been parked away in the corner of the brain and it was probably about time to start to deal with it.

Richard had been trying hard to lead as normal a life as possible. But the strain of travelling by train was making matters worse. He had a heightened awareness of the possibility of another accident happening. Moreover, he was feeling generally hyped up, easily startled by sudden noises and prone to irritability. His concentration was poor and at work he found that he had difficulty making decisions. He felt distanced from other people, tense, irritable and increasingly ill-at-ease. All these are symptoms of post-traumatic stress disorder (PTSD). A major problem for Richard was that he could not prevent the flashbacks from happening. For someone who was determined to get back to normal this was particularly frustrating. I asked him if he knew what the flashback images were.

> 'Obviously I knew I was remembering these events. What I didn't know was how to control these memories.'

'So you felt out of control?'

'Yes.'

'I guess that was difficult because most people find it difficult if they are out of control.'

'I wouldn't call myself a complete control freak, but I do like to be in control.'

In other words, Richard was again experiencing the helplessness he felt on the train, only this time there was no respite, no rescuers to help him get out. Every train journey was fraught. Relaxation was impossible.

You are usually relaxed on a train. That is one of the reasons to travel by train rather than drive. You can just sit back and relax and read the paper, whereas in a car, particularly if you're driving, you have to be alert. There has to be some level of stress. It's a very sudden switch in a train accident, from the state of high level of relaxation, to something completely different.

Fortunately, Richard's GP realized that he needed psychological help and referred him to a clinical psychologist experienced in treating people who have been through trauma. This was when he embarked on a course of psychological therapy that was to help him recover from his PTSD symptoms. I will describe Richard's therapy in subsequent chapters.

The experience of being in a major trauma

Richard's account of his experiences in the Grayrigg rail crash brings out how a sudden and traumatic event can change someone's life. It also illustrates that, even if one is a resourceful and determined person, someone who, in Richard's case, was used to taking risks, and someone with a family tradition of coping in difficult circumstances, it is sometimes impossible to avoid experiencing significant psychological problems. However hard one tries, the problems persist and may even get worse. The moral view held by some that emotional problems should be kept to oneself and dealt with by force of will (stiff upper lip) underestimates the powerful emotional pull that trauma can have. In fact, sometimes this attitude can make matters worse, for persistent failure to control one's emotions is then attributed to personal failings. Self-criticism and shame are added to anxiety and stress. However, I do not want to underestimate the qualities of resourcefulness and determination that Richard clearly had. These can be helpful in treatment where they are properly applied. They helped him in the long recovery from Acute Brachial Neuritis. But it can be difficult, if not impossible, to recover psychologically on one's own, especially if one has little understanding of what the emotions being experienced are about and why they keep reoccurring. We can see that Richard's vivid, distressing memories on the train were symptoms of PTSD, and that, in the 'right' circumstances, these memories were evoked, whatever he tried to do. Richard, an intelligent, determined and resourceful person, found that these qualities alone were not sufficient for him to recover. It was only when he sought help from a clinical psychologist that he was able to put these qualities to work, as we shall see in a later chapter.

Part 2
Aftershocks

Chapter 6: Flashbacks

A Saturday afternoon in October 1989. A police van is parked on the London Road in Headington, Oxford. The driver of the van is PC Graeme Cairns. His sergeant is next to him on the front seat, and in the back are four police officers. They are on duty, doing what police officers do a great deal of, waiting. There is a rap at the window. Graeme Cairns winds it down. 'Very sorry to trouble you,' says a man, 'but there's a bloke with a pistol in the Britannia public house. He's got it stuck in his belt.' This is not long after the Hungerford massacre in which sixteen people were killed and fifteen wounded by a lone gunman, Michael Ryan, who then killed himself. The police are understandably wary about men with guns. Another knock on the window and another man says, 'Terribly sorry but I just saw a man with a gun go into the men's toilets over there.' He points to the public toilets just a few feet away from the van and, as he does so, a man emerges carrying what looks like a Colt .45 semiautomatic pistol in his hand. It is pointed downwards at an angle to the road. Graeme feels the van suddenly jerk as the officers in the back all fall to the floor. The sergeant next to him drops into the foot well. He is left facing the man with a gun.

I met Graeme Cairns in August 2009, twenty years after the incident. He had responded to my request to interview police officers that had been through trauma. Because I had worked in the Thames Valley Police as their psychologist for ten years, I was familiar with the sorts of encounters that police officers have in the course of their work, though men brandishing guns are fortunately rare. Despite the fact that the incident occurred long ago, it was still vivid in Graeme's mind. This is how he described what happened next.

> So I sit there. 'Oh, fuck, what am I going to do? There is a man stood at the side of the road with a gun. I haven't

got a gun. What shall I do? I know what I'll do. I'll run him over.' So I aimed the van at him and, by the time I had revved it up, he's on the pavement on the other side of the road, still with gun in hand. What I wanted to do is drive the van and put him through the window that he was stood next to because I really didn't want to get shot or anybody else to get shot. I couldn't do that because it was a fish-and-chip shop. There was about eight or ten people in this fish-and-chip shop, and putting somebody through the window could have done all sorts of horrible things, like hot fats and fires. It was a nightmare scenario. My heart was racing and I'm thinking: 'What do I do now?'

So I aimed the van at him. I dropped the clutch. I revved the van to the fullest extent that it would go, thinking; 'If he pulls the gun up and pops a shot off, then at least there would be enough momentum in the motor to carry the van forward and take him out and he won't be able to do any more damage.' I shouted in my loudest police voice, 'Drop it! Drop it!' He looked up like a startled rabbit and luckily the gun stayed down, and he did drop it. I shouted, 'Stand back! Stand back!' And then, after what seemed like a hundred years, Duggie from the back of the van jumped out and grabbed his left arm, and the next thing I know, it's like a cartoon, this bloke is in mid-air horizontal, and by the time he hits the ground, everybody else from the back of the van was out and on top of him. By this stage I was staring at the gun on the road, and I knew if it wasn't in his hands, I was safe. I got out and picked up the gun. It wasn't heavy enough to be a proper pistol. It was some sort of flash water pistol. You couldn't tell until you picked it up.

Although the incident has elements of farce, it was not how Graeme Cairns experienced it at the time. It shook him up badly. After all, he had come very close to killing a man. The fact that all the man had was a water pistol made it worse. Had he driven the van into him and killed him, he would have been arrested and subjected to a police investigation. He might well have been suspended or lost his job. It would have been all over the papers. As he put it to me, he had joined the police to help people, not to kill them. That this trauma was not acted out to completion did not diminish its capacity to affect Graeme. Just a couple of weeks later he was on duty, driving with his Chief Inspector, when they received a call from the control room, a report of men unloading shotguns in Jersey Road in the Rosehill area of Oxford. From the address, Graeme knew that these were likely to be stock-car racers undoing their roll cages, which had bits of scaffolding poles that in the dark could be mistaken for a shotgun. Yet although he knew this, he found himself panicking.

All I wanted to do was to shout '10–9, 10–9', which is the police radio code for 'Emergency. Get help here now.' [I had] an overwhelming urge to shout, 'Help! Help!' Then I thought, 'Don't be silly, I'm not in any danger.' But, as I got closer and closer, the urge got worse and worse. It was awful. [I was thinking] 'I don't want to do this, but I've got to go.' I got there and sure enough it was the lads unloading scaffolding poles from their lorry to the cars and vice versa. We had a chat and laugh about what somebody had reported. Then, as I was going back to the car, it all went a bit peculiar. It was like the road moved. I'm looking up Jersey Road and all of a sudden there is another road coming off Jersey Road, which I knew wasn't there. And there, standing in the middle of the road, was this man with a gun. It was weird. It was totally weird. Hang on a minute, that's not there. But it *is* there. I could see this man. I could see this street. I could see the same man I saw at Headington, with a gun. I thought, 'What's going on here?' I was totally and utterly confused . . . There was this street coming out of nowhere . . . I'd still got – what do you call it? – insight

that this was reality and that wasn't. But it was like so real
and what it was doing there, I couldn't tell you.

Graeme had experienced a flashback. In his case it took the form
of a vivid image of the traumatic incident two weeks earlier. The
flashback was brief, lasting only a second or two. It came on him
unawares. It felt real, although in a part of his mind he knew that it
could not be. It evoked the emotions, the panic and stress, he had
previously experienced. And the fact that it had happened worried
him considerably, for he had no idea what it was or if it might
presage something worse. Those who are unfortunate enough to
experience flashbacks after trauma find them very disturbing. In
Chapter 2 I described Elaine's flashback to the image of Stan,
the man in the bombed carriage with his arm stretched out. Until
her therapist worked out what had triggered it, Elaine could not
understand why it should happen, and the fact that it seemed to
come out of the blue made it worse, since she did not know how to
prevent it. The strangeness of flashbacks, the fact that they re-evoke
powerful, often frightening feelings, and their apparent random-
ness, make them one of the most unwelcome legacies of trauma.
A flashback is a form of re-experiencing the trauma, which is one
of the defining symptoms of PTSD, and so it is often equated with
the diagnosis. However, not all flashbacks lead to PTSD; some
will occur early on after the trauma and disappear quite quickly.
Nor do all PTSD sufferers experience actual flashbacks. In many,
the sense of re-experiencing the trauma occurs not in the form of a
sudden, unexpected flashback, but when the individual is asked to
recall the event, or is reminded of it by something on the radio or
television, for instance. In these cases, the person knows that he or
she is recalling the event. The sense of involuntarily being thrust
into the past is absent.

In this chapter I will explain what flashbacks are, how and when
they arise, how common they are, what functions they appear to
serve, whether they are actual memories of the trauma or something more, and where they fit in the underlying neurobiology

of traumatic memory. I will only briefly refer to the psychological treatment of flashbacks, important as it is, as I cover that in Chapters 13 and 14.

The origins of the term 'flashback'

The word 'flashback' first appeared at the beginning of the twentieth century, when it was used to describe a misfiring in a test tube, a flame moving rapidly back through a combustible vapour, creating an explosion ('flashing back'). In the 1960s, when the effects of hallucinogenic drugs were first properly studied, the word was adopted to describe powerful visual experiences that some drug takers had after the drugs had left the system. These were intrusive and frightening images that were similar, but not necessarily identical, to the drug-induced hallucinations themselves. Today we are familiar with a different meaning of the word 'flashback' from films, where it refers to the way the real-time story is interrupted by a replay of events in the past. This cinematic device is a way of looking back to show what actually happened, sometimes in brief episodes or in extended narrative that takes up the whole film, such as in *Brideshead Revisited* or *Little Big Man*. In this colloquial usage of the term it refers to any form of memory or replay. In trauma it has a more specific meaning. Flashback captures the sense of being suddenly and unwillingly catapulted back into the past in the form of a memory that is not like normal memory but more sensory, vivid and immediate. It has also prompted psychologists to think about traumatic memory and suggest that it may involve different processes than occur in normal memory.

Characteristics of flashbacks

Flashbacks are examples of *involuntary memory* (sometimes also called *intrusive memory*). Most of us experience times when our mind wanders and unexpected memories surface. They tend to be about ordinary things, people we know, objects or activities. They occur more commonly when people are in an unfocused state, sitting in a boring meeting or relaxing on the sofa; that is, when the individual's attention is not taken up with the demands of everyday life. Because these involuntary memories are ordinary and common, we tend not to attach much importance to them. Sometimes an involuntary memory may be intense and highly pleasurable. Perhaps the most famous occurs in Marcel Proust's novel *À la Recherche du Temps Perdu*, where the narrator has a sudden recollection of his childhood at Combray, stimulated by the taste of a biscuit (a *'petite madeleine'*) dunked in a cup of tea. But these intensely pleasurable flashbacks are rare. Most involuntary memories are emotionally neutral.

Traumatic flashbacks, by definition, must occur after a traumatic event. They stand out from other involuntary memories in that they tend to be repetitive, unwanted and distressing. They intrude into consciousness often, in brief spurts of vivid sensory imagery. Quite by chance I experienced flashbacks as I was researching this chapter. My wife and I were staying with my elder daughter, Kate, while building work was being done at our house. Early one morning the vet phoned and Kate answered. I was seated nearby at the dining table. Suddenly, Kate broke out into violent sobs and cried out, 'Smudge is dead!' Smudge was one of her two lovely, young cats. He had been killed on the road and his body placed at the door of the vet's. Like Kate, I was shocked and distressed at the news. Later that morning I had arranged to interview someone for this book. During the time of the interview, which lasted about an hour, my mind would flashback to that moment when Kate cried out. The image would occur, brief and vivid. I would suppress it and it would occur again a few minutes later. I must have experienced it a dozen times in the hour the interview lasted. It was a striking personal lesson on the intrusiveness of flashbacks and their capacity to infiltrate consciousness.

Characteristically, flashbacks distort the normal perception of time and place, as happened to PC Graeme Cairns, who saw a street in Headington while in the Rosehill area of Oxford. They

TO HELL AND BACK   87

may also distort a person's normal sense of themselves (for example, by creating a feeling of being dissociated from present surroundings), of things not being real or of feeling 'not real' oneself. Occasionally, a flashback can be powerful enough for someone to lose all connection with present-day reality for a time. This happened to George, a survivor of the 2005 London bombings (see Chapter 2). He was at his office Christmas party about eighteen months after the bombings, talking to a colleague. The party was being held in a nightclub, a dark room with low ceilings, and there were about 200 people crammed into the room. George told me what happened to him.

'It was half seven or eight o'clock. I'd had no more than two glasses of wine, if that. I was on my feet, talking to different people and ended up talking to L, a nice lady. After that, bang. The next thing I know I'm sitting on a bench and there is a woman and a bloke in green overalls sitting opposite me. I thought, "These are ambulance people. What the hell am I doing here?" It turns out – and they tell me this on the way to Outpatients – that as I'm talking to L, almost in mid-sentence, I stop talking, eyes wide open, and they couldn't get through.'

'And you had no recollection of that?'

'No. Apparently I didn't sit down or fall down. I walked out. They are talking to me. No response. And the next thing I know is that I am sitting on the bench and there are these two people.'

George had blanked out. He came round outside the club with no recollection of what had happened or any sense of time having past. He was told about forty-five minutes passed between the conversation taking place and his memory returning. He was taken to Charing Cross Hospital where a medical assessment was carried out but no physical cause was found for his amnesia. The most likely explanation is that George had experienced an extreme dissociative state, brought on by the similarity between his being in a crush of people in a dark, low-ceilinged room (the nightclub) and the tube carriage that he had been in when the bomb went off. Another likely trigger was that he had been talking to 'L' about his experiences in the London bombings. Fortunately, complete amnesia after a psychological trauma is rare. In the vast majority of cases people do not completely lose their sense of themselves or their surroundings. A flashback is most commonly brief, lasting perhaps just a few seconds. But although it may be over quickly, the feelings provoked by it can persist for some time afterwards.

The most common flashbacks are visual ones. One series of research studies of intrusions experienced after trauma showed that between 70 per cent and 97 per cent were visual. Flashbacks can also be experienced through other senses. Smell is a potent trigger. Police officers have the unenviable job of breaking into a room when a strange smell suggests that something horrible is in there. Andy, another police officer I interviewed for this book, was called with a colleague to a multiple-occupancy house in Cowley, Oxford. The man who rented the room concerned had not been seen for some time. It was a very hot day and a distinct, unpleasant smell was coming from it. They broke into the room, which, Andy recollected, was brightly lit, with everything tidy and ordered. In the bed, under the covers, was a body, and when they pulled back the bedclothes, the smell was so horrendous that his colleague ran out of the room to be sick. Two days later, Andy was passing a butcher's shop in Witney when suddenly his mouth was full of vomit and he could vividly smell again the decomposing body in Cowley. The smell of the raw meat had triggered a flashback and his body had reacted automatically, making him sick. Andy did not make a connection with the previous incident until after he had been sick, indicating again that flashbacks can be provoked without conscious knowledge of the cause.

Not all traumas lead to flashbacks. Some traumas, such as road accidents, can lead to loss of consciousness, sometimes for a prolonged period. People then report a loss of memory of both the event itself and of a period of time before it (this is known as retrograde amnesia). In such cases, flashbacks do not occur or, if they do, are in response to either other traumatic events around the incident, such as later hospitalization, or to being told what happened. In theory, given that a flashback is a form of memory, if there is no memory, there can be no flashback. But it is not always that straightforward, as I shall explain later. Studies of the numbers of people reporting flashbacks after trauma (excluding those who lost consciousness) indicate a range of figures, from very high rates (60–80 per cent) in veterans of major conflicts, to less than 2 per cent in experimental studies of students where the 'trauma' is the experience of watching a film of distressing and frightening events. When people are divided into those who developed PTSD after trauma and those who did not, the research evidence shows that flashbacks are consistently higher in the PTSD group. Even so the figures are low. One study of PTSD sufferers reported that only about 10 per cent experienced actual, vivid flashbacks.

Why do flashbacks occur?

The psychologist Nick Grey, who has studied flashbacks extensively and treated many PTSD patients, told me that practically everyone who has been in a major trauma has episodes of vivid memory when, for a moment, it seems as though the experience is being relived. But for many these episodes are not particularly intense, and few have a full flashback. In other words, people experience a sense of 'nowness' along a continuum, with some hardly feeling as though it is happening again and others feeling they are thrust right back into the heart of the trauma. Nick Grey also pointed out to me that we often experience intrusive memories after highly pleasurable events, such as weddings or graduations. The difference is that we tend to engage with them, talking to others about them or looking at photo albums, for instance. In this way, the intrusions become consolidated into our normal autobiographical memory. We do not do the same with traumatic intrusions. In my clinical work, I found that people who had been through trauma almost always reported trauma memories, some of which could be vivid and distressing, just like a flashback. The difference was that they did not come out of the blue but only when the individual was asked to remember the experience, or was reminded of it by, say, something heard on the radio or television.

A flashback appears to come out of the blue but, as we saw with both Elaine and Andy, with careful analysis triggers can usually be identified. These are almost always sensory cues. These cues bypass verbal memory, which is why Andy did not register the connection of the smell of meat to the smell of the decomposing body until after he had reacted by being sick. Sometimes the re-experiencing of similar emotions, such as intense fear, prompts the trauma memory and sets off a flashback. Sensory cues and strong emotions both relate to the parts of the brain that responded automatically when the trauma happened, the amygdala in the limbic system, in particular (see Chapter 3). This has led to a belief that there is an intensity about major traumas that prevents their memory from being fully consolidated in verbal form. Let me use a simple example to clarify this distinction. Yesterday I went to Notting Hill Gate in London to interview a journalist for this book. We met in a café, which was not ideal for the recording as there was a lot of background noise. But it was a very helpful meeting. After the meeting I made a few notes about it – not many, as the interview was recorded – and when I got back home I told my wife about it. In other words, I consolidated the memory in my mind, fitting it into existing structures of my work and my life in general. It slotted easily into my normal autobiographical memory. Suppose, however, a bomb had exploded in the café, wreaking havoc on all of us there, killing and wounding people. I am overwhelmed by horrifying, frightening and unfamiliar sights and sounds. The experience will still be part of my autobiographical memory, of course. But I cannot so easily consolidate it into my normal memory because of its highly charged nature. The experience is still continuing, reverberating in my brain; the flashbacks I experience after it are sharp spikes of unconsolidated memory. This is what happened when Kate told me about Smudge's death. In that case, the intrusive images declined over time and disappeared altogether in a few days, as did the immediate distress. Cats die on the road. Sadly, that is not unusual, and I now incorporate the death of poor Smudge into my autobiographical memory without difficulty. The conclusion is that, when an experience is highly traumatic, particularly when it comes without warning and is extraordinary, flashbacks are to be expected, certainly in the immediate aftermath and perhaps for some time afterwards.

Why do flashbacks persist long after the event has passed?

The idea that the event is still reverberating in the brain might explain the immediate occurrence of flashbacks, but it doesn't tell us why they continue long after the event, sometimes even years after. After all, when a burglar alarm is triggered, we can switch it off and reset it. Why does that not happen in the brain? The truth is that for the majority of people it does. Flashbacks occur only in a minority of those who have been through trauma. Most incorporate the experience successfully into autobiographical memory. Later memories can still be distressing, without having the vivid, present-day quality of a flashback. To explain why some people continue to experience traumatic flashbacks for a long time after the trauma, psychologists have proposed that extreme levels of arousal disrupt normal memory processing, in particular the transition of memories from their raw, immediate, sensory form into a more verbal and contextualized form. Research has shown that, during highly stressful events, the alarm system of the brain – the limbic system and the amygdala in particular – is overwhelmed by stimulation, whereas the hippocampus, the site of verbal learning, is suppressed. This effectively prevents memories from being registered in terms of time, place and context, which is what would happen normally. As Nick Grey told me, 'There is no "time code" on the memory that tells the individual that the event is in the past.' Hence the sense of 'nowness' and the reactivation of the emotions originally experienced.

Psychologists investigating trauma memory have suggested that two separate memory systems explain why flashbacks occur. Sensory and perceptual images are stored at a sub-cortical level in the brain and cannot be accessed voluntarily. They can be triggered automatically by sensory cues. This is exactly what happens when a flashback occurs. Neurons at a sub-cortical level are fired in the brain, just as happened during the trauma itself. They have not been processed in verbal memory. This would explain the way they arise without our willing them, and why they are so intense. Other memories – for example, the recollection of an experience in childhood, or remembering where one put the car keys – are stored at a higher cortical level and involve more than sensory details. The original experiences that gave rise to the memory have been processed verbally and consolidated into autobiographical memory. Although we can try to evoke sensory details, it is more difficult to do, and such memories will not have the intensity of a flashback. But why, given that people are distressed by flashbacks and do not want to have them, are these memories not processed in the same way as other memories?

One of therapies for trauma survivors experiencing flashbacks is called prolonged exposure (I'll address this therapy in more detail in Chapter 13). In this approach the patient is asked to describe the traumatic experience to the therapist in as much detail as possible, and to allow the emotions felt at the time to be re-experienced. Then the process is gone through again, and then again, and then again. Sometimes the session is recorded and the patient asked to listen to the recording repeatedly at home. There is more to the therapy than this, but verbalization and re-experiencing are central. The treatment works, it is believed, by a forced habituation, the feelings losing their power from repetition. It is a direct attempt to shift the memory, to process it verbally, and bring it into normal autobiographical memory. I used this method with Janine and it worked. In her characteristically direct way she told me I had 'hammered' it out of her. The process was hard on her emotionally, but it resulted in a marked decline in her flashbacks.

Before treatment, people's usual response to flashbacks is to try to suppress them or to avoid likely triggers – for example, by not talking to others about the trauma, or refusing to revisit the place where the trauma occurred. The reason for this is obvious: the flashback is upsetting, often inducing high anxiety and other unpleasant emotions. No one wants to have such feelings. But suppression and avoidance, understandable as they are, serve to prolong the flashbacks because they prevent the memory from being processed. People may also try to escape the high arousal of flashback memories by other methods of suppression, notably the use of alcohol and recreational drugs. These too interfere with memory processing. Flashbacks are spikes of raw, unconsolidated memory, brought about by the extreme levels of arousal the trauma produced. It is as though basic biology suddenly takes over and we are no longer protected by the sophisticated ways we have learned to engage with the world. For a brief moment our protective clothing has gone and we are caught naked and shivering.

Replays of the original trauma

If flashbacks are raw spikes of unconsolidated memory, are they simple replays of the original event, or something more? People certainly report feeling that the experience is being replayed, as Graeme did when he saw the man with the gun. Yet flashbacks can incorporate material that was not part of the original trauma. It is also possible for a flashback image to represent what *might have* happened, rather than simply what did happen. A woman trapped in a burning carriage in a rail crash imagined her clothes being burnt, and doctors trying to separate her clothes from her skin on the operating table. This never happened, yet she continued to experience this image for years after the event. Where people have endured traumas over a long period, recall may be in the form of a composite series of images, rather than a single instance. In fact, a flashback, indeed any form of remembering, is not like a filmed sequence running through our mind, despite Janine's striking videocassette analogy (Chapter 4). Memory is an active process of reconstructing reality. We selectively attend to, and therefore recall, what matters to us; we can never see or recall everything. Flashbacks are distinctive not so much because they are necessarily more accurate than other memories, but because they are vivid and distressing. They tend to reflect the worst moments in the trauma, the times when emotions are particularly intense, often called 'hotspots'. In one research study, 79 per cent of people's flashbacks were of such 'hotspot' moments. Other studies have shown that flashbacks recall a particular moment during the experience of trauma, often when the trauma first began, or when there was a change and the trauma became more intense.

It is even possible to have something very like a flashback even if you were not directly involved in the event itself. This happened to Raj, who lost a close friend in the 2005 London bombings. He told me that horrific thoughts about the explosion kept going through his mind in the days and weeks afterwards.

> I kept seeing her body exploding and bits of it spreading. I was imagining bits of it cooking because it was so hot down there . . . I would see a pane of glass on the tube – and you can imagine all the glass and metal there – I would just see parts, like lumps of body material, like lumps of skin and fat and stuff, just like spray. Chunks that big and sizzling and cooking with the heat.

Raj experienced this highly graphic image repeatedly almost every day for several weeks, even though he himself had not experienced the bombings directly. Is it a flashback? It has the characteristics of one – vivid, repetitive, unwanted and distressing. But technically it is not, since Raj was not *recalling* an experience but *imagining* one.

Let me summarize what we know about traumatic flashbacks:

- They are a type of involuntary memory, which is, in itself, quite common.

- They differ from most involuntary memories in that they are unwanted, distressing, repetitive and particularly vivid.

- By definition, they must occur after trauma and, unlike a conscious recollection, seem to come out of the blue, though, with help, people can usually identify a trigger.

- The trigger for a flashback is almost always either a sensory cue or an intense feeling.

- Flashbacks are brief, usually a matter of seconds, and rarely longer than a minute, though there are exceptions.

- Practically everyone in such situations will experience reminders of the trauma with some element of being cast back into the event, a sense of 'nowness'; but only a small minority of people suffer from intense, vivid flashbacks.

- Flashbacks are often about the worst moments – *hotspots* – and often take the individual back to the onset of the trauma or a moment when the trauma started to get worse.

- The experience of flashbacks is one example of the 're-experiencing' symptoms necessary for the diagnosis of PTSD.

- It is possible to have PTSD without experiencing flashbacks provided other forms of re-experiencing are present. Studies have shown that only 10 per cent of those diagnosed with PTSD experience actual flashbacks.

In the next chapter I will consider another important feature of the way we respond to trauma: avoidance; and how that can unwittingly lead to trauma memories persisting after the event is long gone.

Chapter 7: Avoidance

'I don't have a vast amount of detailed memory for what happened [in the first few weeks after the bombings]. People – family and neighbours – said I didn't talk very much. I didn't drive. I opted not to do that . . . I started walking every day. We are very fortunate here; we can walk from the house in at least four directions. I found that quite comforting. And just occasionally when I was out, I remember starting to feel that everybody else was very different to me, a slight distancing from society.'

'You felt slightly cut off?'

'Yes.'

'And you went walking on your own?'

'Yes. I'd always found nature very healing and beneficial. I sought solace in that. I hoped that it would – and to some extent it did – help me to not get into a spiral of depression when I was at home, bored, lack of interest, whatever . . .'

'But you clearly weren't feeling yourself as you were before?'

'No.'

'You were feeling cut off. You didn't feel you could drive. Did you do any activities at all?'

'No.'

'How was your concentration?'

'It was very poor. I remember turning the television off quite a lot because the only above-ground experience on camera was the bus [that had been bombed] and that kept coming up, the Tavistock Square event. I just didn't want to know. I just shunned the whole lot. As far as I was concerned: "Leave me alone, I don't want to know."'

This extract comes from my interview with Tim Coulson. In Chapter 2 I described Tim's experiences in the 2005 London bombings, how he broke into the carriage of the train that had been bombed and how he comforted the injured and dying. His actions on that day received considerable accolades from the press and TV media. Yet he later suffered psychologically from the experience and in the end took early retirement from his job.

What Tim was describing to me, when I visited him in his house near Henley, in July 2009, was a pattern of avoidance. In the first three months after the bombings he stayed at home. He was a college lecturer and it was the long summer vacation. He did not have to go in to work. But the truth was that he had neither the energy nor the motivation to do so. When I asked him about that time, Tim found it hard to remember what he did, other than go for long, solitary walks.

> I healed on the physical level quite easily because it was just cuts and bruises really. If I think about it, from July to the end of September, I don't know what happened a great deal in that time. I was at home. Judy, my wife, had school holidays for the first part of that, so she was at home as well. She fought a battle to keep newspaper, TV and radio reporters away from our house. I have to say I don't really know what went on. It's an odd kind of blank. Somebody said it was nearly the end of September and I thought, 'Oh is it?'

Tim's solitariness, his detachment from others, is not unusual in those who have been through a major trauma. Normal life can be hard to adjust to after a profoundly disturbing experience. The impact of the trauma does not end when the event is over, when, in Tim's case, he emerged from the underground into the light of day. The trauma remains. In the case of a major event it is there in the glare of publicity that surrounds it, in the reporters trying to get a story, in the TV-and-radio coverage that goes on for days and weeks, in the adjustments people have to make to their normal life, and, most significantly, in the memory of what happened.

In this chapter I will consider the part played by avoidance in people's recovery from trauma. In our culture, avoiding doing things tends to be seen as negative; it is better, it is often claimed, to face up squarely to difficulties and try to resolve them. This is in essence a moral judgement. But I believe it is unhelpful to see avoidance in moral terms. It is not usually a deficiency in people's character that makes them practise avoidance. They avoid because they feel that there is no other option. Nor is avoidance always the wrong thing to do. Tim's avoidance of people immediately after the bombings came about without conscious volition on his part; he was responding to something inside himself. He needed the time and the space to come to terms with what he had seen and done.

When I worked as a clinical psychologist, I treated many people suffering from anxiety disorders. Although each person was different, a common factor was avoidance. Those who were claustrophobic avoided enclosed spaces like lifts or tunnels. Those who were socially anxious avoided parties and other gatherings where they had to mix with other people. Those who were agoraphobic would stay at home. Even when someone felt generally anxious with no obvious cause, their heightened emotionality would lead to a desire to avoid people for much the same reason as Tim avoided people. When you do not feel yourself, you do not feel like engaging with the world.

Avoidance has a significant short-term advantage: the likelihood of being seriously distressed is reduced. It is also a way of retaining control. In extreme anxiety – a panic attack, for example – the waves of emotion come crashing down one after the other, and it feels as though there is nothing anyone can do to stop them. This is both frightening and distressing, so it is no surprise that people do not risk putting themselves in situations where those feelings might occur. However, the short-term advantage of avoidance is offset by the longer term disadvantage. Life is inevitably restricted. These restrictions can be practical, such as not going out socially (even not going out at all) or avoiding friends and colleagues. Perhaps more significantly, there is the *psychological* restriction of always being on one's guard, always worrying about something that might happen, so that life is never free of anxiety.

Table 7.1. AVOIDANCE (from DSM-IV (TR) DIAGNOSIS OF PTSD, CRITERION (C))
• Efforts to avoid thoughts, feelings, or conversations associated with trauma
• Efforts to avoid activities, places, or people that arouse recollections of the trauma
• Inability to recall an important aspect of trauma
• Markedly diminished interest or participation in significant activities
• Feelings of detachment or estrangement from others
• Restricted range of affect (e.g. unable to have loving feelings)
• Sense of a foreshortened future (e.g. does not expect to have a career, marriage, children, or a normal life span)

In this chapter I will recount the experiences of Tim and Elaine, who were in the same carriage when a bomb exploded in the neighbouring tube train. Their stories illustrate how a pattern of avoidance can be established and then come to dominate life afterwards. This happened to both of them but in different ways, reflecting their personalities, their backgrounds, and what they did during the trauma. In the diagnosis of post-traumatic stress disorder, avoidance is one of the three defining criteria (see Table 7.1). People avoid talking about the trauma and the thoughts and feelings that it can give rise to, as well as activities and places associated with the trauma. Psychologically, there may be increasing withdrawal from normal life, or from life as it was before the trauma, with a loss of interest in previously enjoyed activities. In addition, there can be a feeling of being detached from other people, and a reduction in positive feelings, or in some cases the loss of all positive feelings. The future is viewed differently, with a sense that it may be cut short. Finally, many find it difficult to remember a key part or parts of the trauma.

Elaine's story

In Chapter 2 I described how, on 7 July 2005, Elaine found herself in a stalled underground train alongside another train, which she believed had crashed, but had in fact been bombed. She had tried to reach out to a man in the other train who had his arm out to her, but she could not reach him. She retreated into herself, even occasionally disappearing under her coat, while she waited for the emergency services to come and rescue her. Eventually, two men in fluorescent jackets appeared and shepherded her and others onto the tracks. All around the train in the tunnel was a confusion of gravel and cables and bits of metal, plus a mess of what were body parts and other fragments from the bombed train. Someone told her to shut her eyes and go for it, which is what she did.

When she eventually got to the platform, pushed up by others below her, she wondered if she should stay and try to help. Elaine worked as an operations manager for the St John Ambulance service. She was involved in emergency planning for events just like this. She would normally be right there, mustering the troops. But her chest was hurting and she could not breathe easily with all the dust and debris. There was no way she would have been allowed to stay, given the state she was in. Yet feelings of guilt about leaving the scene were to trouble her afterwards. From then on, Elaine's journey out of the tube had a surreal air to it. She walked up the stairs until she reached the top.

In the foyer there were people and bodies lying everywhere. I don't know if they were dead people. There were unconscious people, and people in stages of exhaustion and tiredness . . . I just looked and I saw all these people . . . it was like war films, like *M.A.S.H.*, when you see these sort of things . . . There was no first-aid kit. There was nothing with them. They were just using people's clothes and coats . . . and there was a man and he had a big bandage around his head and blood was coming out. He was wandering around looking completely lost. I walked over towards him, but then someone grabbed me, and said, 'No, no. You need to go this way. You're all right. You go into Marks & Spencer.'

Marks & Spencer had been commandeered as somewhere to put the survivors and the walking wounded. Elaine crossed the street and followed people into the store.

There was somebody at the door, and they had a trolley and they were giving people water, which was great, because we'd got all this dirt in our mouths. I grabbed a bottle of water and went and sat down by this pillar. I just sat on the floor. There were other people who came and sat down as well. I sat there and then I rang my husband.

Elaine got through to her husband, Steve, who worked in the control room of the ambulance service. He was given permission to leave and collect her. Then all those in Marks & Spencer were told to move to a hotel.

We walked into the hotel and it was strange. There were two women looking immaculate in their black-and-white suits with their hair tucked back, handing out white towels or flannels. It was bizarre, this raggle-taggle of people going in, and [the women saying] 'Good morning. Would you like to have a towel?' They were in hotel-training mode. They were all smiling, saying 'Here's your towel. Would you like to go and sit over there?' It was surreal.

Elaine took a towel, sat on the floor and tried to clean herself up. When the paramedics arrived, she was given oxygen because her breathing was difficult. Her cuts and bruises were treated and her pulse rate taken. She was told she needed to go to hospital for further checks. She was moved to a place near the door, where she waited, still in shock.

> Lots of people kept asking my name and address over and over again. There was complete chaos. It wasn't organized. There wasn't a reception area. So people kept saying, 'What's your name? What's your address? Is there anyone you want to contact?' So I gave people my name and address over and over again. And I remember being really annoyed by that because nobody seemed to be doing anything with it. It was just hundreds of people getting people's addresses and I don't know who they were, if they were a doctor, or what I was doing there. I hadn't got any choice. I think that was a big thing. I had no choice with anything.

Elaine was eventually taken to hospital, where she was seen by the staff and had a blood sample taken. She told me that she could not remember much of that time. When her husband arrived to take her home, she was still convinced that the train had crashed. Somehow she had not picked up any information about a terrorist attack. In the car driving back, Steve wondered out loud how they would get back. This was how the dialogue between them went, as Elaine recalled it.

> I said, 'You know the way home.'
> 'How am I to find my way home? Half of London's shut, isn't it?' Steve replied.

'Just because of a train crash?'

'What do you mean, a train crash?'

'There was a train crash between Paddington and Edgware Road. I don't know where we are but we are a bit away from it because I came in the ambulance. Roads aren't going to be shut around here.'

And he just looked at me and said, 'You've got no idea, have you?'

I said, 'I know what's happened. The train crashed.'

'No it didn't. It was a bomb. There are bombs everywhere.'

He can be a bit of a drama queen sometimes and I thought, 'Bombs everywhere? Of course there aren't. He's getting himself stressed out.' So I didn't want to talk to him and we didn't have any more discussion about it. I thought he had made it up. I thought he wasn't there so he didn't know what I knew. I heard the crash. Well all right, I thought, maybe there was a bomb somewhere but it has nothing to do with what I was involved in. And I went to sleep on the way home.

Elaine's vivid account of the immediate aftermath of the bombings shows how surreal the experience felt to her, and probably to many other survivors too. Those who saw the television coverage of the people exiting the tube stations will recall how shocked and disorientated they looked. Elaine's account illustrates the defensive nature of avoidance. It was her way of switching off from all the horrors and uncertainty around. On the train, waiting for the emergency services, she did this by hiding under her coat. In the hours that followed, like many survivors, she felt cut off from the world around her, which seemed odd and surreal. She did not even know the true nature of the trauma, clinging on to her original belief that the train had crashed. When Steve tried to tell her the truth, she refused to believe him. In the end, she fell asleep on the journey home, which served to cut herself off absolutely.

Dissociation

Elaine's reactions were not the product of conscious decision-making but driven by her feelings. She was in a dissociative state of mind. Dissociation is described by the psychologist Chris Brewin as 'any kind of temporary breakdown in what we think as the relatively continuous, interrelated processes of perceiving the world around us.' We all experience mild versions of this from time to time, such as daydreaming or the way we can go into auto-pilot when driving a car. What happened to Elaine was both more intense and more prolonged than these common experiences. *In extremis*, people can lose all touch with immediate reality, like George did in the nightclub (see Chapter 6). Dissociation describes the fragmentation of consciousness into separate parts. The normal sense of being actively engaged with the world is hijacked by the feeling of being at one remove from it. Therefore Elaine did not react as she would normally have done to what she experienced in Marks & Spencer and the hotel. The normal Elaine would have taken control, asked questions, wanting to know more. But instead she felt remote, passive and unable to act.

Dissociation can take two forms: *derealization*, which is the sense that the world about you is not real, and *depersonalization*, which is the sense that you are not yourself, and is often accompanied by feeling numb, spaced out or unreal. The two forms can and do coexist. Elaine almost certainly felt both. The feelings of derealization and depersonalization can alternate with sudden intrusive thoughts or images that provoke intense feelings of anxiety and fear. People can cycle through these different states, experiencing numbing on the one hand and then high arousal on the other, and then more numbing, and so on. This is consistent with the notion that during traumatic events consciousness is in a fragmented and unstable state. Dissociation is not uncommon in severe trauma. It functions as a way of protecting those caught up in it from being totally overwhelmed by stress, especially when, as in Elaine's case, the individual feels helpless. Research has shown that 96 per cent of soldiers experience dissociation during survival training, indicating how prevalent it can be given the 'right' conditions. The more severe the trauma, the more likely dissociation is. Although this state of mind is temporary, research has shown that what is called *peri-traumatic dissociation* (experienced in the course of trauma, as happened to Elaine) is predictive of the later diagnosis of PTSD. As we shall see, Elaine went on to develop PTSD symptoms that in the end forced her to leave her work. Before going any further with Elaine's story, however, let me return to Tim and his experiences.

Tim's story

On 7 July 2005, Tim had been in the same stalled carriage as Elaine. In Chapter 2 I described how he forced his way into the bombed carriage in the other train and helped survivors. He cradled the man he later came to know as Stan as he died from his injuries. Here is how he took up the account of what happened next.

> I became acutely aware of somebody behind me to my left on the tunnel wall [who was] returning to consciousness. This was Alison, an Australian woman, who had been, as I now know, blasted out through the door onto the tunnel wall. She'd been crumpled by metal and was in a very poor state of health.

Tim explained who he was and then assessed what Alison's injuries were. There was emergency lighting so he could see reasonably well. He saw that her left eye was very badly swollen, probably due to shrapnel damage, and one leg was 'not in the right shape, bits and pieces that normally live on the inside were on the outside'. He decided it was better to move Alison away from the wall. At a subconscious level, he realized later, he was worried that the tunnel might collapse.

We lifted her onto the floor of the next set of doors down
from where the bomb had been. We brushed the glass and
things out of the way . . . Alison held onto my hand and
asked me if I would stay with her. I still think back to those
moments. Would it have been different if I was a different personality at the time? Because I naturally said, 'Yes,
of course I'll stay' and I genuinely meant it. If I had been
somebody else and said, 'No, there are other people who
need my help, stay here', I speculate as to what might have
happened.

Tim's determination to help was in part driven by the death of
Stan. He did not want another person to die. But it was also something about him as a person. He spent a long time with Alison,
around an hour and a half, during which they talked and shared
personal experiences. He tried to ease her pain by washing her eye
gently and supporting her leg on his shoulder. He reassured her
that help would be arriving shortly, even though he did not know
what would happen. This was pretty heroic, though Tim would
not describe it that way. While he was doing this, he was 'beating down any feelings I might have had . . . about the tunnel wall
collapsing'. In other words, by being as fully engaged as he could
be supporting Alison, he could avoid thinking about the danger
they might have been in. This is another form of avoidance, using
actions as distraction, so as not to dwell on fears. Tim stayed with
Alison throughout her rescue and for some time in hospital. He
held her hand and she held his throughout. That personal touch is
vitally important to people who are seriously injured. It is calm-
ing and acts as a lifeline with the normal world, which seems
to have disappeared.

I have already described what it was like at home for Tim in the
months after the bombings. He sought to recuperate by cutting
himself off from the world. During this time he felt physically
and emotionally drained. He was assailed by vivid flashbacks to

incidents in the tube train and the tunnel. He told me that they were like dreams but more vivid, distressing and persistent. Moreover, dreams end and the feelings go away, whereas the feelings in Tim's flashbacks carried on afterwards. These flashbacks alternated with periods of numbness and withdrawal. All this was exhausting for him. At night he would lie awake and the flashbacks would come and that, too, was exhausting. He took time off his teaching work.

> I didn't miss teaching in the first half of the year, which surprised me. I thought I would, but I didn't. From having been fairly full-on in a managerial role in college, to suddenly have none of that, I expected to have a void, a vast amount of time and I didn't. That space had been filled with other things, albeit I can't enumerate them. They weren't great things, they were much smaller but perhaps more meaningful . . . they satisfied me, the walking, the taking a sandwich and sitting by the river and reading a novel. I was able to manage those kind of things.

Nevertheless, Tim continued to feel exhausted. He went to his GP and was eventually referred to a clinical psychologist, an expert in treating trauma-related problems. He was reluctant to have treatment at first and found it difficult to talk about what he was going through. Yet eventually, through analysing the flashbacks with his therapist's help, he began to make, as he put it, 'some interesting discoveries'. These were some of the specific triggers that would set off the flashbacks:

> 'Loud noise. I remember the first firework night in November, not liking that at all, from the sheer surprise element of the noise. So I was helped to identify a range of things that triggered [a flashback]. Don't watch the TV. If what's on the TV is about the London bombings, it's going to straightaway affect [me].'

'So if you did watch, a flashback might occur?'

'Yes. Or just [being] generally upset . . . That is why I steered away from them, not to avoid them happening, but to avoid any further damage to me. I didn't really need to be that upset. And crowded places . . . the idea of going into Reading town centre on a Saturday being jam-packed with people.'

In Tim's case, avoidance was both protective and problematic. He did not want to be emotionally distressed, which is why he continued to lead the mainly solitary life that he had fallen into. Long walks on his own, sitting by the river, not going to work. But that meant that he rarely confronted essentially normal social situations that he had managed easily when he was well. And although he avoided possible triggers, he still felt exhausted. For he could not avoid the flashbacks altogether. Only when he started therapy did he begin the process of recovery, which proved a lengthy one.

Elaine's story (continued)

Elaine was asleep in the car as Steve drove her from the hospital to their home. She told me that she could not remember anything much about arriving home. She pieced it together later. The next day she began what was to be a lengthy pattern of avoidance. This is how she told me about it.

'Then the following day I didn't want to know what had happened.'

'Didn't *want* to know?'

'I knew what had happened. [I was] walking down the stairs and the television was on and I just switched it off.'

'So you wanted to shut it out?'

'Yes.'

'But you knew by that time it had been a bomb?'

'I knew. I knew there had been some bombs. But I had

no idea the detail of that at all. Up until I saw Martina [her
therapist] I hadn't read a single newspaper.'
    'And when did you see Martina?'
    'The first time I saw her was July last year.'
    'July 2008?'
    'Yes.'
    'So for three years you didn't read anything about it?'
    'I got really clever at that.'

As you can probably tell, I was taken aback by the extent of
Elaine's avoidance. She did not read the papers, listen to radio
news or watch TV news for three years, in case anything about the
bombings was mentioned. Elaine is married. She has grown-up
children and, at the time, her dad was living with them. I wondered what they thought of this.

    'Did anyone try and make you read about it?'
    'No. My family went along with it. But I didn't know
they were going along with it. They realized that if I saw
anything about it, it upset me. And my daughter said [later]
my dad used to buy a newspaper and then when I would
be coming home, he'd pick up all the newspapers and put
them out in the bin . . . I used the Internet for news and I
would select the news I wanted. So I would go onto the
BBC website and on to Oxford or whatever, and if there
was something that was of interest to me, I'd click on that
and read it. But if there was anything to do with terrorism,
bombs, and accidents in general, very bad car accidents,
phew [I thought], I don't need to know about that, it will
just upset me.'
    'So massive avoidance?'
    'Absolutely.'

Much to my surprise, Elaine told me she went back to work one
week after the bombing. She lived in Oxfordshire and commuted

daily into London, as she had done before, a very long journey. Many 7/7 survivors found it extremely difficult to go back on the underground. Some never did. But Elaine returned a week later. How had she done that? Her answer was simple: she shut it out of her mind.

> I got on a train every morning. I was back to games, iPod, puzzles, anything other than being where I was. If my phone battery had run out and I wasn't going to have a game, that meant having a day off; I had to have all these things around me. Immediately I got on the train – even before I got on, actually – I would be doing puzzles, or reading. Get on the train, get to work, get off the train. And then at work, just work like hell.

Elaine immersed herself in her work. As she worked in emergency planning for the St John Ambulance service, how could she avoid hearing about bombings and terrorist attacks? She told me that she delegated all such work to members of her team. She avoided answering the phone, always getting someone else to do it for her, just in case. She told her boss she was fine and to all observers she seemed to be. Except that she was not. Her concentration was shot to pieces. She was coping by virtue of an elaborate and carefully maintained pattern of avoidance. Because she could not bear the thought of being in trains during rush hour, she left home at 5 a.m. and often left her work at 6 or even 7 p.m. She was working seventy hours or more a week. And all the time she was shutting out anything that might remind her of the trauma she had been through. It was almost as though she was pretending that it had not happened.

Elaine had determined that she would not let any reports of traumatic events get through the barriers she had erected both at work and at home. From day one she acted as though the trauma had not happened, as though things could go on just as before. While her avoidance may have been beneficial when she was caught up in the trauma, allowing her to detach herself from the horrors around her, her later avoidance was not helping her recover; if anything, the opposite. She was, in effect, unconsciously deceiving herself. It took a huge amount of Elaine's energy and emotion to do it. Both at home and at work she was constantly vigilant lest any mention of bombs or terrorism got through. It is a tribute to her strength of character that she managed this for three years until one day at work there was a huge bang (a skip had been delivered and dropped with a clang). The sudden noise triggered a lengthy flashback taking her back to her time on the train. Everything went black and she heard vivid screaming. Her elaborate defence collapsed, she broke down in acute distress, and she could no longer carry on. She left work and did not go back.

Is avoidance helpful or harmful?

A few years ago I saw a TV programme on soldiers returning from the war in Afghanistan. It focused on their personal stories and how difficult it was for them to adjust to life at home. One soldier could not or would not talk about what he had been going through to anyone. The interviewer suggested that by bottling up his feelings, by avoiding talking about them, he was making things worse for himself. The implicit message was that everyone needs to talk through feelings, even very painful ones. Is that right? Is avoiding talking about feelings always wrong? I do not think that one can or should make such a categorical statement. So much depends on the context and the person, not to mention their relationships with family and close friends; and on timing. Immediately after the bombings, Tim felt the need to be by himself for a while and found that healing. His avoidance of others then was part of a necessary recovery process. Later, when he tried to go back to work, he discovered that, even with the help of a therapist and a graded programme in which he began with short periods back at work and gradually increased the time he stayed there, he could not manage the job in the same way as he had before. Reluctantly, he took retirement on medical grounds. Would the outcome for Tim have been different had he not gone into the bombed-out carriage and helped the wounded and the dying? It is an impossible question. The help that he provided certainly brought him face to face with sights that were highly distressing and left memory traces that were hard for him to deal with later. But, as he put it, he could not have done anything other than what he did. His avoidance of others in the first three months was essential to his recovery but it also meant that the return to work, when it happened, was not easy. But going back to work right away was not the solution; that was impossible for Tim anyway. In Elaine's case she avoided the horrors around her from the outset. She continued to do this in the hours afterwards, even falling asleep in the car home. Then for almost three years an elaborate pattern of avoidance became her way of getting through the days.

I believe that in both Tim and Elaine's cases avoidance was, so to speak, unavoidable. It was not something consciously chosen by them but rather reflected their personalities and personal histories. I think this sort of avoidance would occur in anyone who has been through a major trauma. The tendency to encourage people to 'face up to' their feelings, as the journalist suggested to the young solider returning from Afghanistan, is well meant. But it can be unhelpful. It underestimates the way traumatic events invade the body and the mind and play havoc with people's lives, making it difficult to come to terms with what they may be feeling. Such pressure does not take into account individual personality and personal history. Most importantly, it fails to recognize that confronting one's demons is a matter of timing. If the protective cloak of avoidance is discarded, it is vital that the person underneath is in a fit enough condition to benefit. If it is done too early, then it can make matters worse. In the treatment of people with PTSD and other trauma-related problems, therapists take great care to establish a safe, trusting relationship before seeking to do anything specific, aware that avoidance should not be relinquished too soon and that the process of facing up to what has happened is more complicated than talking about one's feelings.

Chapter 8: Guilt, shame and anger

'In 2008 I went to Paris and found a place. I moved into it in November and I was there till February. It was really a bit of a dive. I just wasn't that happy in general really. I went to work nine to six, it was winter, and everybody in Paris goes back home and they live in the suburbs. It was just boring and I felt lonely. But I was quite proud so I didn't really want to say, "I don't like this, I want to change." I just thought, "Let's carry on." That was all involved in everything that happened really, because I love walking in the street. It was, like, ten . . .'

'Ten at night?'

'Yeah. It was pretty central so I wasn't thinking that anything would happen in the street. There were these three guys sitting on the Pont Neuf near Notre Dame. And they just called me. I think they wanted a light or something. I went over and they started talking. So I chatted to them for forty minutes. I guess quite a lot of people wouldn't have done that in the first place. Then I got up to go home and they followed me. They said they were going to the tube and, I don't know, I quite enjoyed their company. It was quite fun really. We were joking around. Yeah, it was a bit stupid of me . . . and then they ended up in my apartment. They followed me through the door, the outside door. It didn't have a lock actually. It was broken. But they weren't threatening. There were a lot of people there so I just thought . . .'

'They came into your apartment?'

'Yeah. They were outside the apartment door. I said, "I don't think you should come in. No, no." But they just ended up coming in and it was, "Oh all right, I guess you can." I didn't envisage anything was going to happen . . . I guess I was pretty stupid, looking back on it. But it depends what state of mind you are in. I was really depressed and lonely at the time. So yeah, that happened. We sat down and chatted for a while and then it all went from there. I finally got up and said, "Right, I'm quite tired. It's been nice knowing you. I'll meet you another time." I'd got a little bit of trust in them because I'd been talking with them for over an hour . . . and then it all happened. They weren't violent, like physically. I mean they were physically threatening. But they didn't have a knife or anything. And there were three of them. It was like, "Oh shit."'

This extract is from an interview I had with a young woman called Georgie, in London in November 2009. She was describing the events that led up to her being held prisoner and repeatedly raped for several hours by three men in her apartment in Paris. She was twenty-three years old at the time and was on a work placement as part of her languages degree at a university in Britain. She had come to me through a psychologist friend of mine. Georgie had never met me before and so it could not have been easy for her to talk about something as personal and distressing as rape. Yet she did it creditably. It had helped her, she told me towards the end of the interview, that she had had to repeat her story many times to the French police and courts as part of the legal process that led to the conviction and jailing of the three men.

In this chapter I will discuss feelings of guilt, shame and anger, all of which were experienced by Georgie. They are part of the process of secondary appraisal, the term that I introduced in Chapter 3. While primary appraisal is how the trauma is viewed and understood as it is happening, secondary appraisal is when the trauma is put into context and evaluated. In other words, secondary appraisal is the very human process of trying to make sense of what has happened, including one's own reactions at the time.

Rape can give rise to many psychological problems, including the symptoms that make up the diagnosis of PTSD; these include high levels of arousal, flashbacks and other forms of reliving the trauma, feelings of numbness and dissociation, and avoidance. On her return to England, Georgie experienced all of these to some degree. Important as these are, I will not focus on them in this chapter, since they have already been covered in earlier ones. Instead I will be looking at the other intense emotions that can arise from major trauma, and what part they play in people's reactions to this trauma.

The trauma of rape

Rape is an assault upon the person, a physical attack that subjugates one person to the actions and pleasures of another person or persons. Although the abuse of power is a significant feature, and needs to be taken into account in understanding the effect upon the person, the defining feature of rape is that it is sexual. It is a gross violation of the physical intimacy that many of us enjoy with people we are close to. Not surprisingly, one consequence of rape is that the enjoyment of sex can be severely compromised, as can close relationships in general. Both non-sexual physical assault and rape are personal traumas, that is, they are deliberately directed against the individual, whether the victim is known to the attacker or a complete stranger. Unlike terrorist attacks, natural disasters or major accidents, where someone just happens to be in the way, the rape victim is chosen, and in many instances known to the attacker. In 85.7 per cent of recorded rapes in the UK in 2007 the suspect was known to the victim or identified following investigation.

The incidence of rape in the UK or any other country is difficult to estimate with any accuracy for two reasons. Firstly, there is the question of definition. As Joanna Bourke points out in her thorough account of the history of rape, there is no single, agreed definition of it. Is the use of brute force a necessary feature of rape? But this excludes more subtle forms of coercion. Has there to be penetration of the vagina or anus? Not according to current legal definitions in the UK. Thus, the 2003 Sexual Offences Act defines a rapist as someone who 'intentionally penetrates the vagina, anus or mouth of another person with his penis where the victim does not consent to the penetration and where he does not reasonably believe that the victim consents'. But other jurisdictions have different definitions. Societal and cultural differences shape what is seen as rape and how rapist and victim are treated. Bourke chose to define sexual abuse, including rape, 'as any act called such by a participant or third party', thereby bypassing the problems of finding an agreed objective definition. But her subjective definition only pushes the problem one step back, since people will have different understandings on which they base their claim of being raped.

The other difficulty in forming an accurate picture of the nature and extent of rape is the under-reporting of sexual assaults. It is estimated that between 75 and 95 per cent of rapes are never reported. There are several reasons for this, but not least is the depressing statistic that, in the UK for the last few years, only a very small percentage of rapes reported to the police (5 per cent or thereabouts) resulted in a successful conviction. The figure is higher for those cases that are taken to court, though still only just over 50 per cent. But neither figure is encouraging to victims of rape, and many decide it is not worth the stress of seeking redress in the courts and so do not report it. The scrutiny that rape victims are put under in a formal investigation and, later, at the trial has been shown to be more intense than for any other crime. There is a risk that the victim becomes retraumatized as a result.

Despite the difficulties in collecting accurate statistics, there is little doubt that sexual violence in general constitutes a major trauma, particularly for women. According to the World Health Organisation, nearly one in four women worldwide may experience sexual violence from an intimate partner in their lifetime, with figures ranging from 15 per cent to 71 per cent, across ten countries. In the UK, studies suggest that around 50,000 women are raped every year, although, given the under-reporting of the crime, the true figure is likely to be much higher. North American research data show that rape and sexual molestation before the age of eighteen are the two commonest traumas experienced by women.

Unsurprisingly, being raped can lead to psychological problems. In the 1970s, prior to the formulation of the diagnosis PTSD, the term *rape-trauma syndrome* was used to describe what seemed to be the typical psychological problems that women experienced after rape. The syndrome was described as having two phases, an *acute phase* that lasted a matter of weeks, and a *restorative phase* that went on for months or sometimes years after the trauma. In the acute phase the symptoms were virtually identical to those now seen as diagnostic of PTSD, namely intense fear at the time, followed by feelings of agitation, distress and anxiety, sometimes feelings of numbness or dissociation, difficulties in concentration and decision making, fatigue, nightmares and sleep disturbance, and a sense of reliving the trauma. In the restorative phase people sought to resume a normal life and, outwardly, many seemed to have done so successfully. However, below the surface, a range of psychological symptoms persisted, including anxiety, depression, mood swings, relationship problems, sexual problems and insomnia.

Rape-trauma syndrome is now generally seen as a subset of PTSD. Research has shown that rape not only gives rise to PTSD symptoms in the acute phase, but also that a substantial number of rape survivors are formally diagnosed with PTSD. In one study, two-thirds of rape survivors had PTSD one month after the rape and almost half (47 per cent) at three months. In a community study of rape victims followed up over a long period, 16.5 per cent still met the PTSD criteria on average seventeen years after the rape, indicating that, for a few, their problems were not resolved. The trauma of rape has multiple consequences. In one study, sexual problems occurred in over 70 per cent of women. In another study, 42.6 per cent of victims of rape reported having other physical problems. Depression is a common reaction and for some can be a long-lasting problem. Suicidal thoughts occur to many survivors; the figures for those victims of rape who consider suicide range from 2.9 per cent to 50 per cent. Being raped can give rise to intense distressing feelings that can persist for a long time.

What Georgie felt

When I asked Georgie about her feelings during the time the men were in her flat, she told me that when they started coming on to her she did not react at first, as she thought she might just be able to turn the situation round. 'I can still control this,' she thought. 'I was just really proud, and I couldn't scream. I couldn't. [I was] just frozen and then your mind kind of shuts down a bit.' Then it became obvious that the men were not going to be deflected. They pinned her to the bed and forced her to give them oral sex repeatedly. I asked her if she had been very frightened at that point. To my surprise, she said no.

> That's the thing. I'd got really logical. You know in a way you think you're being logical and perhaps you are. I guess it's about surviving really. I just thought, 'Oh my God.' You can't actually think the word 'rape'. I didn't realize I was raped until I went to the police station and I started screaming out. I kind of froze . . . I just thought, 'This is happening and now there is nothing I can do about it.'

Georgie's account of her initial lack of emotional response is less surprising when we think of the way the trauma developed. This was no sudden event that shocked her to the core. She had become friendly with the men and had chatted to them for over an hour. So when they started sexually assaulting her, she thought at first she might be able to get out of the situation. Very soon though she realized that that was not the case and there was no way she could resist three men. She described being in two states of mind: firstly that she was *logical*, by which she meant trying to remain calm and find a way out, and secondly that she *froze*. Freezing is one of the responses animals have when in extreme danger and it may be that Georgie was doing something similar, shutting her body down. This is akin to the dissociative state that I described in earlier chapters, where the traumatized person feels numb and cut off from the world. The three men repeatedly raped Georgie for about an hour, leaving her feeling pretty traumatized. But still a part of her mind was being logical, seeking a way out.

> I thought I had never actually been hit by a guy and I thought, because I could see they were pretty aggressive, I needed to get out of this somehow. I didn't actually want to end up on the bed bleeding to death . . . I am pretty sure they didn't have a knife. [But] I am sure they wouldn't have hesitated to do whatever they had to do. So I kind of just, like, I don't know, I just ended up lying there, just being complicit.

Being frozen and in 'survival mode' very likely protected Georgie against extreme emotions, at least at first. But then the situation changed. Two of the men left, leaving one behind. This man, whom Georgie took as the ringleader, continued to force himself on her sexually and at this point she fought back.

> I started to kind of fight a bit. One time I kicked him and he fell on the floor and he was very pissed off. I didn't really help the situation obviously . . . I don't know he was like obsessive, he just wouldn't stop, and he went on for about forty minutes and then there was some respite. I don't know what he was doing then. All I know is my bag was quite close to me and I just reached for my phone but it was gone and then I noticed all my stuff was gone.

The two men who had left had stolen her money, phone, credit cards, iPod and camera from her bag. Georgie seized onto this.

She shouted she would call the police. The man was annoyed about what had happened. She thought afterwards that he realized that the stolen items would undermine any story they might concoct that it had all been a bit of fun and that she had consented to sex. By this time Georgie's emotions had flooded in and she became, in her words, 'frantic', determined to get out of the situation. The man told her he could get her stuff back but insisted she accompanied him to do this.

> 'By then I had lost everything. I was made to give all these blow jobs. I just wanted my stuff and everything. I was obsessed with my stuff because that was the only thing that seemed to create a reaction. I thought that was my way of getting out really, and he was like, "Oh yeah, in another half-minute." And he would say, "No. I want another blow job." That was the most humiliating part.'
>
> 'Why was that the most humiliating part?'
>
> 'Do you know why? Because it wasn't like anything was being forced on you. It was like, "Give me another half-minute and you can go . . . I just want another minute" or whatever. He must have repeated it ten times. It was really humiliating because you felt like you're being forced to be complicit.'
>
> 'You were trying to find a way out of the situation.'
>
> 'I was doing it not because I wanted to. But it was like I was giving some customer service to get out of my apartment.'

Guilt and shame

Georgie felt guilty because she thought she had been complicit (a word she uses twice in the extracts above) in what had happened to her. Because she had felt bored and lonely, she had chatted to the men in the street and allowed them to accompany her to her flat, where they had more or less forced their way in. Her guilt was about having been naive or 'stupid', as she put it, though she recognized that 99 times out of 100 in a similar situation nothing traumatic would have happened. She felt ashamed at having engaged in sexual plea-bargaining to get the man out of her apartment. Listening to her account, I was aware of how little choice she had. Georgie understood this very well. But understanding why one behaved as one did does not take away the feelings one has about the experience.

There has been much debate in the psychology literature about the difference between guilt and shame. Most theorists take the view that guilt is about the commission or non-commission of a specific act, while shame is about what is revealed more generally about oneself. Guilt arises from doing things against one's conscience or that one knows to be wrong because of cultural and ethical rules, while shame occurs when we realize that we have not lived up to our idealized version of ourselves, that we have let ourselves down and that others have seen this. Shame is very much to do with exposure, just as it was in the story of Adam and Eve in the Garden of Eden. It occurs when we are seen to behave in ways that are less than ideal. Once I was caught out dropping the name of a famous person in conversation, as though he was well known to me, whereas I had only briefly met him a couple of times. I felt acutely ashamed. I did not like this attention-seeking side of me to be revealed.

Georgie's traumatic experiences continued after she and the man left her apartment, ostensibly to find the two men who had stolen her possessions. It was the middle of the night and she was totally exhausted. She was too tired to try and run and anyway she had no one to turn to. She felt she just had to go along with the plan to get her stuff back. Eventually, after a taxi ride across the city, being forced to surrender her bank-account pin-number and having had money taken from her account, and then having stopped to buy alcohol and got into a second taxi, she saw her chance to escape.

We got to this big boulevard and then it stopped at these traffic lights. And I don't know, I just had a moment of clarity, jumped out, ran in the middle of the road. I waved my arms, saw a taxi stop and jumped in. And then the guy ran after me and opened the door, but the taxi drove off. So he was left behind. I ended up at the nearest police station. It was strange actually because in the taxi it was the first time I felt safe and it was actually the first time I cried from emotion. I was just screaming that everything had been lost, that I had been raped, I'd been attacked.

Georgie had escaped from the man. But her experiences at the police station proved traumatic in a different way. She was now visibly distressed and having to tell the police officers what had happened was not easy. Recounting the events to me, she recalled struggling to speak at all, let alone in French. The officers were distracted by her loss of credit cards rather than the rape and wanted her to cancel the cards first. They inevitably raised the issue of how the men had got into her apartment.

This inspector was saying, 'Why did you let them into your apartment?' You know, it took a while when I was back in England to get over that. I lied at first. I said I didn't . . . I didn't want to let them in and they pushed in. The police made me feel so guilty, so terrible. It was probably obvious to them that wasn't what happened. That kind of made them think that I was lying.

This act of equivocation was to trouble Georgie hugely afterwards. While it was true the men had not physically forced their way in, they had undoubtedly pressurized her. Listening to her account, it seemed to me that the difference was minimal: the men had very probably set out to assault her sexually, and if she had refused them entry they would have forced their way in. But it was what Georgie felt that mattered, and she felt guilty at having

allowed herself to get into this situation at all. Her guilt was compounded by the lie she told the police. It added to her sense of
having let herself and other people down. The focus on something
one did or did not do is at the heart of guilt. Elaine, who was
in the 2005 London bombings (see Chapter 2), felt guilty about
not doing anything to help others. Even Tim, who cared for the
wounded and dying, felt guilty that he had thought only of himself
at first, checking to see if he was physically all right. These are not
rational assessments. They are part of secondary appraisal and are
coloured by intense feelings.

A tragic example of the effect of guilt occurred to one of the
survivors of the capsizing of the *Herald of Free Enterprise* in the
port of Zeebrugge in March 1987, which resulted in the deaths of
193 passengers and crew. On the vehicle deck, all the trucks and
lorries were thrown on their sides and piled on top of each other,
while water flooded into the hold. The drivers were trapped in their
cabs. One lorry driver managed to smash the cab window with his
suitcase, climb out and over the bonnet of his truck, and swim to
safety. Courageously, he went on to help other passengers trapped
elsewhere in the boat to get out. But despite his resourcefulness
and courage the driver could not forget the cries of his fellow lorry
drivers whom he could not save from death. Tormented by guilt,
he committed suicide three years later.

It is difficult to dispel feelings of guilt. Reasoned argument
rarely has an effect. This is because the feeling of guilt continues
to haunt people as they replay the trauma in their heads, just as
those feelings of fear and distress do. 'If only' thoughts occur, as
though the mind is looking for a way of magically undoing the
trauma. *If only* she had not chatted to the men for forty minutes
or allowed them to accompany her back to her apartment, then
the rape would not have happened. The assumption of responsibility provides an explanation and is a way of making sense of
the experience. It gives the person back some control, albeit at
a huge cost. When Georgie returned to England, she stayed at
her parents' home for five months, mostly lying in bed. She did

not want to do anything or see people. She told me she was in 'this very big bubble of pain and guilt'. She experienced frequent distressing flashbacks to the rape. Her guilt tormented her as she thought of the pain and distress she had brought to her parents and others. She was in despair and had thoughts of killing herself. She became significantly depressed. The specific self-condemnation at the heart of guilt developed into a more general feeling of self-loathing and despair. The helplessness Georgie felt at the time of the rape was replicated as she found herself staying in bed unable to do anything. In her case, there proved to be an underlying physical problem that was discovered only when she went to her GP for a blood test. Her haemoglobin levels had fallen to a dangerously low level, leaving her zonked out, hardly able to pick up her handbag. After several blood transfusions, Georgie's haemoglobin levels rose and her physical condition improved. Whatever its cause, her physical illness must have affected her emotional state, adding to her depression and making recovery more difficult.

When I asked Georgie if she had felt shame, she referred in particular to the twenty-four hours after the rape, when she was in the hands of the police, still in the same clothes she had been wearing in her apartment. She felt unclean and disgusted by the physical aspects of the rape, the semen, the marks on her body, the thought of their hands all over her. Her disgust at what she had been put through was not helped by the failure of the police to look after her properly. She was not allowed to shower, she had to continue to wear the same clothes, she was closely interrogated, she was driven to an awful police hospital where criminals and drunks were in evidence, and finally taken back to her apartment. Georgie had to wait outside while the police conducted a forensic examination of the premises. Then she was abandoned there without anyone establishing if she had any friends or support of any kind. In fact, having no money, Georgie had to go out again and use her Metro pass to get to the house of a work colleague, who took her in. In other words, not only had the three men treated her as an object to be degraded sexually and used for their own pleasure, but the police had equally treated her as an object in their investigation, failing to respond to her humanely as a traumatized and vulnerable young woman. In this way, the investigation compounded the trauma.

In the case of both guilt and shame the victim turns the spotlight on herself: *she* was at fault and *she* behaved in ways that made her feel ashamed. This can be reinforced by cultural and societal attitudes towards women and men. In some societies the woman is severely punished, even killed, for being raped, as though the act itself is enough to condemn the victim, whatever her behaviour. The shame is felt by the family and the community and, totally unfairly, the woman is held responsible. Shame in this case arises out of the mores and religious codes of a community, and so the victim suffers doubly, first from the act and second from the social consequences of the act. Lest we in the West feel superior to other cultures in this regard, we should remember that it is not long ago that women's behaviour at the time of the rape and her sexual history were used as a means of defence for the rapist, a way of condemning the woman for the rape (*she asked for it, didn't she?*). The shocking statistic that only about 5 per cent of reported rapes reach successful conviction in the UK epitomizes the failure of our culture to treat the victims of rape properly.

Anger

On a quiet morning in July 1990, Susan Brison went for a walk along a French country road and was savagely and mercilessly attacked by a stranger. He dragged her into a ravine, sexually assaulted her, beat her, strangled her and left her for dead. Her recovery from this terrible attack and how it changed her life is the subject of her book *Aftermath*. It is one of the best books on trauma and recovery that I have read. Brison is a philosopher and her thoughtful and moving account benefits from her ability to analyse and understand both herself and society. Being a

philosopher, unsurprisingly, did not protect her from the emotional ravages of the attack in the months and years afterwards.
Like other rape victims she was assailed by flashbacks and intense
feelings of fear, shame and anger. Her anger, however, was not
directed at her attacker. While her husband wanted to kill him,
she could not feel any anger towards him. The reason for this, she
thought, was that it was too terrifying to be angry with him, as it
required her to imagine herself in proximity to him. But while she
may have not have felt angry with the attacker, she did feel anger.

> The anger was still there, but it got directed toward safer
> targets: my family and closest friends. My anger spread,
> giving me painful shooting signs that I was coming back to
> life. I could not accept what happened to me.

Eventually she attended a self-defence class and the confidence
she gained from learning to fight back 'gave me back my life',
though it was a changed life. Brison found that many of the
rape survivors she subsequently encountered failed to feel anger
towards their assailants. Instead they tended to blame themselves.
She attributed this to their urgent need to regain the control they
had lost, even if the cost was guilt, self-blame and depression. It
may also reflect the character of the person. Jo, a young woman
I assessed in my clinical practice, had been in a horrendous road
accident that had left her with severe injuries requiring many painful operations over several years. When I asked her if she had felt
angry with the young man who had caused the accident by reck-
lessly overtaking on a blind bend, she said no. She did not want to
concede any space to him but, rather, to concentrate exclusively
on her own recovery. Anger would only get in the way. When I got
to know her better, I saw that she was a determined and resourceful woman and, although her life had been completely turned
upside down by the accident and its traumatic consequences,
she persevered at the hard work of getting better and in the end
made a remarkable and successful recovery. In contrast, Danielle,

another young woman I saw in my practice, who also had been in a road accident where she was not at fault, could not let go of her anger at the other driver, to such an extent that it dominated her life. Nothing could help her, since her pain and suffering continually reminded her of what she had lost. I could see that she had always been someone with a strong sense of entitlement and, after the accident, she felt entitled both to redress (which was minimal as the driver received merely a fine and some points on his licence) and to the restoration of her previous, pain-free self. As the latter could never happen, her anger could never be assuaged (for more discussion of Jo's and Danielle's experiences, see Chapter 18).

As Brison noted, anger is often directed at others. When Georgie talked to me about the way the French police treated her, her anger suddenly flared up like a fierce burst of flame. 'I fucking hate the police,' she told me. 'God, they were so stupid.' They had treated her in a way that demeaned her. When I asked if she felt angry later – when she was back at university, for example – she said she had felt angry a lot of the time.

'Was the anger directed at [the rapists]?'

'No. It wasn't even directed. I never felt that I wanted to hurt them or I wanted revenge. I don't know why. I really don't know why. I just felt angry. Actually, I felt really angry at myself for ages . . . and there is nothing you can do when you feel angry at yourself. I didn't cut my wrists or anything but I did quite a lot of [stupid things]. It's not like you think consciously, "I'm going to bang my head", but I did quite a lot of that. I remember one time getting furious because my brother said something really stupid . . . and I got absolutely ballistic. I can remember I was just jumping up and down like this little child, literally jumping up and down. I ran into the hall and I started crashing my fists on the floor and banging my head. And it took me literally about two minutes before I realized what I was doing.

Conclusion

It is unsurprising that experiencing a major trauma can lead to a range of intense emotions, not just fear. We are human beings and subject to many different feelings. This is especially true of the process of secondary appraisal, where the trauma is evaluated in terms of our view of ourselves and how others see us. Like fear, other emotions are intensified by the nature of the traumatic experience. Anger, guilt and shame can take hold afterwards, and can cause problems in themselves. Feelings cannot be simply willed away. Being told that one should not feel guilty or angry or ashamed is unhelpful, as it assumes that the person can switch their emotions on and off like a tap. With the help of her therapist, Georgie eventually came through her feelings of self-blame and despair and was able to view the experience very differently (see Chapter 16). In other chapters I will describe what treatment can do and how therapists can help someone through such intense and distressing emotions. The first step is to acknowledge that these emotions can be experienced by anyone and do not represent personal failings. This is not as easy as it sounds, but it is important. Another step is the recognition that how we *feel* affects and is affected by how we *think*. A major trauma changes our view of ourselves and the world. This is what I will discuss in the next chapter.

Chapter 9: Shattered illusions

'I haven't come across any trauma quite like that, of one person in a car, a plane coming over, hitting the car down one side, spinning the car off the road and you, the driver, being physically 100 per cent all right. You might not have been but you were . . . so it was remarkable in two senses, one that it happened, and one that you survived in the way you did.'

'Yes.'

'Now looking back on it, how do you think that it's affected you having had that experience? Has it changed you as a person in any way or are you much the same person as you were before?'

'I think it's changed me. In a strange sort of way I think I'm a little more calm about things now. Things wouldn't excite me and upset me quite as much now because, I suppose, having been through that, I'm not going to match that again in a hurry. So other things now don't seem quite so serious and troublesome as they might have done before that accident. I can look at things with a slightly calmer view and take things in my stride probably a little easier than I could have done before that. I feel that it's almost a life-changing experience.'

'That's what I'm interested in, that sense that some people find it changes their life . . . and the transformation sometimes has both positive and negative features. I don't know if you can relate to that, can you?'

'I think I can. I think I understand myself a bit better now because of it. I know who I am a bit better now. I'm probably lucky to be here, I know that. And I don't take things for granted quite as much as I used to. I can enjoy the

world around me a bit better . . . It's that things don't seem
quite as bad as they would have done normally.'
   'It puts things more in perspective.'
   'It puts things more in perspective. Yes.'

This is an extract from my interview with Steve, who had a most
remarkable traumatic experience, which I mentioned briefly in
Chapter 1. When travelling home from work in his car, he heard
the sound of a plane flying very low. The noise got louder and
louder. Puzzled, he looked up and there, through the car's sun
roof, he saw the whole body of a plane, a Harrier Jump Jet, almost
sitting on top of his car, but going in the opposite direction. Out
of the windscreen he saw a parachute disappearing behind the tree
line to the left; the pilot had ejected from the plane. Suddenly
there was a huge explosion, everything went black, the car's
windscreen caved in and the car began to wobble. Through his
rear-view mirror, Steve saw a fireball in the road behind. His car
spun out of control, turned 360 degrees and rolled backwards
into a ditch by the side of the road, where it stopped. Looking
to his left, he could see the plane burning further down the road.
Fear gripped him. He thought that there might be another, larger
explosion that would engulf him. He scrambled his way out of the
car and sprinted up the road to get as far away from the burning
wreckage as he could. This was the beginning of a long period of
psychological difficulty for Steve, as the realization of his narrow
escape from death hit home. When eventually he retrieved his car,
he discovered that it had been damaged all the way down one
side, the passenger side. Part of the plane must have hit his car.
Just a few inches' difference and he and the car could have been
obliterated. He was both extraordinarily unlucky, to have been in
the way of the crashing plane, and extraordinarily lucky, to have
escaped physically entirely unharmed.
   In the interview Steve talked about having gained a changed
perspective on life as a result of surviving this incredible accident.
He was better able to take things in his stride and he felt he was

calmer than before. This was not always the case. In the immediate aftermath of the accident he suffered characteristic post-
traumatic symptoms of anxiety and difficulty sleeping, with his
sleep punctuated by dreams in which he relived the accident. He
was tired and irritable. He was off work for six weeks during which
he spent most of his time going for long, solitary walks, rather like
Tim in Chapter 7. Any noise would startle him, particularly, and
not surprisingly, the sound of planes in the sky. He lived within a
couple of miles of an airstrip and so planes were common. Steve
would always look up at the plane and check that it was not going
to crash down on him. This became an obsession; he could not let
a plane pass without looking up to check its progress. Eventually,
he was formally diagnosed with PTSD and a long litigation case
began. It was three years after the crash that the case was finally
settled in his favour, and only then did Steve begin the process of
making a full recovery.

Steve's case illustrates how trauma can change a person's
view of himself and the world. In his case the change was positive as he came to terms with his narrow escape from death and
began to see life as something to be lived and savoured. I came
across several other examples of this positive personal transformation in my practice (see Chapter 16). But more commonly,
those who had been through major trauma suffered negative
consequences, at least at first. They became sensitized to a world
that felt unsafe, where danger could lurk round the corner, and
in which vigilance now had to be a way of life. Steve's obsession with the noise of planes is a specific example of this. In this
chapter, I will consider how trauma can change the way we see
ourselves and the world. This is what psychologists call *cognitive change,* that is, it describes what happens in our minds, the
mental processes of perception, appraisal, thinking and believing. These are so much part of our human life that we take them
for granted, that is until something happens that derails these
automatic processes and forces us to reappraise ourselves and
the world.

In psychological terms cognition can be broken down into three main inter-related processes. I have illustrated these schematically in Fig. 9.1.

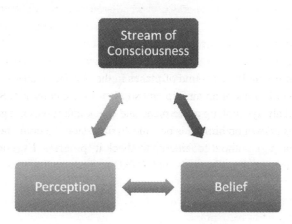

Fig. 9.1. Dynamic interaction between appraisals, perception and beliefs.

Firstly, there are the immediate thoughts and images we have in our mind at any one time, what is known as the stream of consciousness. Secondly, there is the way we perceive the world and ourselves, which can be compared to a set of filters reflecting our personality, experience and personal history. Thirdly, there are our fundamental beliefs or values. Trauma can affect cognition at all three levels and, as Fig. 9.1 shows, there is a dynamic interaction between the processes. In the rest of this chapter I will illustrate how this works and why understanding these psychological processes can help recovery from trauma.

The stream of consciousness

In earlier chapters I introduced Janine, the police officer who had cradled the man who had been shot outside Milton Keynes police station. In the days and weeks afterwards she experienced vivid flashbacks to the incident, which she described as like having a videocassette in her brain that was playing continuously. Her stream of consciousness had been invaded by trauma memories that she did not understand and that distressed her hugely. As she put it, 'I got to a phase which is what I refer to now to my close friends as *my mental phase*, because it got so intense that I couldn't string a sentence together. I didn't want to leave the house. I didn't want to talk to anyone.' Janine's experience describes how normal thinking can be disturbed by the emotions generated by the trauma. The stream of consciousness that we take for granted is fundamentally changed and, with that change, it feels like we are no longer the person we were. In Janine's case she thought she was going mad. When I interviewed her in February 2010, this is how she recalled what her mental state was like during that time:

> 'You felt a bit frightened or worried that you might end up in a psychiatric home and go mad?'
> 'It's true. Yes.'
> 'It's very frightening that sort of thought . . .'
> 'It does seem ridiculous now . . .'
> 'Yes, but at the time you believed it very strongly . . .'
> 'But at the time it was very real. Because I had these tapes playing in my head. I couldn't communicate properly and I probably didn't know what day of the week it was. So to all intents and purposes, I was pretty insane.'

In psychological terms what Janine and many others felt after trauma is perfectly explicable, although it does not feel like that to those suffering at the time. In normal life, thoughts and images flit through our minds all the time, some of which we attend to, most of which we do not. As I write this chapter I am running possible phrases through my mind while at the same time wondering whether Janine's experiences might be good to use as an example here. At the periphery of my thoughts is the awareness that the sun is shining and that it might be nice to make time for a walk this afternoon. A quick glance at the clock tells me that I have a half an hour to go before I break for coffee. I have other vague thoughts and feelings that I do not attend to. Writing can trigger considerable self-doubt and on occasions this comes to the surface, especially as I struggle to write something tricky. But today this is not in evidence, though I know it lurks just below the surface. This is the stream of consciousness. The writers Virginia Woolf and James Joyce tapped into it when they wrote their acclaimed novels, turning the churning, erratic, confusion of memory, thought and feeling into something illuminating and insightful. But to the ordinary person this is normal, everyday experience.

Idiosyncratic negative appraisals

One of the major cognitive theories of trauma begins with the stream of consciousness, and what psychologists call *idiosyncratic negative appraisals* that occur within it. Flashbacks and other forms of trauma memory intrude into the stream of consciousness. They give the impression of 'nowness', as though the trauma is happening again. As human beings, we try to make sense of our experiences, to understand what is happening and what part we play in it. This is the process of secondary appraisal that I outlined in Chapter 3. It describes the way the trauma is assessed and evaluated, including the appraisal of one's own actions and reactions. Because trauma memories are distressing and, to many, inexplicable, the appraisal tends to be negative. 'I must be going mad' was Janine's negative appraisal of her experiences. In addition, the trauma has disrupted the normal process of consolidating memories into autobiographical memory and so the negative appraisals derive from spikes of unconsolidated memory, repeatedly interrupting the stream of consciousness, causing distress. The feelings generated by these memories – often these are feelings of threat and insecurity but other emotions may also be experienced – provoke specific negative appraisals. For example, one specific negative appraisal for a survivor of the 2005 London bombings might be that travelling on the underground is now too dangerous. Although this is not objectively true in terms of risk, the feeling imbues the negative appraisal with a strong conviction that is difficult to shake off. The person no longer travels on the underground. In this way negative appraisals can come to influence a person's life.

A negative appraisal can be about the outside world (*external*) or it can focus on oneself (*internal*). The two types often occur together. The experience of trauma can give rise to the belief that the world is now no longer a safe place (an *external* attribution). Thus, Steve worried about planes dropping out of the sky. Janine thought that her fellow police officers were going to forcibly place her in a psychiatric hospital. Richard, who had been in the Grayrigg train crash, worried that there might be another derailment. Veterans returning from conflict often report an almost paranoid state of hyper-sensitivity, as though danger were lurking on every street corner. It is clear that these are not rational appraisals, not a cool, detached consideration of risk and probabilities, but fuelled by fundamental feelings of insecurity. Feelings and thoughts are closely intertwined, which is why, when feelings are very strong for whatever reason, our thinking is shaped by them.

The experience of flashbacks and other trauma memories also shapes how we see ourselves (an *internal* attribution). Janine was convinced she was going mad. She understood the intrusions as a sign of mental breakdown and her thoughts flew ahead to madness and incarceration in a psychiatric hospital. A key feature is often the feeling of things being out of control, because the intrusions appear to come into the mind for no discernible reason. One of the flashbacks Elaine experienced occurred occasionally at supermarket check-outs: she would suddenly be thrust back to her time on the London underground when she was waiting to be rescued. It was inexplicable to her why this should happen in an ordinary situation such as a supermarket. She felt at the mercy of forces outside her control. With the help of her therapist she recognized that her flashbacks were triggered by certain sensory cues like the lighting in the supermarket or, in another case, her grandchildren holding out their hands to her at the same height as Stan, the dying man in the other train, had. Once there is an explanation, and it is believed by the individual concerned, then the negative thoughts begin to lose their power. In Janine's case, once she was told her that her reliving of the trauma was a characteristic symptom of PTSD, she was able to relinquish the idea that she was going mad. The diagnosis made sense of her experiences and offered her the possibility of recovery.

Negative appraisals interact with negative feelings in a downward spiral of thoughts and feelings. For example, a trauma memory elicits feelings of distress and anxiety. If these feelings are interpreted as signs of madness or as personal weakness, this in turn provokes more anxiety and distress. A characteristic of negative appraisals is that they seem to have a life of their own. People desperately want to stop thinking such negative thoughts. But the thoughts cannot be wished away, and the failure to stop such thoughts can lead to further negative feelings and even stronger negative thoughts such as 'I am a weak person; I must be going mad; I am different from normal people; there is something seriously wrong with me.' In other words, these negative thoughts can change our perception of ourselves and the world, and they shape our beliefs about ourselves. Elaine made huge efforts to control what came into her mind by refusing to read newspapers, listen to the radio or watch TV, in case terrorist attacks or similar were mentioned (see Chapter 7). For three years her family and her work colleagues complied with her efforts. When she eventually broke down, it was because she was exhausted, unable any longer to maintain the rigid control she had put into place. She finally acknowledged that she was unwell. Because she was forgetful, had difficulty concentrating and felt emotionally detached from her family, she thought she had Alzheimer's disease. It was only when she was eventually assessed by a psychologist that the diagnosis of PTSD was made.

Without an objective explanation of what the feelings are about, it is scarcely surprising that many people come to believe they are at fault or have some awful illness or are going mad. This does not apply equally to everyone. The term '*idiosyncratic* negative appraisal' points to the importance of individual differences. Exactly how a person's thinking is coloured by feelings to some extent reflects who they are and what their personal history is. In Janine's case the feeling that she felt most strongly was anger, something that she only came to understand much later.

> The anger built up to such an extent that it almost rein-
> forced [the flashbacks] . . . I think it was because it fuelled
> the anger, it kept the anger going. I often wonder why did I
> hold onto it so much and I think it's because, as a person, I
> do have quite a strong sense of what's right and wrong, I do
> think that it is my personality . . .

Janine acknowledges that what made her angry was her strong sense of right and wrong, coupled with her feelings of being let down by her employers. As we have seen. this was not just to do with the shooting, after which she was upbraided for putting herself at risk, but also an earlier incident where she had developed problems with her feet because she had been left to stand too long in the heat. Because of the person she is, the overwhelming feeling she had was anger. Her idiosyncratic negative appraisals were all about being let down by those who should have looked after her.

The value of this cognitive model is that it provides a straightforward explanation of what people are feeling and thinking after trauma. It links strong feelings like anxiety, anger, shame or guilt to certain types of thoughts (negative appraisals) and detaches these thoughts from our general sense of who we are. They are, after all, just thoughts, part of the stream of consciousness. It is important to recognize that they do not define us as certain types of people, however much they seem to give that impression. Once recognized and labelled, such thoughts can be changed. The therapeutic method known as cognitive behaviour therapy (CBT) has been successful in helping people do just that.

Idiosyncratic negative appraisal describes one feature of the cognitive model of trauma. As we saw in Fig. 9.1 it is intimately linked to two other cognitive processes, how we perceive the world, and our fundamental beliefs.

Changes in perception

Kerry was living in New York on 11 September 2001, when two hijacked planes flew into the Twin Towers and brought them down. I interviewed her in London in May 2010, and the story she told me illustrated how a major trauma can transform both the external and internal landscape. Kerry worked as a location scout for a photographer and on the morning of 9/11 was due to attend a fashion shoot with a colleague in the Plaza area around the Twin Towers. At the last minute her colleague phoned her to say he had changed his mind about the venue, deciding he would go to Central Park and that he no longer needed her for the shoot. Her flat was about half a mile from the Twin Towers and shortly after her colleague phoned, she heard the sound of a plane flying low overhead and then another a few minutes later. She turned on the television and, like many people around the world, gazed in horror at the images of the planes smashing into the Twin Towers. Hesitating for a long time in her flat, she wondered what to do; in the end she decided to go out to see what was happening.

'Finally I made it out of the door and from the corner, literally a couple of houses away, you could see straight down to the Towers. And I just stood on the street and tried to understand what was going on. The first thing I noticed as I came out of the door was that people had started to walk uptown past the end of my street.'

'Was that away from the Twin Towers?'

'Yes. There were groups of people walking and their heads were kind of [bowed], they weren't saying anything. There was no talking and that is one of the things that stayed with me for the first couple of days, the silence. You know, everyone was very quiet. The airspace had been completely cleared. No one quite knew what was going on. But there wasn't panic and hysteria. There weren't people running to and fro. There was just this kind of silent walking . . . It was just about fleeing and people were covered in white, they were all covered in this white [ash].'

'It must have looked very strange.'

'It was really strange. There was a man sitting on the ground with his cell phone. There were no cell phones. There were no phones so he couldn't use his phone. But he had his cell phone pressed to his ear, his head in his hands with his cell phone, not talking, completely covered in white and sitting there. I remember that really clearly.'

For Kerry, the familiar world of Manhattan was transformed into a surreal scene, something that has since become familiar to us from the television coverage at the time. The physical landscape around her had changed and with it came a feeling of dislocation. She tried to get nearer to the Twin Towers but was stopped. Her memory of exactly what she did after that is disjointed. But what she remembers clearly is standing watching the Towers collapse, one after the other. This event had a marked effect on her.

I stood on the corner as close as I could get with a group of people, and no one saying anything except sighing, 'Oh my God, oh my God, what's going on?' And I watched the Towers fall. That was devastating. I just crumbled inside. There was a real sense of collapse . . . it marked the end of Manhattan, this kind of edge, and suddenly to have this open space, it was really like all the containment fell away.

Kerry's experience on the day of the 9/11 attack echoes the description of those in the 2005 London bombings in Chapter 2. A

familiar world is suddenly changed and the effect is felt emotionally, often with feelings of detachment, confusion and uncertainty.
After 9/11, New York was not the same city as before. America
was not the same country as before. A horrific, deliberate, murderous series of assaults had been committed by, at the time they were
perpetrated, unknown enemies. The effect was felt nationwide.
The nation's defences had been breached with the result that the
sense of security that most Americans felt had been shattered. This
represents a change in perception. 'Things can never be the same'
is commonly said after such a trauma and the cliché captures the
basic truth. The world is seen differently. As Kerry's experience
shows, her internal world mirrored the external changes: she herself no longer felt contained, safe.

The way perception can change after trauma is intimately connected with negative appraisals in the stream of consciousness.
For a long time after the trauma of being raped Georgie felt guilty.
She thought she had to some extent brought the trauma on herself.
This reflected her view of herself as having been too proud to
acknowledge her loneliness, with the result that she chatted to the
three men for a long time and allowed them to follow her home.
Her guilt was also about having let her parents down. It was only
after being in therapy that Georgie began to see things in a different light; that is, her perception of herself changed. When I asked
about this, she told me that it was now clear in her mind that the
men were responsible, not her.

> 'I thought "They are in my apartment". I definitely felt the
> guy who was with me at the end [would not listen]. I clearly
> shouted at him and told him 'no' and 'go away'. But the
> others I felt, you know . . . but I did ask them to leave the
> apartment. I said I didn't want to do anything and I said it
> quite repeatedly. But then when it started, I think now I did
> cry but it was not actually emotional. It was more like tears
> from just pressure and the stuff. It was horrible not being
> able to breathe.'

'Do you feel guilty now?'

'No. Perhaps guilt can never go away totally but I just
think guilt is really a pointless feeling, unless it teaches
you anything . . . so I kind of distance myself from it a
bit. [It was] quite brutal. OK, it happened. It wasn't my
fault. It's their fault. But I was pretty stupid as well and
there were reasons why I was stupid because I was actually
really depressed in Paris. [I was] very stupidly proud so I
wouldn't tell anyone.'

Georgie's appraisal of herself now is far less negative. While she
recognizes that there were contributory factors in what happened,
such as her loneliness and pride, she knows that the three men
were the ones who were guilty – as was, in fact, proved conclu-
sively by the court. She no longer feels at fault. Moreover, as she
read more about women and rape, she was able to see a broader
context, and this changed her perception of the event and led to
her feeling much better about herself.

Shattered illusions

The psychologist Ronnie Janoff-Bulman coined the term 'the
shattering of illusions' to describe the change in fundamental
beliefs that follow trauma. She pointed out that 'much of the
psychological toll [after trauma] derives from the shattering of
very basic assumptions that victims have held about themselves
and their world'. The world comes to be seen as unsafe and dangerous and the sense of invulnerability that most of us have is
shattered. The change to beliefs is the third element in the model I
presented in Fig. 9.1. It gets to the heart of what matters to people,
their sense of themselves, their identity, and how the familiar,
cosy world that they took for granted has fundamentally changed.

Shortly after the coroner's inquest into the 2005 London bombings had ended in March 2011, I asked Tim Coulson to reflect on
how he had been changed by that traumatic event. He told me

that he had become less confident about taking on new things, especially if they required active decision making, and that he was a more serious person than he had been before, less capable of simply having fun. He continued to feel somewhat detached from other people, which was the state of mind he felt very strongly in the immediate aftermath of the trauma. Yet on the other hand, his basic beliefs and values had, if anything, been strengthened, particularly in terms of his belief in the importance of proactively helping others, which was what he had done so memorably at the time of the trauma. He believed the world was a less safe place as a result of the bombings and he was acutely aware of how national attitudes reflected this. After 9/11 and the London bombings, the western world no longer feels as secure as it was, or, to put it psychologically, the West's illusion of safety has been shattered by those events. He told me that the trauma had had both positive and negative effects on him: on the one hand it had led to a greater separateness from others, particularly professional colleagues, but on the other it had given him greater freedom to plan and do new things. Tim's summary will almost certainly resonate with other survivors of trauma who, like him, feel that the traumatic event changed them, and that the change has both positive and negative features.

In Georgie's case, psychotherapy helped her to shed the critical, self-judging, negative thoughts that she experienced so acutely after the rape. Her psychologist's nonjudgemental acceptance of her helped her to feel good about herself again. On returning to university she found that her flatmates, whom she told about the rape, accepted her and respected her for her strength in seeking redress through the courts. At a psychological level she came to better understand herself and that the vulnerability which she had experienced during the rape was not a personal failing but simply a part of who she is as a person.

I think emotions can be good or bad depending on how you look at them. It's like OK, I'm really strong. That's a good

thing. I can carry on with this. And I can also be strong
enough to be vulnerable and that was quite a big thing . . .
if you don't make yourself vulnerable, you can't really be a
human, to be honest.

Both Tim and Georgie went through personal transformations
as a result of the traumas they experienced. Neither wanted to
go through those horrendous experiences, of course, but having
gone through them their beliefs about themselves and the world
changed. Acknowledging this change is a key to recovery. There
are some who resist such changes, desperately wanting things to
be as they were before. But because this can never happen, their
lives remain blighted by the trauma. In the next chapter I will discuss how the experience of a trauma can trigger off the memory of
past traumas. I will also look at the importance of understanding
this, if a person is to make a full recovery.

Chapter 10: The past and the present

'It was a big church. [It] had capacity for 1,500 and there were 1,300 people in the church that night.'

'So what was your first apprehension of the attack? What do you remember about that?'

'I just remember seeing these men coming in and not knowing what it was at all. I remember thinking it was kids up to mischief. I remember seeing what obviously was a grenade. I thought it was a water bomb. I could see stuff coming out which I thought was water, but it was in fact a grenade packed with nails.'

'So this visual image, you see these men. Black men?'

'Four black men wearing blue boiler suits and I can still picture the one chap crouching down to lob the grenade. I can still see that very clearly.'

'Where were you in the church?'

'I was about half way. It was laid out like a cinema, steps up, wooden pews in between. But I was probably midway up from the stage and I remember at the time it happened, there were musicians playing on the stage. There was a woman playing the piano and someone singing. Suddenly the door next to the stage opened, just as the duet was ending and I can remember seeing a man crouching down to throw something and then there being a lot of noise. I can remember feeling dust and something showering over me. Then I don't think I remember terribly much. I was knocked out for a while, a short while . . . I do then remember coming round, being aware that something had happened, and smelling, I suppose it must have been, gun smoke . . . I noticed that my friend was lying with his head on the back of an upturned pew and it was very strange. He was twitching and moaning and then I began to get really frightened because I could see his heart beating. He was quite a fit rugby player. I could see his heart beat and every time his heart beat, blood gushed out of his head and started to pool in the overturned pew. So I tried to do what I could to stop the wound, but I remember a feeling of absolute helplessness. I just didn't know [what to do]. I was about thirty-two and I remember wanting my mother. She was the one person I wanted to be there and actually she would have been useless in those circumstances. She says that herself to this day. But I do remember that quite clearly, wanting my mum.'

'So you felt really helpless. What about the men? Were they still there?'

'No, they'd gone by then and at that stage we were waiting for the emergency services . . . and I can remember people then coming around to help. And then I remember the church emptying, someone talking through a megaphone and saying, "Please clear the area unless you are attending to wounded."'

'And you were attending to your friend?'

'I was attending to my friend and then there was a man on the other side of me . . . He was a surgeon from New Zealand I think, and he'd been shot in the arm quite badly. He was conscious but he was wanting help. I think someone had splinted it for him, actually, if I remember back now, I do remember helping him to tie a sling because he was uncomfortable. And him telling me to be calm. He said I looked absolutely terrified.'

'And that's how you felt, was it?'

'No, I don't think I really did feel terrified at the time. I felt helpless. I'll never forget that, that feeling of utter helplessness.'

On 25 July 1993, a cold, wet winter's evening, Kathryn was in St James's Church in Cape Town, South Africa for the Sunday evening service when four men broke into the church, throwing grenades and spraying it with gunfire. The four were part of the Azanian People's Liberation Army, a terrorist group and the military wing of the Pan Africanist Congress. In the attack eleven people were killed and fifty-eight wounded. Kathryn suffered minor grazes and the explosion affected her hearing in one ear, but she was otherwise physically uninjured. Yet, as the extract from my interview with her shows, she was caught up in the middle of the violence, tending to her friend who was severely injured, unconscious and bleeding profusely from a head wound. Not surprisingly, she was badly shaken and her predominant feeling at the time was of utter helplessness. With the help of the surgical team at the local hospital, her friend's life was saved, but he was brain damaged and was left with considerable handicaps.

This is exactly the type of major trauma that, in some people, leads to the diagnosis of PTSD. It was a sudden, unexpected, catastrophic event. It instilled feelings of terror and helplessness. It is hard to imagine a more frightening situation than a group of armed men throwing grenades and indiscriminately spraying the congregation of a church with machine-gun fire. But although Kathryn did have psychological problems after the trauma, it was not PTSD that she suffered from but claustrophobia and depression. Her example illustrates how important it is not to assume that the psychological effect of trauma will always take the form of PTSD. How someone is affected is, in part, a product of their personal history – their past, in other words.

In this chapter I will consider the importance of the past in shaping people's response to trauma. Who a person is and the experiences they have been through will influence how they respond to a major trauma, as I illustrated in Chapter 7, with the differing stories of Elaine and Tim in the wake of the 2005 London bombings. Sometimes being caught up in a major trauma can evoke memories of an earlier trauma. I described an example of this in Chapter 1, when a man who was badly beaten up by a gang of youths outside a supermarket was plagued by nightmares that reminded him of the constant physical abuse he had suffered from his father when he was a child. The past trauma might have been completely forgotten until the present trauma triggers its memory; or it might be part of autobiographical memory, as in the case of the man who was beaten up by the gang of youths. Either way, to fully understand the reaction entails recalling traumatic events from the past, something that people can find difficult to do. A major trauma can have a disruptive effect on the mind's capacity to function properly in the present and that in turn can release past memories that have been repressed or forgotten. Psychoanalysis, the psychological theory that began with Freud, focuses on anxiety-provoking experiences in childhood, often unconscious, that are tapped into at times of extreme fear. I will describe how these ideas help to illuminate the psychology of people's reactions to trauma. The present always encompasses the past, to some degree. How this happens and what part it plays in trauma is the subject of this chapter.

Kathryn's experiences after the massacre

I asked Kathryn how the trauma had affected her in the days and weeks afterwards. She told me she did not sleep well and that she kept having flashbacks to the trauma.

> 'As soon as I drifted off into sleep I could see a guy crouching down. I still could draw that now.'
>> 'So you had a very strong visual image as you were falling to sleep of that man crouching there. And that would jerk you awake?'
> 'Yes. So sleep became absolutely terrible and a dread.'
>> 'So you weren't sleeping at all well?'
> 'No, and to this day I don't sleep well.'
>> 'Did you have dreams or nightmares as well as this particular flashback?"

'I did have nightmares initially.'

'Do you remember what their content was?'

'Feelings of claustrophobia and of struggling to do something. I still get them nowadays. Running but my legs don't want to move.'

'Feeling trapped, really.'

'Getting to an airport and finding I haven't got my passport. At that time I did quite a lot of trail walking. [I was] having dreams that I would go on a trail and hadn't got food or hadn't got my sleeping bag or had forgotten my hiking boots. You know that sort of feeling that everything was against me.'

Flashbacks and traumatic nightmares, provided they persist beyond a month after the trauma, are prime indicators in the diagnosis of PTSD. Kathryn told me that it was vaguely suggested that she might have PTSD but she did not recall receiving a formal diagnosis. That she did not was probably more to do with the fact that PTSD was not so well known in the 1990s. Yet her specific symptoms are interesting in themselves, irrespective of the diagnosis. Kathryn told me that the flashbacks occurred only at night and just before she was going to sleep. They are more correctly described as *hypnagogic phenomena*. These are vivid perceptual experiences that occur at the transition from wakefulness to sleep, interrupting the process of falling asleep. They are not particular to trauma. In one study, 37 per cent of a population sample of almost 5,000 adults reported experiencing hypnagogic phenomena. It is clear that the trauma provoked these intrusive, disturbing images. The stress of what Kathryn had been through affected her peace of mind. The disruption to sleep added to the strain. But other than these images at night she had no vivid flashback memories.

In sleep, when her defences were lowered, she had nightmares. However, they were not about the massacre she had just been through, but about other situations in which she felt trapped and helpless. For a long time it was assumed that traumatic nightmares were simply unalloyed repetitions of the trauma. But research studies have shown that they commonly contain other material not obviously related to the event itself, just as Kathryn's did. Nightmares are different from normal dreams. Dreaming occurs naturally during the sleep cycle and, on awakening, the memory of the dream rapidly fades. Unless we write the dream down or tell someone immediately about it, the memory of it is lost. Even when we do try to capture the dream, we are often unsure that our dream report is accurate. Dreams are elusive. Nightmares are not. In the wake of nightmares there is detailed and vivid recall of what is an extended and disturbing dream. We wake up in a state of fear and anxiety. The dream material stays with us rather than fading away. The commonest feeling in a nightmare is of helplessness in the presence of some sort of danger that threatens our survival or security.

Kathryn's nightmares were undoubtedly prompted by the trauma she had experienced. The link is provided not by the memory of the event itself but by the feeling of helplessness she experienced in the church. Her friend was seriously injured and she had to tend to him. She described a harrowing scene as she tried to do that.

> 'I'll never forget that feeling of utter helplessness. I became very frightened for my friend because I could see he was horribly injured. And then I tried to stop the wound from bleeding . . .'
>
> 'You put your hand over his head wound?'
>
> 'I got a T-shirt and tried to stem the bleeding. I later learned that he had sustained a bullet wound to the temple that had exited at the top of his head. I remember how spongy, warm and sticky his scalp felt and I realize now what must have been little bits of brain all over my clothing, little jelly-like whitish-grey bits. [I remember] being afraid that the emergency services weren't attending to him first. They were there at this stage. I could see the stretchers

coming in. He didn't seem to be getting any attention. I remember getting quite sort of panicky and shouty, you know, "You've got to come here now!"'

Unlike many others in the church, Kathryn could not leave, because she was tending to her friend. She was trapped. She could see how seriously he was injured but she had little idea of what to do to help him. She felt helpless. These two feelings came out in the nightmares she experienced – wanting to run but not being able to; being on a walk and forgetting her boots or other key equipment; or being at the airport without a passport. The panic she felt was not so much to do with any threat to her life, but an acute anxiety about being trapped in an impossible situation and not being able to get out of it. Looked at this way, it is not surprising that Kathryn developed claustrophobia.

Claustrophobia

It was only when the ambulance came that Kathryn was at last able to leave. Later, she and her parents went to look for her friend in two different hospitals, not knowing if he was alive or dead. With his brother and sister she trawled through the various cubicles looking for him, not knowing what they would find. It was at this stage that she was overwhelmed by a feeling of panic.

And then when we were in the hospital, I think my mother was probably fussing over me, and I suddenly felt terribly claustrophobic. I think by that stage we'd found him and we were waiting to be called by a consultant who would tell us what the prognosis was. I remember the man was kindly and gentle and said that, although his injuries were significant, they had experience of bullet wounds and would do their best to save his life. They gave him a 50/50 chance. It was a long night and when eventually we left the hospital, a pharmacist friend gave me a tranquillizer to help me to sleep.

A few days after the attack the local police ran a series of group
therapy sessions in which Kathryn was encouraged to participate.
She went only once.

> There were about fifteen people in the room and none of
> them had directly dealt with an injury like me, so I felt a
> sense of detachment from the group. I had such an over-
> whelming feeling of claustrophobia during the group ses-
> sion that I had to leave the room. A police psychologist
> followed me out and encouraged me to have one-on-one
> counselling, which I eventually did with a local clinical
> psychologist and her psychiatrist husband who had offered
> their services free of charge.

In the weeks that followed the event, Kathryn found crowded
places difficult to be in; in shopping centres, for example, she felt
pressed in by the lights, the music and the crowds. She wanted
to run away. She began avoiding them. Even to this day, almost
two decades after the trauma, she can find that such places make
her uneasy, though by no means to the degree she experienced in
South Africa. She reminded me that, in the 1990s, an armed struggle was occurring in South Africa, so the danger of being attacked
was real. Eventually she left the country and came to England. But
a feeling of detachment from other people persisted.

I asked Kathryn if claustrophobia was something she had been
prone to before the massacre. She thought she might have had
a tendency that way. She recalled locking herself in a toilet as a
child and panicking and being unable to take instructions from her
mother, who was outside. But her experience in the church was of a
different order, far worse than anything she had experienced before.

> In the church, I wanted to run away. I actually did want to.
> I wanted my mother there but I also wanted to run away
> because I didn't know how to cope. I didn't know what to
> do. I felt useless. I do remember that feeling of just wanting

to run away. I'm glad I didn't because I think I would have suffered guilt for a long time afterwards.

Kathryn's desire for her mother, even though she knew rationally that her mother's presence in the church would not have helped, was, in effect, a young child's yearning for the security of a parent. It illustrates nicely how past feelings can be evoked in the present.

Guilt and depression

The day after the trauma, Kathryn went to see her friend in hospital. He had been operated on and was in recovery. But he was clearly in a bad way. This is how she described that visit to me.

> 'He did look pretty horrific. He was black and blue. Obviously his whole head was bandaged. He had black eyes. His arms were in a sling and he was attached to all sorts of beeping machines. He looked pretty horrendous. They had badly shaved his head so he just looked awful ... I remember I was there with him when his parents arrived – they had flown in from the UK. It must have been a huge shock for them and I can still picture his mother's face when she saw him ... It was weird, I knew I wasn't responsible but I did have what I have read about since, survivor guilt, I'm pretty sure I suffered from that. I just didn't know whether I could face his parents. I didn't really know what to do, what to think.'
>
> 'When you said you felt guilty, were you thinking that you might have done something differently?'
>
> 'Yes. I was worried that I hadn't done my best for him. I didn't know anything about first aid. I just didn't know where to start.'

Kathryn mentions 'survivor guilt'. In Robert Lifton's account of the survivors of Hiroshima, he explains that many experienced guilt simply about having survived when so many others had died. People also experienced guilt about what they had done or not done. Parents found it heart-wrenching not to have been able to prevent their children from dying. Sometimes the individual's focus narrowed to something small. One man was asked by his son to remove a nail from his shoe. The father told him he would do it after school. His son did not survive and the father felt terrible guilt, thinking that perhaps his son could have run faster had he taken the nail out. Guilt is not rational. Ruminating about what one might have done differently is like magically seeking to undo the trauma. 'If only' thoughts are replayed in the mind, without bringing any real comfort or relief.

Why should survivors of major trauma feel guilt at all? After all, survival is often entirely a matter of chance, as it was with Kathryn. The men on either side of her were hit by bullets. She was simply fortunate not to have been. But feeling fortunate and experiencing relief at being alive and not seriously injured can be regarded as inappropriate feelings, given the horror that has been inflicted on others. The profound shock of the trauma can also affect how people behave, sometimes in ways that they later regret. In Lifton's interviews with the survivors of Hiroshima, many regretted having 'selfishly' put their own survival above that of neighbours or even strangers. The cries of the dying and injured echoed in their ears. One man, searching for his family, felt accused by the eyes of the anonymous dead, as though they were reproaching him for living.

Guilt can reach back to difficult past relationships and to resentments and arguments that cannot now be resolved because the person has died. In my memoir I recount the therapy of a woman I called 'Laura' who could not come to terms with the death of her mother. She was plunged into feelings of guilt and depression, blaming herself for not being there when her mother died. Throughout her life she had had a difficult relationship with her mother who, being depressed herself, had failed to look after Laura when she was a child. Her guilt was in a large part about the anger she felt towards her mother, something she had buried deep inside her. Her mother's death meant there was no chance for reparation or forgiveness.

In the hospital, Kathryn worried that she had not done her best for her friend. In the presence of his parents she was acutely aware how badly injured he was and how she, conversely, had survived relatively unscathed. Along with her nightmares, these thoughts disturbed her sleep, causing insomnia.

'I was given sleeping tablets and then I was given antidepressants as well. I don't know if I did feel very depressed. I don't know now looking back whether I perhaps was depressed anyway.'

'What, before the incident?'

'Yes, I think possibly I was a little.'

'What makes you think that? Do you remember, then, periods of feeling very sad?'

'Melancholy, yes. I think depression probably runs a little bit in my family. So I took these antidepressants and some sleeping tablets and then I seemed to feel OK.'

When feelings of guilt are intense, depression can follow. In Chapter 8 I described how Georgie was plunged into depression when she returned to her parents' home after the rape. Looking back, Kathryn is not sure if she felt more depressed than usual at that time. She was aware of having a history of depression and that her mother had been depressed. Her example illustrates how the past shapes the present, how the shock of a trauma affects people where they are most vulnerable, like a fault line that causes the earth's movement to become a massive earthquake. Kathryn's pre-existing depression was accentuated by seeing what had happened to her friend. She told me she visited the hospital daily for several months.

Once he came round, it was very difficult to see him because it wasn't the person I knew, who was funny, sociable and always game for a party. He couldn't speak properly. He

was paralysed down his right side. He was very confused
and anxious. He had these dreadful headaches which were
relieved by drilling small holes into his skull.

It was shocking to see this transformation of her friend, who now
seemed like a shell of himself, struggling to do ordinary things and,
later, becoming quite disinhibited and childlike, a different person,
in effect. Seeing him every day seared the huge loss into Kathryn's
mind. In addition, her attendance at the head-injury ward brought
her into contact with others who were also suffering terribly.

'So you were seeing people at their very worst in some
ways, in terms of injuries and lots of young people whose
lives were being completely transformed.'
    'That's right. He was in the ward at the same time as
a nineteen-year-old girl who'd been in a terrible, dreadful car accident. Some people had died and she was brain
damaged and she couldn't move her limbs. I used to see
her parents at her bedside and you know you became quite
close to these people because you'd see them every day.
"How is yours getting on? Any progress?" . . . and I think
also at that stage the state hospitals in South Africa were
grim, really. I mean I think the surgical procedures were
top-notch. The surgeons were great, but some of the ward
was pretty ropey. The food was awful and he just didn't
seem clean at times.'

Kathryn visited her friend daily for seven months, visits that seem
to have been driven by her feelings of guilt.

'I felt it was something that I needed to do. I think I was
at that stage [when I was] probably processing the guilt. I
pretty much went most days, in the evenings after work.'
    'A huge commitment, really.'
    'It was.'

'Was there some sort of reparation in this visit, in going back?'

'Possibly, I'm not sure. It was just something that I felt I needed to do, but it was a strain.'

I have described Kathryn's experience to illustrate the way the past influenced how she was affected by a major trauma. The feelings of helplessness and anxiety she felt in the church came out as claustrophobia, something she recalled having as a child. Her guilt at being uninjured when her friend was badly brain damaged played into her propensity for depression. The huge commitment she undertook to visit her friend every day was an expression of a desire for reparation. It also says something about Kathryn's personality that she took her responsibilities seriously. Another person might have behaved very differently. It is not hard to imagine someone else perhaps visiting the injured friend in the first few days but then much less frequently or not at all. I wonder what I might have done myself. I doubt if I would have been so conscientious.

Past traumas

In Chapter 9 I recounted the experience of Kerry, who witnessed the destruction of the Twin Towers on 9/11. Looking at the devastation in the first days, she experienced a feeling that the world had changed and that she herself no longer felt 'contained'. She recalled trying to give blood and seeing people standing in line to identify the dead, seeing bodies and body parts arriving in black bags, and the desperate 'Missing' notices with their photographs of lost loved ones. It was a strange, surreal time. In the US there was a general level of fear and anxiety mixed with a resurgence of patriotism, as many people hung the American flag from their houses. I asked Kerry how she was feeling during this time.

'I was really grateful for my meditative practice. Whenever I felt panic or hysteria coming on, I would sit there and meditate.'

'Did that tend to happen quite a bit, that you would feel panic or hysteria?'

'I'm not a hysterical person and I'm not an overly panicked person, due to the nature of my childhood and how I was raised. I grew up in quite an intense childhood home and internalized everything and so I have a tendency to keep things contained really well. I function really well in a crisis situation. And the meditation really helped to contain that.'

Kerry volunteered to work for the Salvation Army, expecting to be sent to JFK airport to unpack boxes. Instead, she and some of her fellow volunteers were driven to the site of the Twin Towers, now known as Ground Zero. They had been selected to distribute food and whatever was needed to the people working there.

'It was a really alarming experience. I was there for two days. I finished that day and came back the next day. For me it was, on one level, a gift. It brought it home and I really understood. I went straight into automatic pilot in production mode, into organizing and sorting and fixing, into crisis-management.'

'Is that something that you were familiar with?'

'Yes. Familiar with and also that is how, childhood-wise, when things were in crisis, [I] sorted it out.'

Kerry's account of how she felt and what she did immediately after 9/11 reveals how much her reaction was shaped by the past. She told me that, as a child, she had had to learn the importance of being in control. She came from an Irish Catholic family that believed in disciplining the children by beating, while her mother had occasional bouts of violence that were fuelled by alcohol. Her mother's moods were mercurial and Kerry sought to mitigate their effects by controlling her own behaviour, becoming a quiet, good girl. In his writings, the psychoanalyst and paediatrician Donald Winnicott described the way children cope with this sort of childhood; he stated that they form a *false self*, the persona of a good, compliant, well-behaved child. Their anger and despair are buried deep in the unconscious – a *true self*, which at traumatic times threatens to break through into consciousness. The way Kerry responded after 9/11 was once again to seek control. She controlled her fears by meditating. She went into 'organizing' mode as she worked for the Salvation Army at the site of the Twin Towers, and later at JFK airport. She did a lot of reading about PTSD and the effects of war. She also took a job in a large advertising agency, hoping that this would give her a sense of security. But this proved to be another source of anxiety, as she tried to adapt to a corporate culture that was driven largely by fear.

A major trauma breaches the mind's defences and allows deeper and more primitive fears to flood in. There is a loss of trust both in the external world and, internally, in the mind's capacity to protect itself. Just as New York City's defences were shattered by the action of the terrorists who brought down the Twin Towers, leaving the city and the country feeling vulnerable, so the experience of intense fear breaks through normal cognitive processes of thinking and feeling, flooding the mind with anxiety that reaches right back to the powerful fears of childhood. This is not a conscious or rational process. It shows itself in the way people react and behave. The sense of detachment or estrangement, which Kerry and many others felt in the immediate aftermath of 9/11, represents the mind initially shutting down in the face of intense emotion. After a while the emotion floods back and it is at this point that the past and present become fused. The link comes from the intensity of the feelings and the way they provoke ways of behaving that were evident earlier on in the individual's life.

Conclusion

The experiences of Kathryn and Kerry illustrate the importance of the past in gaining a full understanding of the psychological effects of trauma. It is easy to overlook the past. After all, a major traumatic event, whether an earthquake or a terrorist attack or something more personal, is so vivid and immediate that the tendency is to attribute the problems that follow entirely to it. This is the limitation of the diagnosis of PTSD, which is arrived at *ahistorically*, that is, without taking into account the nature of the person and their personal history. Robert Scaer, a neurologist with over thirty years' experience working with trauma victims, argues that we all experience many traumas during our lifetime, including experiences that are regarded as culturally normal, and that it is essential to relate the present trauma to those past experiences, because if we do not, we fail to understand what the current trauma truly means. This is entirely sensible. The psychoanalytic account of trauma has long recognized that it is the coincidence of the external threat and our internal, unconscious fears that makes traumatic anxiety so overwhelming. Not only is the world outside unsafe but we come to doubt the world inside, which is why people often report a feeling of disintegration or a sense that they are not quite real, or wonder if they are going mad.

I am writing this chapter a couple of weeks after the 2011 Japanese earthquake that triggered off a tsunami devastating the east coast of Honshu island. In my mind's eye I can see the televised pictures of the huge tsunami wave barrelling its way over the coastline, sweeping houses, cars, trees, walls and roads before it as though they are mere children's toys. This image captures the transformational nature of a major trauma, how the normal landscape of our customary thoughts and beliefs is suddenly and irrevocably altered, creating a new and uncertain world.

Part 3:
Recovery

Chapter 11: Revisiting

On 27 August 1979, off the west coast of Ireland on a lovely sunny morning, a small boat, *Shadow V*, was blown to pieces by a 5 lb gelignite bomb placed under the deck and activated by remote control by members of the IRA. Lord Mountbatten was at the helm. Also on board were his daughter and son-in-law, Patricia and John Brabourne, two of their children, 15-year-old twins Timothy and Nicholas, John's mother Lady Brabourne, and Paul Maxwell, a 15-year-old Irish friend of the family. The bomb killed Lord Mountbatten, Lady Brabourne, Nicholas Knatchbull and Paul Maxwell, and seriously wounded Timothy and his parents. The IRA regarded it as a blow struck against English oppression in Ireland. To the bereaved families it was a devastating tragedy, the deliberate, cold-blooded murder of innocent people on a family outing to check on the lobster pots around the coast. This was no ordinary tragedy, if such a thing exists, for the Mountbattens were relatives of the Queen and the shock of the outrage reverberated around the world. Those of us who were living at that time can recall the event, even if, like mine, one's recollection of it is hazy. I recalled that Lord Mounbatten had been killed but little else. I did not know anything about the personal consequences to the family, and had it not been for a meeting with Tim Knatchbull over thirty years later I doubt if I would ever have known anything more.

I first came across Tim at the 2010 Oxford Literary Festival when he talked with great candour about the trauma he had suffered. He had just published a book, *From a Clear Blue Sky: Surviving the Mountbatten Bomb*, in which he gave a detailed account of the events leading up to the murders, as well as recounting his experience, decades later, of returning to the west coast of Ireland, a journey that was as much psychological as it was geographical. I bought the book and asked Tim if he would grant me an interview, which he kindly did. I was interested to talk to him about several aspects of the trauma he had been through, the huge change it had made to his life at a young and impressionable age, the loss of his identical twin, Nick, and the long process of mental and emotional recovery that he went through. But most of all I was interested in his conscious decision to return to Ireland, and what that had meant to him.

In this chapter I will consider what may be gained from revisiting the site of a trauma and what the risks may be. As far as I can discover, there is no psychological research specifically on revisiting; that is, there are no studies evaluating whether or not returning to the trauma site is either beneficial or detrimental. In truth, it is difficult to do such research. There are so many confounding variables. Much depends on the nature of the person, the type of traumatic experience, the stage the person has reached in his or her recovery from the trauma, whether or not he or she is undergoing treatment, whether or not support is provided, what expectations the person has with regard to revisiting, and what actually happens during any revisiting. However, what we know clinically about the psychological recovery from trauma suggests that revisiting a trauma site could be an important part of the process of moving on, a way of putting the original trauma to bed – of achieving 'closure', to use an American term.

During 2003–4 Tim Knatchbull carried out a carefully planned series of visits. These proved enormously helpful to him, as I will describe. However, returning to where the trauma took place is not always beneficial. There is a misconception that the traumatized person should quickly 'get back on the horse', to use an old saying. In my work with the police, I saw a young WPC who had been in road accident in which the driver of the police car she was travelling in lost control at speed, going over a hump-backed bridge. The WPC injured her back and suffered considerable pain and anxiety. She told me that, a few days after the accident, on the advice of her GP, she returned to the accident site. But this had not helped her. The advice may have been well intentioned but it was psychologically inept. Revisiting the site of a trauma is not something that should be undertaken without careful preparation. Even more important is finding the right time to do it, if it is to be done at all. A few days after the trauma is often the wrong time, as the person is usually still suffering physical and/or psychological effects. There is a risk of making matters worse.

Revisiting is one component of certain trauma therapies (sometimes called 'exposure' or 'reliving' therapies) in which the trauma sufferer is exposed to trauma memories in order to aid the processing of those memories. At some point in the treatment the therapist and client may return to the trauma site together, often with beneficial results. Some trauma sufferers return of their own accord. This can be part of a self-help programme, as it was with Tim, or it may simply be a matter of necessity. George, who was in the 2005 London bombings, told me that he went back on the underground just five days after the explosion. He did not want to lose his job, which required travelling to properties all over London. The underground was the best way of getting around and so he forced himself to go back, getting through the initial fear. For a long while he found travelling on the tube difficult. He remained apprehensive, alert to possible terrorists amongst the passengers, sometimes leaving a carriage if someone looked suspicious.

In this chapter I will present the stories of two exceptional people who, for different reasons and at different points in their lives, made a deliberate return to a place where they had undergone harrowing traumatic experiences. Their stories illuminate the human desire for making sense of difficult and painful experiences and to mould those experiences into something new.

From a clear blue sky: Tim's story

When Tim and his family left Ireland shortly after the bombing, it seemed unlikely that any of them would return. The family would be too much at risk of another attack. But Tim thought otherwise. In the car leaving Classiebawn Castle, his late grand-father's holiday home, he announced that they would be back. His siblings told him that this would be impossible, but he stub-bornly held on to the belief that he would one day return. It is not hard to understand why Tim should want to return. He had lost his beloved twin brother and because of his own injuries and those of his parents, there had been no opportunity properly to say goodbye to Nick. The west coast of Ireland had been a magical place for the brothers; it must have been difficult to imagine that all of that was gone forever. The effect of the atrocity was felt most directly by the people immediately involved, by those who had been killed, those injured and their relatives and friends. But the bomb also exploded a childhood, a happy way of life and, in Tim's stubborn determination to return, there very probably lay a wish to recover that.

Tim revisited Ireland at two different times in his life. The first time was in 1987 when he was twenty-two and had finished his degree at Cambridge. In his book he described how he was feeling at the time.

> I decided to make 1987 a gap year in which I would travel and work. I also wanted to return to Ireland for the first time since the bomb; I did not know what I would do there but I felt drawn to half-developed thoughts lingering at the back of my mind. I had an uneasy feeling about the hole in my life left by Nick's death. I was aware that I needed to sort out my incomplete and confused emotions but I did not know how to proceed or how to explain my feelings to others.

He took an Aer Lingus flight to Shannon and had the impression of 'landing behind some form of invisible barrier, a sort of emo-tional Iron Curtain'. On his own he drove around, visiting once-familiar places. Throughout he felt a cold, raw numbness. He was aware that painful feelings were somewhere beneath the surface, but he could not get in touch with them. Having just received his pilot's licence, he hired a Cessna and flew out to the island of Inishmurray and back over Classiebawn. Later, he drove to the castle where he had stayed as a boy and viewed it from a distance, all the while feeling numb. In my interview I asked Tim about this first visit.

> I just couldn't make sense of the place. I didn't have the support, didn't know how to do it, didn't have the courage of my convictions, didn't have the wherewithal. Apart from anything, my life wasn't set up for me to be there for a week at a time and I knew that I wasn't making the progress that I needed to. And in 1987 people were still shooting and blowing people up.

Tim knew, emotionally, that he needed to revisit Ireland, but his return in 1987 did not lead to any catharsis or other emotional change. It is possible to see, with hindsight, that this revisiting came too soon in his life, when his feelings were still uncertain and confused, and when he had not established himself in a career or long-term relationship. He returned on impulse and alone. Though the return did not achieve what he had hoped, he wrote that it had 'started something difficult but necessary'. It reinforced in him the conviction that he needed to return for something important – though, at that time, he had no idea what that might be.

The next time Tim returned to Ireland was in August 2003, sixteen years after his first visit. This was the start of a series of many short trips over a year in which he revisited places and people, allowing memories to resurface, and discovering 'pieces of the jigsaw' that had been lost. This experience was very different from his first visit. One reason was that *he* was different, an older man, more emotionally mature, with a wife and family and a firm sense of himself. He was also *ready*, a term that is difficult to define precisely, in this context. He had spent some time in psychotherapy and the neutrality of that relationship had allowed

him the space to begin exploring his feelings. Tim told me about
the importance of this in our interview.

> My relationship with the therapist was very much, well,
> she was quite old school. So I didn't form a deep bond
> and attachment with her. But there was a certain degree
> of healthy environment in her consulting room for me to
> know that I could experiment with what I was saying and
> feeling and thinking, articulating without risk to myself or
> others. I think there were some things I said to her that I
> would not have said to anybody else other than to a profes-
> sional . . . and I think that there were probably half a dozen
> ingredients that I needed to get into my life before I was
> able to go through the process I describe in my book, the
> final process of saying goodbye to Nick, the feeling of tak-
> ing off my rucksack.

Tim used the phrase 'taking off my rucksack' to describe the
process of at last getting rid of the burden of unresolved grief for
his twin's death. The significant difference from the earlier visit
lay, he believed, within himself.

> On my first trip back in the 1980s . . . I found that I didn't
> have what I needed to have inside me; the tool kit inside me
> was woefully lacking to make sense. It was like an opera-
> tion that I needed to do and I didn't have the scalpels for
> it. It took me years to find the tools and put them together
> and go back.

In his book Tim describes the various visits he undertook in
2003–4 and what he gained from them. He returned first of all to
Classiebawn Castle, which had been leased to a local Irishman
who made him welcome. Driving through the castle gates he
noticed his grandparents' initials and crest still on the gate pillars.
As he walked into the castle, he saw the wooden-handled nets in

which the family had caught prawns. 'A rush of memories and emotions swept over me,' he wrote. 'I felt I had dived in at the deep end and I needed to go back outside to acclimatize.' This was the start of rediscovering objects and places that immediately brought him back to his childhood. Walking around the castle he found many such evocations. 'Each of these places – a room or a spot offering a familiar view – has something locked up in it, like a sweet fragrance. On opening it up for the first time, there is an evanescent and fragile sensation, soon scattered to the wind. From every corner the rooms whisper memories of sensations, noises and smells.' This is one of the keys to revisiting, the sense of rediscovering the past through objects or places that were either long forgotten (from conscious memory at least) or were not remembered in any detail. Throughout his many visits, Tim found his memory jogged by these rediscoveries and that allowed the past back in – both the happy times and the painful ones.

A major purpose in revisiting a trauma site is to fill in the gaps in knowledge. Tim, like any other survivor of trauma, experienced the event only from his own perspective. He had been badly injured and so had lapsed in and out of consciousness. He had heard of certain events only later – the rescue of the wounded and the recovery of the dead, for example. And so he meticulously sought out people who had been there, so that he was finally able to piece together the sequence of events as described by witnesses. One benefit of doing this sort of reconstruction is to correct worrying misconceptions. For example, Tim had experienced flashback memories to when he was pulled out of the water by a couple in another boat. These included the vibration of the engine, the cold, the taste of saltwater and diesel, the smell of oil on his skin. But the flashbacks were never visual. He dreaded the moment that the visual memories might suddenly return. This anxiety was alleviated when his rescuers told him that he had been unable to see when he was pulled from the water, and that his sight returned only when they came ashore. There would be no visual flashbacks to that time.

Tim had never properly said goodbye to his brother, Nick. Because of his own injuries he had not been able to attend the funeral. He did not know in any detail what had happened other than that Nick's body was eventually found in the water, several hours after the explosion. He talked to the people who had taken him from the water and heard exactly what they had done. He was shown a photograph taken at the time. 'It was as terrible a photograph as I have ever seen,' he wrote, 'but it also gave me what I wanted: a sense of being there.'

The details were being filled in. In his book, Tim describes a highly charged moment when he is granted an interview with the pathologist who had examined Nick's body. A 'bulging red folder with "Mountbatten" written in large handwriting across its front' is produced and together they go through it. I cannot do justice here to how Tim felt during this interview; it is beautifully and sensitively described in his book and I can only recommend that people read it. Revisiting the circumstances surrounding his brother's death enabled him to say a proper and emotional goodbye, to lay aside the rucksack at last. Moreover, it released him from a feeling that he had scarcely been aware of. 'I later realized that there had existed in my mind, even if subconsciously, a feeling that I had somehow abandoned Nick in this final duty. That trace of unreasoned and unreasonable emotion now disappeared.'

Tim encountered many places and many people on his frequent returns to Ireland. He kept a diary, which was to form the basis of his book. This project not only gave his visits a purpose beyond his personal need to revisit the site of the trauma, but it also allowed him to create something entirely new. In interviewing other trauma victims I have come across a few who have done something similar, making a film or setting up a website in memory of a loved one. Psychologically, I see this as an important part of the healing process. It enables people to take something positive from an awful loss and take control over events that, at the time, they had no control over. Tim described to me what it meant to him (for more on this see Chapter 16).

Some people find it unfathomable that I would want to talk about it and share it with others. But I have certainly come to the conclusion that it wasn't just going back to the island; it was the ability to articulate it to myself and to be able to articulate it to others that were extra levels of healing. The ability to write it down, document it, share it with others is in itself a therapeutic thing to do.

A return to Colombia: Mark's story

When people ask me what it's like to be kidnapped, I always find it hard to put it into words, how to explain the not knowing, the sense of powerlessness, the very real proximity of death, the total lack of freedom and any sort of choice in the way your life progresses. It's all these feelings but it's all these feelings constantly. It never lets up. The shadow of your kidnap is always hanging over you. You go to bed with it, you wake up with it, and it's only in those first few seconds of the morning that you forget where you are and for a few precious moments you are free.

These are the words of film director Mark Henderson, who was one of eight tourists kidnapped and held by Colombian guerrillas in 2003, in Mark's case for 101 days. It was a gruelling, exhausting and at times terrifying experience. At first, the hostages believed that they were being held for money. Later, it became clear that the kidnappers had a political motive. They were part of the Ejército de Liberación Nacional (the ELN, or National Liberation Army), a Marxist guerrilla group that has been at war with the Colombian government for more than 40 years. Mark decided from the outset that the best strategy was to try and bond with the kidnappers.

Our captors didn't actually beat us but they were cruel and would hold guns to our heads, threatening to shoot us. I'd

do anything I could to ingratiate myself with them. You
want them to like you – you don't want to be the one who
they shoot.

When two new guards arrived, Antonio and Camila, Mark found
in Antonio someone he could more easily relate to. Unlike the
other guards, these two were kind to the hostages. They were more
educated and more politically aware.

Camila was the camp commander's secretary and Antonio
was effectively in charge of training new recruits, teaching
them about the ELN's Marxist doctrines. I got the impression that, out of all our guards, Antonio was the one who
really believed in what he was fighting for.

Antonio and Mark talked about the situation in Colombia, the
struggle of the poor and oppressed against a corrupt military
regime. They shared the same taste in films and music. In this
way, a bond was established which was to play a significant role
in what happened to Mark when he was back in England. The
hostages were eventually released following negotiations through
a Catholic priest working for the Catholic Overseas Development
Agency. Seven years later, Mark returned to Colombia for a
reunion with Antonio, a journey which he made into a remarkable
documentary film for Channel 4. I watched the film and decided
to get in touch with him and ask him why he had returned to
Colombia to make the film and what he had got out of it.

In April 2011 I met Mark in his flat near Clapham Common. We
were surrounded by boxes and furniture as he and his partner were
in the throes of moving. It was kind of him to spare me an hour
at this busy time. As soon as the recording got underway, Mark
settled easily into telling me the story of the making of the film. I
was intrigued by the fact that he and Antonio had entered into an
email exchange just under a year after Mark had been released,
an exchange that went on for six years. The initial contact was

brokered by the Catholic priest who had helped negotiate their release. When he was being held as a hostage, Mark had talked to Antonio about making a film about the ELN's struggles. Mark told me how Antonio referred to that in his first email.

> I think the words were, 'I hear you are the star of the media over there now.' And it was all quite weird wording because there was no apology, no specific reference to the kidnapping. He never used the word 'kidnapping', if you actually look at all the emails. He always talks about 'your experience', 'your time in Colombia', things like that.

In his second email, Antonio mentioned making the documentary about the ELN that they had talked about. Mark's initial reaction was unequivocal; there was no way he would ever return to Colombia. Apart from anything else, it was not fair to his family to put himself at risk again. He had only been released just over a year ago. In 2010, when he eventually returned to make his film, the situation in Colombia was very different, and he too was different. This underlines the point I made when discussing Tim's visits to Ireland, that timing is crucial. If a person is not *ready* (vague though this term is, it is important), the return might have adverse effects. From a psychological perspective, the key to revisiting is that it should be a success. But what does 'success' mean? What did Mark want from his return to Colombia? What did he actually gain? In our interview, I asked him how he had come to the decision to make the film after all.

> I suddenly thought: 'I want to go back and meet him. I want to find out what [actually happened].' I spoke with everyone else about the kidnapping. It really is a cliché but you want to put all the pieces in place. I knew this bit and then my parents could give me this bit and the Met Police tell me this bit and the priest told me this bit and there was still a good quarter over here, which is their story. And because

we had always been lied to during the whole process of the kidnapping, we could never actually tell when they were telling the truth. I wanted to sit down with him and say 'Right, what was the truth?'

It helped that Mark was a television producer, familiar with the business of making documentaries.

I think once I got into the process – because making televi-sion is my profession – sometimes I would almost put on the director's hat or my producer's hat as opposed to the actual ex-hostage's hat. [But] sometimes I had to step back from it and think about me, and this especially happened when I went back. When people say, 'Why did you make the film?' [I say] I just wanted to tell the story . . . I just wanted to have a testament of what happened to me. Now I understand why people write books. And actually having something physical I've realized means you can actually distance yourself from it. Even more, you can actually give it to someone and say, 'That's it'.

The film would be a tangible record of the kidnapping. Like Tim's book, there would be something to show, something that others could see. Moreover, it would give Mark back the control he had lost when held hostage. Shortly after he was released, Mark began writing a book about his experiences. He had kept a diary from about day 8 or 9 of his kidnapping, but wanted to recapture what had happened, during the first few days in particular. He wrote about 80,000 words, a huge amount, but found the process of reliving the experience through writing made him feel anxious and weak. It affected his sleep so that he woke up screaming, or was jolted awake by disturbing dreams. He saw a psychologist, who advised him that these were symptoms of PTSD, and although he did not fit the complete diagnosis, the nature of his experience was essentially the same. That helped, Mark told me. It helped because, like Janine (see Chapter 4), Mark now knew he was not going mad and that he could get better. Writing the book almost certainly came too early in Mark's recovery, and the very length of it suggests it had become a bit of an obsession. He abandoned the book and decided he needed to go back to the normality of work. Later, when he was stronger and had obtained some distance from the trauma of the kidnapping, he could revisit it in a form that he was more familiar with – film.

When Mark and another of the hostages, a German woman named Reini, finally met Antonio, they had prepared a series of questions to ask him. For security reasons Antonio was filmed in silhouette. In the film we see a short extract of this encounter, just a few minutes. But Mark told me that the meeting went on for seven hours, as Antonio was determined to answer all their questions.

> '[There were] four of us and one of him. And it really did feel like the tables had turned, like we were the ones in control. And then by him saying "No, I want to answer all your questions", he was suppliant, what's the word?'
>
> 'Submissive?'
>
> 'Submissive. He was almost being submissive. It really felt like a shift of power. He'd always been this kidnapper and now he wanted to give us whatever he could . . . and it wasn't so much necessarily what he said, but it was the fact that he did it. That meant more to us.'

I asked Mark what he thought Antonio's motive was in meeting them. Was he seeking to apologise, to make reparation?

> I think so. I always wanted to believe in the humanity of all of our guards and yet with some of them I could never see it. With him I could. And that is why I never understood how he could do what he did and then live with himself . . . I think he met up with us because actually we did connect

as people. He almost wanted to say 'Look, I am not the person you think I am. I am a human being. I do care.'

In the film we see Antonio making an apology. At first he rationalizes the kidnapping in terms of the political struggle for human rights of oppressed people. But when Mark makes the point that he had violated *their* human rights, he admits the truth of this. He says what he did was wrong and asks for their forgiveness. In South Africa, the Truth and Reconciliation Commission enabled former enemies to meet and make atonement even for some of the most horrific crimes. The Forgiveness Project is a website that explicitly encourages and empowers people to explore the nature of forgiveness and alternatives to revenge by telling their stories. It is possible that, for Antonio, the act of meeting Mark and Reini began a process of making atonement for his part in the kidnapping. For Mark it was a very important part of regaining control through 'filling in the pieces' of the events, essentially providing different and better memories of that traumatic time. Mark put it very well in our interview.

By making the film and by being together we were almost overriding any memories we had of that place. And when we all came out, and even now when we speak to each other, we don't talk about the kidnapping. We talk about when we made the film. It's almost like we've replaced it.

Conclusion

Tim and Mark's experiences show, in their respective ways, how it is possible to gain a great deal from going back to revisit the site of a trauma. Not all traumas lend themselves to this, of course; in some cases it is simply not possible to return. Both individuals had the same motive, to fill in the missing pieces of information that came from being physically back in the place where the trauma had happened, and interviewing people who had been there at the

time. Mark told me that when he first met up with three of his fellow hostages again, the four of them were able to explain in detail
what had happened or what they did at particular times. We know
that memory is reconstructive and one consequence of the revisiting process is the realization that our memories do not always
match the reality of the event itself. This is very much part of what
happens in reliving therapy, when the client and therapist together
return to the site and actively disconfirm irrational fantasies or
beliefs (see Chapter 13). As Mark put it, new memories can now
replace the old ones. These are more positive and, moreover, are
in the control of the person: it is what they have deliberately set
out to achieve. Another important feature of returning to the site
of the trauma is emotional. Tim wanted to remember his brother
Nick's last moments, and in doing so say goodbye to him. Mark
wanted to talk directly to Antonio and tell him how he felt. This
is not just a matter of emotional catharsis, but something more
active. Tim could finally lay down his rucksack and grieve for his
lost brother. Mark could now see his Colombian experience in a
different light. Finally, both achieved something memorable and
creative, one a book, the other a film.

Chapter 12: Psychotherapy

'I was out running when it happened. I run most days, usually in the early morning before work. But that day was a Bank Holiday and it was almost eleven before I started.'

Val hesitates. I sense something not being said.

'Was there anything unusual about that day? Anything particular that happened?'

'Max and I had had a row. A stupid argument.' Sadness shows briefly on her face. 'He doesn't want kids. I do. Well, we just got into it.'

'So you were feeling upset when you left?'

Val nods. 'Yeah. Angry as well. He's so fucking stubborn.'

I wait for her to say something more but she doesn't.

'Tell me what happened when the dogs appeared.'

She sighs, runs her hand through her hair. Her reluctance to talk about it is obvious. Being savaged by two large dogs must have been a terrible experience.

'I know it's hard to talk about so take your time. Tell it to me slowly and we'll stop whenever you want.'

'I wish *I* could stop it whenever I want. I have these flashbacks. They come back suddenly, unexpectedly. They can be so vivid.' She shudders. 'I dream about it too, wake up screaming, according to Max. He's the one who said I should see a shrink. But I don't really believe in all that therapy stuff. Sorry, don't mean to offend.'

She smiles and I smile back. I don't feel offended. There is something disarming about Val, her directness, her candour. At this moment I am aware of a number of things. I know from her GP's referral letter that she was badly mauled by two large dogs and had to be treated in hospital for lacerations, some pretty deep. Complications developed, an infection, and she had to be readmitted. In all, it took four months and three operations. The GP also told me that she has taken out a civil action against the hospital trust. I need to bear all this in mind. The trauma is not just the dog attack but everything that followed. And it is still going on.

The vignette above is a reconstruction, based on an example from my clinic. This exchange, or something similar, could be how an initial interview with a psychotherapist might begin. In this and the following two chapters I will discuss the psychological treatment of trauma-related problems. It is possible to be overwhelmed by the number and variety of different therapies available. Strange-sounding names abound: exposure, reliving, cognitive restructuring, imagery rescripting, mindfulness meditation, energy psychology, somato-sensory psychotherapy, eye-movement desensitization and reprocessing (EMDR), neurolinguistic programming (NLP), emotional freedom techniques (EFT) . . . not to mention the broad schools of therapy, such as cognitive therapy, psychoanalysis, systemic therapy and person-centred therapy.

Therapy, however, is not just about techniques. It is a personal relationship where the qualities of the participants are as important as what they do. We can see this in the brief exchanges I had with Val. From the outset I found her easy to relate to. I noted her candour and her directness. I was also aware of the ambivalence demonstrated by her sceptical attitude to psychotherapy in general and by her admission that her husband, Max, had persuaded her to seek help. First impressions of people in therapy are extremely important. Despite Val's ambivalence, I felt that I could work with her, even though I did not yet know what that work might entail. She, too, would have formed an opinion of me based upon the way I related to her. These kinds of impressions will influence the therapy, determining whether or not it succeeds, whatever techniques are decided upon.

It is essential that the client comes to trust the therapist, and all good therapists want to create a sense of safety, a feeling that whatever is said in therapy will be met with seriousness, respect, genuine interest and, eventually, understanding. To me these are the *sine qua non* of psychological therapy. Some therapists fail to show these qualities; their approach is very different, aggressive even, telling the client what is wrong and what they (the client) must do to put it right. Others work in an explicitly medical way; their message is that the *techniques* are what matters, irrespective of the personal qualities of the therapist. To me, though, the personal relationship is vital, something that I learned in almost forty years of being a psychotherapist.

In this chapter I will describe what are sometimes known as the non-specific factors of therapy. These are what all good therapies should include and what anyone who seeks psychological help for trauma-related problems should look out for. In the following two chapters I will describe two broadly different treatment approaches, the first based on reliving the trauma in words and images, the second focusing more on bodily reactions and discharging pent-up energy.

Non-specific factors

Fifty years ago the psychotherapist Jerome Frank published a highly influential book on the commonalities that exist in all psychotherapies and methods of healing. He argued that therapies work not so much because of the specific techniques used but because of what they have in common. Every therapy depends upon a therapeutic relationship in which the therapist inculcates hope and optimism through his or her expertise and experience, thereby restoring the client's morale and fostering recovery through the client's own resources. Frank described the main non-specific factors as:

•   The therapist's belief in his or her capacity to help

- The client's expectations of recovery

- The therapeutic relationship

- The place of safety, e.g. the therapist's consulting room

- The rituals involved in carrying out specific techniques

- The restoration of the client's morale

A crucial part of Frank's thesis is his belief that the therapeutic *relationship* is more important than the specific form of treatment offered. Nevertheless, techniques are important, since the therapist needs to be convinced that what he or she does is going to be helpful (which Frank termed the 'ritual' of therapy) and the client needs to invest their hopes and expectations in something definite. But, he argued, the non-specifics outweigh whatever specific effects might be derived from the techniques. This controversial conclusion was not generally welcomed by therapists, most of whom had a vested interest in the specific methods they had trained in. It was asserted by those who disagreed with Frank's hypothesis that, on the contrary, identifiable psychological problems like PTSD, anxiety or depression should be treated by specific treatment methods, preferably those that research studies had shown to be effective. This quasi-medical model has dominated psychotherapy research for more than fifty years. It is one reason why so many different therapies for trauma exist. Each new therapy wants to prove that it is the best, the most effective and the most cost-efficient.

In my view, Frank was essentially right to point to the importance of non-specific factors, and in particular the therapeutic relationship. But it is not necessary to discard the view that a particular psychological technique can have marked beneficial effects in its own right. We are beginning to understand more about how the mind copes with the legacy of major trauma – the persistence of trauma memories, for example – and this knowledge can inform the practice of therapists. Techniques allied to scientific knowledge can make a huge difference, just as has happened in medicine. I will discuss this more in the next two chapters. Whatever therapy is offered, the quality of the therapeutic relationship will make a significant difference. It is this relationship that clients most commonly refer to when asked about what was helpful in therapy. When it comes to trauma-related problems, it is essential to establish a good therapeutic relationship at the outset.

Judith Herman's three stages of trauma therapy

In one of the best and most influential books on the treatment of traumatized people, *Trauma and Recovery: The Aftermath of Violence – from Domestic Abuse to Political Terror*, the psychologist Judith Herman divided trauma therapy into three broad stages. The first stage consists of creating a secure base, ensuring that the client feels safe enough to disclose emotionally laden material; it is about establishing a good therapeutic relationship. With some people this happens in one or two sessions but in others it may take weeks or months. The second phase corresponds to the active therapy, the form of which will depend on the nature of problem, the skills, experience and orientation of the therapist, the hopes and expectations of the client, and their mutual understanding and agreement about the goals and methods of therapy. Here specific problem-solving techniques like eye-movement desensitization and reprocessing (EMDR), reliving, or emotional freedom techniques (EFT) could be used. Or more traditional psychological treatments might be employed, like those based on psychoanalysis, in which client and therapist verbally explore what the trauma has meant in terms of the client's background and early history. The third and final stage is about the client's reintegration into the normality of ordinary life, a process that begins in therapy and needs to continue after it has ended. Here the focus is on how the changed person – changed both by the trauma and by the therapy – can successfully pick up the threads of his or her life. Herman's tripartite model acts like a template that can be placed on very different therapies, dividing them into the same three discernible stages. She argues that all three stages are necessary in any effective therapy.

The first phase: a secure base

The first phase is about knowledge and safety. The therapist seeks to find out about both the client and the trauma. This should include the option that therapy is not what the client needs at this time. It is important not to assume that therapy is appropriate for everyone who suffers psychological problems after trauma. Most people will recover from the psychological effects of a trauma, even a major one, without any formal treatment. Val, however, seems to be stuck, and I have already learned several things about her that should enable me to work out whether or not psychotherapy is likely to help her. She has told me that the initial trauma, the attack by two dogs, is not over. Not only does she still have flashbacks and nightmares, but she also had a traumatic time in hospital. Moreover, this additional trauma has not been fully resolved; she has taken out a civil action against the hospital trust. Sometimes, legal actions prolong the problem because they keep the trauma (and the emotions) alive. In Chapter 9 I presented Steve (the man who was almost flattened by a Harrier Jump Jet), who recovered fully only when his compensation case was resolved. This might be an issue for Val too. She also told me that she had had a row with her partner just before she went out running. This is interesting for two reasons. It probably put her in an emotionally charged state of mind, and this could well have interacted with her body's reaction to the attack, perhaps making the physical reaction more powerful. It is also of interest in its own right. Is her relationship with her partner a serious and continuing problem? I once took on a young woman recovering from the trauma of a serious road accident, whose husband abandoned her after the first treatment session, thus adding an acute personal trauma to the chronic one.

sufficiently confident of her ability to cope should such an attack actually happen. That confidence, I suspect, has been significantly dented by the attack. She has not done much running since. This hints at something that will be important: the *meaning* of the attack. A trauma is not just an objective event, but has a particular meaning to the person undergoing it. In previous chapters I introduced the terms primary and secondary appraisal. Val's comment 'How wrong can you be?' suggests that the trauma has had an impact on her sense of self (secondary appraisal). It may be that she blames herself in some way.

> 'You don't run much now. Is that because of the physical injuries or . . .?'
>
> 'I couldn't run at first. Then when the ops went wrong, that made it impossible for a while.'
>
> Val stops. I wait. I want her to tell me about it, to hear what matters to her.
>
> 'I could run now, I guess. But I don't know. I don't want to, if you know what I mean.'
>
> She looks directly at me and I sense something in the look. Desperation, perhaps. Certainly something unsettling. I take a risk and fill in the blank. 'It's not the same now, is it? It's shaken your confidence, the attack.'
>
> She nods. Her eyes are brimming. She is close to tears. 'I used to love running. It was my life. Now that's been taken away from me. By those bloody dogs. They were not killed, you know. They were given one more chance. They're still there in that yard. It's not fair.'

A good therapist tries to understand and empathize, to put himself or herself in the client's shoes, to feel what the client is feeling. The best approach is tentative and slow. Rattling off a string of questions, however pertinent, can make the client feel like an object of investigation, as though the therapist's sole aim is to tick the boxes that will lead to a diagnosis of anxiety or PTSD. I am genuinely interested in Val, in the attack, in her suffering and how her life has been affected. I want to know more and for her to tell me. This is what creating a good relationship is about. Genuine interest, empathy and a desire to help. At this stage, if I were to step back from the interview and take stock, I would see that the attack has badly shaken Val, and her response has something of the characteristics of phobic anxiety. There is apparently no prior trauma, certainly no previous dog attack, though there may be other traumas that, however indirectly, may have been evoked by this one. There will be time later to find that out, just as there will be time for her tell me more about the actual attack.

Here I am highlighting the non-specifics of an opening exchange with a client, which can be summarized as creating a sense of safety and trust. This is done, in part, by how the therapist reacts to the client. It is also the phase when his or her experience and expertise come into play. The therapist's knowledge about psychological traumas, about how people are affected, about the secondary appraisals, and the fact that they have seen and helped many clients before, these all send a message to the client that this problem can be handled. 'Containment' is the word that many trauma therapists use. The client's experience during the trauma was uncontained; it spilled over into her internal and external world. Recalling it later triggers that sense of being uncontained, often expressed as helplessness or feeling out of control. If the therapist shows, through his or her knowledge, both calmness and a conviction that the client's emotions can be contained, then the client experiences a huge sense of relief. As I described before, in relation to Janine (Chapter 4), a specific diagnosis can also convey that conviction and understanding to the client, and provide the foundation on which therapy is built. But the diagnosis alone is not enough; the therapist's manner, his or her empathy and personality, play a significant part. It is the difference between ticking off a checklist of symptoms and showing care and understanding. This is why the personal relationship is vital in the first phase of trauma therapy.

The second phase: active therapy

It is in the second phase that the therapist and client actively combat the effects of the trauma, often by using specific treatment techniques. For example, in reliving therapy the client is encouraged to recall the trauma in specific detail, while the therapist listens and prompts. This may be repeated several times. It may even be recorded on an audio recorder for the client to listen to at home. Reliving is designed to elicit the emotions felt at the time, with a view to allowing them to be processed, so that they are no longer felt as so raw and sensory. It is the method I used with Janine (see Chapter 4). She told me I had 'hammered the emotions out of her', indicating how hard this process was for her. But it helped her recover. Reliving is just one of several treatments that have the aim of moving the client on from being stuck with powerful and distressing trauma memories. I discuss this approach in more detail in the next chapter.

Before getting to the second, active phase, two questions need to be addressed. Is the client ready for the treatment? What sort of therapy is it best to employ? Neither of these is straightforward and a mistake that some therapists make is to rush into active treatment before these questions are answered. In the extract below I have completed my initial assessment of Val and am ready to broach treatment.

'From what you told me so far, Val, I have a strong sense of your being stuck. Is that right?'

'Definitely.'

'As I see it, there are two aspects to this – there may be more, but two stand out to me – first, that running is no longer a pleasure for you but has become a source of fear and anxiety . . .'

Val nods.

'. . . and second, that the attack has affected you as a person. You have lost your normal self-confidence, which is not surprising. Oh, and there's one other thing. You are angry about what happened; not just the attack, but what happened afterwards, the way you were badly treated in hospital and the fact that nothing was done about the dogs.'

'I *am* angry. That's true. It also comes out at home. I'm snappy with Max. He seems to think I should get over it. I wish I could but I can't. And how can that man continue to keep the dogs after what they did? It's totally wrong.'

'So three things. Your fear, your lack of confidence and your anger. Is there anything else, anything you feel I have left out?'

The therapist, however experienced he or she may be in treating trauma, needs to understand the individual in front of them. This is known as arriving at a *formulation*, which is a way of expressing that understanding verbally, and sometimes visually in the form of diagram, and communicating it to the client. In the extract above I am beginning to do that, concentrating for the moment on delineating what the main psychological problems are. Listing problems is only a part of the formulation. There should be some understanding of how these problems have arisen and in what ways the person's history and circumstances may be significant. For example, had Val suffered a previous trauma of a similar nature, this might have predisposed her to a stronger reaction, and would need to be taken into account. Or had she been an anxious person in general (perhaps having had a difficult, frightening childhood), past anxieties might have been reactivated. Or had it emerged that her marriage to Max was on the rocks, the trauma of the attack could well have been mixed up with the trauma of a close relationship that was in trouble. Therapists are not omniscient and it is not always the case that they have all the relevant information to arrive at a formulation in the first sessions. Formulations can be wrong. But it is vital that a formulation is arrived at: it will make it clear to the client what the therapist thinks about the problem and, importantly, it will lead on to a blueprint for the active therapy.

It is essential that the client feels safe before moving to the next, stressful stage. With some people this can be a major issue, and a long time is needed to develop that sense of trust. With others it can happen quickly. Asking the person directly if he or she is ready to proceed is an obvious thing to do, but people may not know until they try. A good therapist develops a sensitivity both to the client's motivation and to possible confounding factors, the presence of high general anxiety, for instance, or the complication of having other pressing problems to contend with. The desire to change can be accompanied by considerable uncertainty. Therapists have different understandings of how change comes about, reflecting their particular theoretical background. In psychoanalysis, for example, resistance to change is expected, for the focus of the therapy is on uncovering unconscious mental conflicts that emerge in the form of conflicted and difficult emotions. This is very different from the problem-solving therapies, which are predominantly rational and more superficial (but nevertheless useful). To choose to embark on twice- or thrice-weekly sessions of psychoanalysis over the course of a year or more is very different from agreeing to six to twelve sessions of EMDR or EFT. Therefore the therapist needs to explain what the aims and requirements of therapy are, so that the client can make an informed choice.

The boundary between the first and second phases is not always clear-cut. Therapist and client will learn more about the problem from how the active therapy goes (or fails to go). This may lead to a reformulation and possibly a shift in the therapy. The process of assessment can in itself be therapeutic, helping reduce anxiety as the problem is aired. One of the major non-specific factors that Frank mentioned in his book was the way a supportive, interested therapist can boost the client's morale, prompting recovery regardless of what is done. The value of seeing a professional therapist was highlighted by Tim Knatchbull in the last chapter. He found that he could discuss highly personal matters with his therapist, which would have been far more difficult to do with family or friends, perhaps even impossible. The neutrality and professionalism of the therapist are crucial factors in helping clients through distressing and difficult experiences.

The final phase: reintegration

In my account of Tim Coulson, who was caught up in the 2005 London bombings (Chapters 2 and 7), I described how, after receiving therapy, he attempted to go back to his work as a lecturer. However, despite having benefited from treatment, he was unable to carry on working and took early retirement. Elaine, who had been in the same carriage as Tim, resolutely went back to work and for two years tried to cope, by avoiding any mention of bombings or terrorist attacks. However, she broke down at work, went off sick and was eventually treated by a psychologist colleague of mine. Elaine recovered but she never went back to her work with the St John Ambulance service. She has since embarked on a new career running shops that sell burlesque costumes. Richard, who was in the Grayrigg rail crash (Chapter 5), found he could no longer manage the train journey to and from Swindon that his busy job demanded. He too left his job and began a second career as a freelance consultant. These examples illustrate how a major trauma can result in a significant change in a person's life. In all three cases they changed their work and found a way of making a living that was less stressful or, in Tim's case, took retirement and found pleasure in other activities. All had had psychological treatment with clear benefits in terms of the reduction of PTSD and other symptoms. Yet the trauma had changed them as people. They felt that they could no longer do the work they had done before. But this is not always the case. George, who was also in the London bombings, returned to his old job even though it meant travelling on the underground. He did so because he thought he was too old, at sixty-two, to seek a new job, and eventually he found he could cope with the fears travelling on the tube gave rise to. People who resume their work after a major trauma may find that they themselves are different in many ways. In the paper this morning I read a piece about the Barcelona footballer Eric Abidal, who had an operation to remove a cancerous growth from his liver. He remains a footballer and has again played games for his team. However, he is no longer attracted to the celebrity lifestyle; he has sold his fast, expensive cars and is looking to use his money to help other people. His brush with potentially life-threatening illness put football's values in perspective and opened up a different way of being in the world.

In this third phase of therapy the therapist and client work together on returning to some sort of normality. Val had a short course of therapy that successfully reduced her phobic anxiety about dogs. Some dogs can be dangerous and together we worked out which ones to avoid or be wary of. As any dog owner knows, there are clear signs that dogs make when their intentions are unfriendly. Val learned these. She resumed running, choosing a different route and always carrying with her a can of mace. She had one awkward encounter with a dog, which upset her, although the dog did not attack and she was not injured. With my prompting, she refused to let it put her off running. Gradually, she regained confidence in herself and took on board the message that she could be in control of her life rather than letting her fears dominate. She arrived at a settlement with the hospital trust, which helped her to move on. In Val's case, the effects of the trauma were quite specific and successfully treated by anxiety-management methods. Reintegration into normal life did not mean a major change to her life. Her marriage to Max was solid despite their differences over whether or not to have children. He attended some of the later therapy sessions and was instrumental in supporting Val as she resumed running. In more complex cases, the third phase of therapy can raise significant psychological issues, over and above the specific effects of the trauma. Therapist and client need to decide how to proceed, whether or not it is appropriate to work on these issues, and, if so, how that might be done.

Conclusion

Many people feel unsure about going to a psychotherapist, perhaps because they worry that the process will reveal their inner-
most secrets, or feel doubtful about trusting a complete stranger.
Others may think that psychotherapy is a form of self-indulgence,
simply a chance to waffle on about oneself interminably. One of
my children gave me a book of psychotherapy cartoons in one of
which an indignant client is saying to his startled psychoanalyst,
'Well, I'm paying for these sessions so, as I was saying, I hit a
birdie on the fourteenth.' But good therapy is far more than talking about oneself, and a good psychotherapist combines empathy
with shrewd understanding of what may be helpful and what may
not. As I have shown in this chapter, psychotherapy is, at heart, a
personal relationship, and so the qualities of the people involved,
both client and therapist, are hugely important. But it is also true
that what the therapist does or does not do, the techniques he or she
uses, will make a significant difference. In the next two chapters
I will discuss two very different ways in which psychotherapists
have sought to help trauma sufferers.

Chapter 13: Reliving

'I first met Anne in September 2007, so that would be seven months after the train crash. I really didn't know what to expect but I remember where we met was a very calm environment, very relaxed. Anne had a gentle style of questioning and one of the first things that she did was to get me to describe my experiences of the rail crash while she taped them, and then she gave me the tape so I could take that home and listen to it.'

'And when you were describing the experiences were you getting distressed in remembering them?'

'Yes, I was.'

'So that was also on the tape, presumably?'

'Yes. Then the exercises were to listen to my tape two or three times a week and note down when I was feeling particularly emotional and upset . . . What I would do is go into the bedroom, sit on the bed and put headphones on and listen to the tape. I made a little box chart on a piece of paper just so I could note things down as I was listening to it. And over time you start to realize that by the ninth or tenth time you don't seem to be getting as upset as frequently as you were to begin with. I don't know if that's just the fact of getting bored with hearing it.'

'Did Anne explain the rationale to you?'

'I think she would have done. The ability to process and essentially understand and file away the [trauma] memories.'

This extract is taken from my second interview with Richard Blakemore, who was in the Grayrigg rail crash (Chapter 5). Richard spent some time recovering from the physical injuries he sustained in the crash and then developed an autoimmune illness, Brachial Neuritis, which also laid him low. Shortly after the trauma, he refused his GP's initial offer of psychological help, feeling that it might be too much, as he was still recovering physically. But when she contacted him again some months later, he agreed to a referral to a clinical psychologist (Anne).

The type of therapy Richard received is known as prolonged exposure or reliving. There are several variants of this approach with different names: for example, emotional processing, imagery rescripting and cognitive restructuring. Although there are differences in the way each variant of the approach is conducted, all these therapies have in common the aim of getting the client to access trauma memories and process these memories from their raw, fragmented sensory form into verbal memory. This is consistent with the neurobiological theory that I discussed in Chapter 3, which states that sensory memories are located primarily in the amygdala (the 'alarm system' that has become highly sensitized) and need to be shifted to the hippocampus, the site of verbal memory.

These reliving therapies are examples of a broader therapeutic approach, cognitive-behaviour therapy (CBT), which is a practical, problem-solving, educational and collaborative approach to the treatment of mental-health problems. Research into CBT suggests that it is a highly effective form of psychotherapy, although the evidence is not as definitive as proponents of CBT argue. But there is no doubt that it is a pragmatic way of helping people, one in which therapist and client work closely together to achieve agreed goals. In CBT the therapist draws upon a cognitive model in which feelings are shaped by the thoughts, perceptions and beliefs that people hold (see Chapter 9). These cognitions are in turn shaped by feelings. For example, persistent depressed mood can make someone feel that they are a failure, which in turn deepens the depression, resulting in an interacting spiral of low mood and negative thoughts. Learning to recognize, interrupt and then challenge the negative thinking and thereby change mood is the central task of CBT. Other techniques are also used, such as counteracting avoidance and setting up behavioural experiments in which the client is encouraged to put his or her negative thinking to the test. Because the focus in CBT is on collaborative action, an agenda is agreed at the beginning of each session, the procedures used in therapy are described and explained, and specific homework tasks agreed on, to be undertaken before the next session. Less time is given to personal exploration than in other forms of therapy, though a good therapist will ensure that this happens to some degree. CBT is particularly suited to self-help, and there are many CBT self-help books for trauma-related problems. It has also been adapted for use in a computerized form.

Richard's therapist, Anne, used CBT to help him overcome his PTSD symptoms and also to try to conquer his fear and distress when travelling on trains. A key part of the therapy was the recording that was made of his recounting his experiences in the rail crash, which he later listened to repeatedly at home. This technique is known as *prolonged exposure*, and the American clinical psychologist Edna Foa is credited with developing and evaluating it, although its origins go back to early behaviour therapy. Foa uses both imaginary exposure, in the session itself, and real-life exposure, in between sessions. The therapy is relatively short, between nine and twelve sessions, and has produced positive results for clients with PTSD and other problems. The theory behind the approach is simple: it is assumed that the main problem is excessive fear, which is maintained largely by avoidance. Prolonged exposure in both imagination and reality prevents avoidance and thereby allows the fear to decline over time. I asked Richard what the therapy felt like and how much progress he made.

I think it was a gradual process for me. It wasn't a sudden switching on or switching off of lights. During the first three months that we were meeting I was still travelling in and out of Swindon on a train, and then at Christmas or

New Year I decided I wasn't going to do that any more. I started driving in and out of Swindon.

Despite the reduction of fear Richard experienced when listening to his recorded account of the crash, he was still suffering anxiety on his regular train journeys to and from work. He decided not to take the train but go by car. This was certainly avoidance but it was not necessarily the wrong thing to do. As I discussed in Chapter 5, the problem was that Richard's anxiety was regularly reinforced by his daily train journeys. It was never given the chance to decline. But driving many miles every week proved exhausting, and moreover did not give him time to read papers and prepare for meetings. In the end Richard decided he needed to change his job.

'[While] I was trying to deal with the PTSD from the rail crash, [I had] conversations with Anne about what I should be doing about the job. Anne was being absolutely scrupulous in not telling me what she thought I should do. Although when I finally reached the conclusion, it was perfectly clear that she felt that I had reached the correct conclusion.'

'She gave you the space to talk about it which was helpful.'

'Yes. That was not an easy process. It was a job that I only started in September 2006 [one year before the crash]. It was a challenging job that had its frustrations which I was enjoying and you have that dreadful feeling of giving up on something.'

This illustrates the importance of the therapeutic relationship and shows the therapist's flexibility in not sticking rigidly to the techniques. It helped Richard that Anne allowed him space to talk about this difficult decision. He had come to trust her and she was careful to refrain from giving him direct advice. Yet once Richard made his decision, she gave him her support. The therapy continued with real-life exposure, focusing on getting Richard to make some train journeys without excessive anxiety.

'I started off doing a variety of different journeys, started off with short distances, gradually trying to [increase them].'

'So you and Anne worked it out together?'

'Yes. And to give a bit of focus I had the idea of linking them with visiting cathedrals over the South of England. Winchester and Bath, Bristol, Worcester.'

'Something positive at the end.'

'Yes.'

'So that was a graduated programme of getting used to being on a train again and trying to overcome your anxiety?'

'Yes.'

'Was there anything else involved? Did you do any exercises in particular when you were on the train?'

'When I felt myself getting a bit stressed, I would try and relax my breathing. I would try and take a step back from the situation. What I found was that I got to the point where I was more comfortable travelling by train if it was essentially a journey that I didn't have to take at a particular time of day, if there were no deadlines, and if I was feeling relaxed getting on the train, then I was less likely to have any problems during the journey.'

Relaxation techniques, including progressive muscular relaxation, breathing exercises and meditation can help to counteract distress as well as acting as a distraction from anxious thoughts. One consequence of the CBT was to return control to Richard; he could decide what train journeys to take and how to manage them without undue distress. His change of job to a freelance consultant also enabled him to control what work he did and where he travelled. I asked Richard what he saw as the benefits of the therapy as a whole.

I think I have pretty much come to terms with everything that happened in the Grayrigg crash. It was pretty much processed, put away in a nice, neat file and slid into one of the drawers of the brain, a rather large filing cabinet! And I can bring it out if I want to and look back to it. But generally I don't feel any great need to do that. It's all in the past pretty much as far as general day-to-day activities are concerned.

He was also more relaxed about rail travel, although he would hesitate about doing anything that involved regular train journeys. That was an enduring legacy of the trauma; it was a major reason why he changed his work. Richard's experience illustrates the benefits of a CBT programme that has prolonged exposure as the main technique. It also underlines the importance of the therapeutic relationship, as Richard came to trust Anne, while she ensured that he had the space to talk about his life-altering decision to change his job.

Hotspots and trauma memories

In April 2011 I interviewed Ann Hackmann, a clinical psychologist who has done extensive therapeutic work with traumatized people over many years. She uses a CBT approach that incorporates reliving but, in contrast to prolonged exposure, the focus is less directly on fear reduction than on describing the trauma memories in detail. Her therapy derives from a theoretical model of PTSD, developed by the psychologists Anke Ehlers and David Clark. In this model the key to the persistence of traumatic anxiety lies in the fragmented nature of trauma memories and their association with specific triggers. This combination gives rise to the feeling of 'now-ness', the belief that the trauma is, to some degree, happening again (a sense of current threat). The therapist's job is to work directly on the fragmented memories, put them in context and give them a proper time code. Ann Hackmann explained how this works.

'The patient goes through the memory in a sequence as best they can in the first-person present tense, from when they think the trauma began to a time when they felt more safe and settled. They do that with their eyes closed, bringing the imagery to mind as clearly as possible, and talking about not just what they see and hear but what they feel in the body, what their emotions are and what the thoughts are. From time to time the therapist will ask questions like "How do you feel?" or "What are you thinking now?"'

'So it would be talking as if it were actually happening rather than talking about it in the past?'

'Yes. We find that once they get into the reliving, something very different happens. It becomes much more sensory, much more emotive. And we also get bodily changes. We've seen people start vomiting or shivering, or getting very hot, body memories of what happened in the trauma, pain, even bruising sometimes.'

'So it's very much being back into the trauma?

'Yes.'

'And do you record that?'

'Yes, we record every session on an audiotape.'

The procedure up to this point is essentially similar to prolonged exposure, the method Anne, Richard's therapist, used with him. But here the focus is on trauma memories, what is happening in the mind, rather than the fear reduction.

'We give the patient the tape to take home. They listen to it just once. [This is] because we are not then going to move into any kind of habituation type rationale. We simply want them to bring awareness to the material.'

'Is that how it differs from the traditional exposure?'

'In traditional exposure therapy you do repeated reliving in every session and they might have to listen to the tape every day for homework. In our approach what we are trying to do is capitalize on the benefits of actually getting in touch with more of the material through reliving, looking out for what we call the hotspots, the worst moments, because they are going to be the focus of our work. But also helping the person get things in a correct sequence and begin to piece together the material, elaborate it in that way, because often you've just had the fragments protruding but you haven't had any clear memory of the whole thing.'

In other words, the reliving procedure is the vehicle for getting to the worst memories, the 'hotspots'. It is designed to allow the trauma memories to be fully accessed, sorted through and then integrated into normal memory (or 'emotionally processed' as it is sometimes called). Ann Hackmann employs a useful metaphor to illustrate what is involved.

Imagine a cupboard where everything's been thrown out and jumbled about after a burglar has been. If you just stuff everything back in, it keeps bursting open. You have to learn to take everything out, sort it out and then put it back in properly so that the doors stay shut.

Richard used a similar analogy when he talked of the brain's filing cabinet and how, by the end of therapy, he could file away the memories of the Grayrigg crash.

Repeatedly imagining the trauma in therapy can lead to the client recalling details that were not apparent the first time they imagined the event. The fragments of memory tend to cohere into a more integrated narrative and there can be clues to the trauma's deeper meaning. I used reliving on a police officer who had been traumatized when an operation to capture drug smugglers amongst kebab sellers went wrong. He was trapped in the front of the kebab van, while the owner lunged at him with a long carving knife. Somehow he managed to escape without serious injury, yet the incident affected him badly and he could no longer work on front-line duty. Asking him to imagine the sequence of events pro-voked distress at first, but this lessened over repeated imaginings. At the same time more and more details of the scene emerged with each repetition. On the fourth occasion, he remembered for the first time that, after he had got away from the van, he walked back through a cordon of his fellow officers, who were completely silent, as though he was some sort of pariah. He felt let down by the police and he was very angry at having being exposed to such risk. This is a negative appraisal arising out of the meaning he gave to the experience and, as can sometimes be the case, it linked in with other occasions that he felt the police had let him down (see Janine's anger in Chapter 4). He also felt ashamed at having broken down in front of fellow officers. The different meanings gave rise to different emotions, anger on the one hand and shame on the other.

Ann Hackmann described her approach as 'finding out what the different hotspots in the memory actually meant, and then building a broader context in which we can modify those toxic meanings and bring them together with something else, like self-compassion'. In other words, the therapist guides the client towards cognitive change, starting with the distressing memories, the hotspots, understanding what they are about (exploring the meaning), and then moving on to arrive at more realistic, updated and less negative meanings. Some reliving therapies use guided imagery to do this, in which the therapist asks the client to imag-ine different scenarios to the ones recalled. For example, had I been using this technique, I could have suggested to my police officer that he imagined walking back past his fellow officers and looking at each of them, discovering that they are sympathetic, not hostile. He was in a highly dissociated state at the time, which had cut him off from everything and everyone around him, and was almost certainly not attending to what the officers were doing. He perceived their silence as judgemental, whereas it was quite likely to have been supportive. The recast image could help change the meaning of the memory and thereby reduce or even eliminate feelings of anger and shame. Obviously, the change needs to be towards a perception that is realistic, and the therapist's skill and experience come into play to ensure this.

There are times when the meaning of the trauma memory is not so much to do with the index trauma (the one that provoked the immediate distress) but more to do with a previous, sometimes forgotten, trauma or a deeply held belief. Ann Hackmann told me of a man she had seen who had been in a car crash; he believed that he had caused the accident and that he had killed someone, neither of which was the case. This belief was revealed during the reliving. Ann explained what she did in the therapy.

> 'I examined it [the hotspot] very carefully and tried to challenge the idea that it was his fault, which it wasn't. I came across the meaning that this had happened because he was bad and attracted bad events. So then we worked on that specific hotspot but it turned out that I couldn't do anything about changing that meaning in the present. I then did something that we call following the emotional bridge back to the past. [I went back] to the time when he first decided he was a bad person who attracted bad things. It was a memory of when he was aged seven, and he was in his fifties. Then we worked on doing something to change it.'
>
> 'This seems to be important. It is something to do with the personality and experiences of the individual . . .'
>
> 'Which colour the meaning of the trauma memory.'
>
> 'And that seems to be because quite a few trauma memories will tap into pre-existing ones.'
>
> 'In cognitive-therapy terms, it is a significant piece of evidence for a negative belief that is still around today.'

There are some who maintain that a current trauma always links back to earlier experience. The neurologist Robert Scaer came to this view late on in his career, after treating many traumatized people (see Chapter 10). This suggests that, rather than treating a trauma as a discrete event, however extreme, we should view it in the context of an individual's traumatic history, and that will help us understand the individual's reaction. It is right, in my view, to consider the individual's personal history, especially when there have been earlier traumas. It is obvious, for instance, that someone who has been sexually abused in earlier life is likely to react differently to a rape than someone who has not been abused. There are people whose lives have been pretty brutal, who have suffered more than their fair share of traumas, and any new trauma will have a meaning in that context. The reliving method allows access to earlier experiences via hotspots and what Ann calls 'building an emotional bridge to the past'. However, she rejects the idea that this is necessary for everyone. Some major traumas will affect people in a similar way, regardless of their personal history, as those caught up in the 2005 London bombings will testify. Extreme events provoke extreme reactions. There is a qualitative difference between the ordinary slings and arrows of our lives and the sudden explosive effect of a major trauma. There are commonalities in the physical and psychological reactions in the latter, as I have shown. How these events are processed will certainly reflect personality and personal history. (For example, see Chapter 7 on the different experiences of Elaine and Tim to the 2005 London bombings). A good therapist will always take these into account when exploring the person's reaction and working out the best way to help them.

Revisiting and behavioural experiments

One strategy that CBT therapists use is to set up behavioural experiments, going into real-life situations, often where the trauma originally took place. Sometimes the client does this on his or her own, as an agreed homework assignment. But it is commoner, and in many ways preferable, for the therapist and client to do this together. Behaviour therapy, as this used to be called, was something I did early on in my career, taking agoraphobics (those with a fear of leaving the safety of their homes) on increasingly long journeys around Camberwell, where I then worked. My aim was simply to reduce their anxiety and restore their self-confidence, and usually the therapy achieved this. It is a very different experience when therapist and patient leave the cocoon of the therapist's office and venture into the real world. As a therapist, you learn so much more about the person and their reactions, what affects them and what does not. The client will learn things, too, and this is one of main rationales for using this approach in CBT. Trauma memories hold a particular picture of what happened in the past. The time code on the memory is distorted, so that the event feels like it is happening again. Being in the actual place provides new information and that can change the trauma memory, updating it and reducing its emotional power. It is also a way of discovering what triggers a flashback memory. A simple example of this was told to me by Elaine, who had been treated by a colleague of mine, Martina, for PTSD and other problems after the 2005 London bombing (see Chapters 2 and 3). Elaine felt inexplicably stressed out when she arrived one day for a treatment session.

'I wasn't stressed on my way there. But I was stressed when I got there and Martina just nailed it straight away. She said, "I think we need to pop outside and I just want to show you [something]." Somebody had been having a bonfire, and so it was all smoky and you could smell it.'

'And that triggered it off?'

'That triggered it off. And I guess from what I had said a few days previous, Martina would realize that. I had absolutely no idea when I arrived. I said, "I feel really quite tense." I was worried I was going to have flashbacks and I was going to be sick in her office.'

'So you actually had some action to take. You went out and looked.'

'We went out and saw the bonfire and that helped. She actually used that. [It was] her way of saying "tune into the things that are likely to [disturb you]" . . . and I did a huge long list because I was desperate to find out what was causing the various flashbacks. It was about being more observant, because I walking through life everyday and had no idea about what was going on around me.'

Martina's behavioural experiment enabled Elaine to realize what had triggered her increased stress that day. It also confirmed the value of the strategy of paying attention to what was around her, for Elaine had been highly averse to doing this for a long time. Crucially, it restored her feeling of control. She had felt at the mercy of the flashbacks because they seemed to come out of the blue. Now she had a strategy for working out their causes.

If it [the flashback] happens what I would do then is go with it rather than come away from it, which I did previously. And then at a certain point, if it's apparent that I am not where I think I am, then I try and get my bearings. Rather than just move on, and think it's happened again, how embarrassing, it was to actually go back [and think], 'Oh that's interesting. Why did that happen?' and working it out.

Behavioural experiments are frequently used in CBT to test out whether the client's beliefs are correct. This may be allied to overcoming avoidance. Some survivors of the 2005 London bombings avoided travelling on the tube or on buses afterwards. In some cases this was an irksome restriction on their lives. Rachel Handley, Ann Hackmann and others describe the successful treatment of two survivors of the bombing, in which therapist and client together went back on public transport. Here the key to success was in arriving at a cognitive formulation of what the survivors' respective problems were and devising the revisiting programme to put what they believed might happen to the test. One woman believed that, should she go back on public transport, two things might happen. Firstly, she would be in danger of another bomb going off, and secondly, she would become hysterical and lose control of her emotions. Her gut feeling was that the chances of a bomb exploding while she was on a tube train was 1 in 100. When she and her therapist calculated the probabilities accurately, it came to 1 in 72,000,000. When travelling, she was encouraged to look at others rather than bury herself in a paper or book, so that she could access reality rather than her trauma memories. Then she was asked to allow the trauma memories to surface and directly test whether she got hysterical, which she did not.

The value of being in the situation, as opposed to talking about it, is that the client has immediate feedback, the impact of which can occasionally be dramatic. I once took a client who was claustrophobic about travelling in lifts to a store where there were lifts that went up and down several floors. After initial hesitation she got on a lift to go one floor up and found she had no difficulty at all. She then travelled up and down the lifts and was amazed that she could do this without any anxiety. The whole session took less than half an hour.

In reliving therapy, revisiting the trauma site will usually occur towards the end of treatment. The therapist's presence not only provides support, boosts morale and prevents avoidance, but it also means that therapeutic work can be done on trauma memories *in situ*. Triggers can be identified, imagery can be accessed and changed and the benefits experienced immediately. In his interview with me, the psychologist Nick Grey summarized what was to be gained from revisiting the scene:

- **'Then' versus 'Now'.** Revisiting the site and realizing that it looks different from the time when the trauma occurred provides powerful updating information that the trauma is over.

- **Reconstructing the Trauma.** Visiting the site provides very specific memory cues that help in accessing the memory and in adding greater detail to the client's account. Sometimes during a site visit new meanings may emerge that the patient did not access in the other memory work.

- **Finding Updating Information.** The site visit is also helpful in generating updating information for some of the patient's problematic appraisals, especially those concerning their belief that they might have prevented the event from occurring.

- **Testing Meanings in Behavioral Experiments.** For some patients, it is useful to set up the site visit as a behavioral experiment to test specific appraisals about impending danger.

In Chapter 11 I described how two people, Tim Knatchbull and Mark Henderson, revisited the sites of their respective traumas off their own bat and how beneficial they found the experience. Both made their trips several years after the trauma and when they felt ready to do so. Clients in therapy are not usually confident enough to tackle revisiting until some preparatory work has been done, and even then they may hesitate. The presence of the therapist is important. It ensures that the experience is more likely to be positive than negative. The therapist acts as a guide, supporter and mentor, and the meaning of the experience can be explored both at the time and later. Reliving has emerged as the treatment of choice for many people's trauma-related problems, certainly those where fear, anxiety and post-traumatic stress play a large part. It can seem deceptively easy; just closing one's eyes and remembering the trauma. But as I hope I have made clear, it needs to be done properly, carefully and sensitively. Ann Hackmann told me that her therapy sessions are one and a half hours in length, longer in the real-life work, and care is taken to allow the client time to recover towards the end of the session. The close contact that comes from the real-life work undertaken together can make a huge impact in terms of the non-specific factors that I described in Chapter 12. Therapist and client may travel long distances to revisit a trauma site: Ann described going from Oxford to Wales with one client. Sometimes people are seen every working day for one or two weeks to maximize the therapeutic gains. This flexibility is unusual amongst therapists, who tend, for their own professional reasons, to stick to weekly or twice-weekly fifty-minute sessions. It is a particular strength of CBT.

In the following chapter I will describe therapies that focus directly on bodily reactions, generically called *somato-sensory therapies*. Bodily reactions occur during reliving; the vivid imagining often provokes shivering, vomiting or feelings of hot or cold, as Ann mentioned. Some forms of reliving, such as eye-movement desensitization and reprocessing (EMDR), use body movements (for example, the movement of the eyes following the therapist's finger as it moves from side-to-side) to aid recall of trauma memories. But most reliving therapies do not specifically address the physical, with the exception of the use of relaxation methods to combat anxiety. In somato-sensory therapies it is the body that is primarily addressed, sometimes with startling results.

Chapter 14: The body remembers

'I had fantastic treatment . . . The treatment was basically reliving the events [of the trauma of giving birth] and recording my reliving of those events . . . We had one big session where I'd just go back and remember it all. That lasted about two hours.'

'And was it upsetting during those two hours?'

'It was exhausting. I was basically in a slightly hypnotic state. I have the recording of it and there were times when I could feel the pushing, and there were times when I was screaming exactly as I would have been at the time. And there was a point where I lost all the sensation below my ribcage because that is when I had the epidural. I kept trying to lie down in the chair.'

'So you were physically in your body? You were reliving the experiences?'

'Yes. And I also had a lot of somatic memories. And they were also combined with other events from my childhood. One of the weirdest ones was when I was reliving the moment when they finally pulled him out, and they had to pull really hard because he was really stuck down there in my pelvis. And I remember thinking at the time, "It's just like when I had my teeth pulled when I was eight". I had four canines removed and they had to pull so hard. It was that same feeling of pressure followed by relief. And at that point in the reliving my whole head went numb and I couldn't speak. I was talking like this, exactly the same as when I had the anaesthetic in my mouth [she talks slowly and indistinctly]. I couldn't talk [properly] and it was so peculiar . . .'

This is an extract from my interview with Annie, a woman who had a highly traumatic experience giving birth to her first child. She had planned to have a home birth, expecting that, while it would be painful, it should, in the end, be a wonderful experience. However, it was far from that. At home, after many hours of painful contractions, complications set in. There was meconium (faecal matter) in the waters, she was still only 7 cm dilated and the baby was in a transverse position. She was rushed to hospital where, after a nightmare of pain, anxiety and more problems, a c-section was performed and the baby delivered. Annie was very cold, exhausted, unable to see clearly because her glasses had been removed, and in a vulnerable state. In fact, as she discovered when she revisited the trauma in therapy, she was convinced she was about to die. She remembered thinking that she should name the baby right away as 'it felt like I was about to go out like a light or like a candle'. The expectation that the birth of her first child would be a joyous and happy occasion led to a very different, terrifying reality, the experience of which was to haunt her for years afterwards.

Annie was eventually diagnosed with PTSD, which was a relief to her, in the same way as it was to Janine (see Chapter 4) because her condition had finally been recognized and given a name. She underwent a course of intense reliving therapy, which, while hard work, proved beneficial. During the process of reliving, Annie re-experienced physically what she had been through at the time of the trauma, as the extract above shows. Reliving can sometimes have such effects, as Ann Hackmann mentioned in the last chapter. In reliving, bodily responses are a by-product of the therapy, an indication that it is making an impact. They are not targeted directly. However, there is a group of therapies that do just that, *somatic* or *sensorimotor psychotherapies*, as they are called. The therapist starts with the body's reactions, rather than what is happening in the mind. The direct focus on the body, it is claimed, allows trauma reactions to be processed more swiftly, sometimes in a single session, and without necessarily reliving the trauma in any detail. One of the leading therapists of this approach, Peter Levine, has suggested that the current emphasis on reliving is misconceived. 'Just exposing a client to his or her traumatic memories and having the person relive them was, at best, unnecessary (reducing integration in feelings of mastery and goodness) and at worst re-traumatizing for the individual.' Knowing about the body's reactions is crucial both to how the therapy is done and whether or not it will be of help.

In this chapter I will present trauma therapies that specifically use physical techniques. I will begin with eye-movement desensitization and reprocessing (EMDR), a treatment that emerged out of cognitive-behaviour therapy (CBT), in which reliving remains an important component. I will move on to consider two well-established treatments, Pat Ogden's sensorimotor psychotherapy and Peter Levine's somatic experiencing. Finally, I'll introduce newer and more controversial therapies, emotional freedom techniques (EFT) on the one hand, and the energy-psychology movement on the other. Here practitioners use a range of body-based techniques and draw explicitly upon eastern ideas and methods of healing. In my career as a psychotherapist I learned nothing about the body and, beyond using physical relaxation and breathing techniques in anxiety management, I paid it no attention in therapy. Looking back, I realize how limited this was. In concentrating entirely on the mind and predominantly on verbal methods of therapy, I behaved as though the body were just an adjunct, a vehicle for expressing thoughts and feelings, unimportant in itself. Reading about somatic psychotherapies, and through contact with colleagues who practise this approach, I have come to see that a comprehensive understanding and treatment of trauma must include the body and, arguably, should begin there. In Chapter 2, the accounts of those caught up in the 2005 London bombings showed just how physical the experience was. The body reacts first, the mind follows. What happens if we do the same in therapy, and begin with the body? Will the mind follow? This chapter will show that it does.

Eye-movement desensitization and reprocessing (EMDR)

On a sunny afternoon in the spring of 1987, the psychologist Francine Shapiro went for a walk around a small lake. Then an odd thing happened. She had been thinking about something disturbing, 'one of those nagging negative thoughts', as she put it, and suddenly the thought disappeared.

> I started to pay careful attention as I walked along. I noticed that when a disturbing thought entered my mind, my eyes spontaneously started moving back and forth. They were making rapid repetitive movements on a diagonal from lower left to upper right. At the same time, I noticed that my disturbing thought had shifted from consciousness, and when I brought it back to mind, it no longer bothered me as much. I was intrigued. I tried doing it deliberately. I thought about something else that was causing me mild anxiety, and this time I did rapid eye movements intentionally. That thought went away, too. And when I brought it back, its negative emotional charge was gone.

The technique of EMDR was born. In the twenty-five years since Shapiro discovered that making certain eye movements, during the recall of a trauma or other emotionally disturbing experience, seemed almost miraculously to dissipate the emotional distress, EMDR has become one of the best-known and most researched techniques for treating traumatized people. Its success has not been uncontroversial, partly because it seems almost too good to be true. How can people get better simply by moving their eyes in a certain way? It smacked of the mystical manipulations of stage hypnotists: *just follow my finger and you will fall into a trance*. In fact, EMDR is more complicated and far more interesting that any magic trick. Shapiro's serendipitous discovery led to an increasing awareness that just talking about trauma was not necessarily helpful. It also challenged the idea of emotional catharsis, that is, that the full re-experiencing of all the distressing sensations and feelings that the trauma caused, was necessary in order to get better. This remains a prevalent belief today, often expressed to trauma sufferers in terms of 'you need to get it all out' or 'only when you allow your feelings out will you recover' or, simply, 'you need to talk about what you went through'. Reliving is sometimes conceived in that way. It was what I put Janine through, and it was how Annie was successfully treated. It is a part of Foa's prolonged-exposure technique. Yet, as Peter Levine noted, it may not be necessary to do this, and if not done carefully and sensitively, it may cause re-traumatization. EMDR offers a less distressing way of getting rid of trauma memories.

Shapiro and other EMDR therapists are at pains to stress that the therapy is more than a technique; it is a comprehensive package. In the first phase the therapist takes a detailed assessment, including a full history. A safe therapeutic relationship is established, as in all trauma therapies. Then an appropriate target memory is selected to be worked on using the EMDR technique. This needs to be a carefully chosen, specific memory (a dream image, a person, an event, a fantasy, a body sensation, a thought) that will unblock the flow of emotional experience like, as the EMDR therapist, Laurel Parnell, puts it, 'a single log that is blocking the flow of a stream'. Finding the right memory can take some time, occasionally weeks, depending on the complexity of the trauma. In addition to the target memory, the client is asked for a negative thought or belief associated with it that affects their daily life, and then for a positive thought that they would like to believe about themselves. Finally, they are asked what they feel in their body when they visualize the memory. Laurel Parnell described how this was done with a woman who had seen a man drown in front of her during a canoeing accident and was traumatized by her failure to help him.

- L: What image from the incident disturbs you most?
- R: The image of the man looking at me and saying "help!"

- L: What do you believe about yourself when you look at the picture?

- R: I killed him. [negative cognition]

- L: What would you like to believe about yourself?

- R: I did the best I could. [positive cognition]

- L: What do you feel in your body?

- R: I feel spacey and frozen.

(From Laurel Parnell, *Transforming Trauma: EMDR* (New York: Norton, 1997). Reprinted by permission of the publisher.)

In the EMDR procedure the client is asked to bring up the disturbing image with all the attendant disturbing sensations, feelings and negative thoughts and hold it in mind while following the movement of the therapist's finger with their eyes as it makes rapid sweeps back and forth. This can lead to a range of experiences. Sometimes highly emotional, intense sensations are experienced. Sometimes past-traumatic memories are recalled. Sometimes horrific images come to mind. Whatever the experience, the client is encouraged 'let whatever happens happen' and to stay with it, reassured that it will all pass. The procedure continues until there is a shift that indicates the material has been processed and the image no longer causes distress. This may happen quickly or take a long time. The client is then asked what they are thinking, the therapist anticipating that the elimination of the distress will give rise to a more positive thought. In R's case it led to the realization that there was truly nothing she could have done to save the drowning man, which was a great relief to her. There are variations to the EMDR procedure. Studies showed that other forms of bilateral stimulation (alternating hand-taps, flashing lights or a chime that pans back and forth from ear to ear) work just as well as the stimulation of eye movement. If a client gets stuck and is unable to process the memory any further, the therapist may suggest a new perspective or image (known as an 'interweave'), bringing in new information to jump-start the processing.

Research studies have shown EMDR to be effective in treating trauma-related problems. It is particularly successful with single-incident (Type I) traumas, where it can work in one or two sessions. Shapiro explained its way of working as 'accelerated information processing'. Certain trauma memories get stuck and remain unprocessed. The recall of the target memory combined with bilateral stimulation (eye movements, tapping or similar) triggers a mechanism in the brain that frees the blockage very rapidly, more rapidly than simple recall on its own, allowing emotional processing to occur. The idea of accelerated information processing is not new; it underpins reliving, for example, and can be derived from the neurobiological theories of trauma memory (see Chapter 3). EMDR differs from reliving in two ways. Firstly, only a part of the memory is focused on, not the whole experience, and secondly, it uses specific bilateral stimulation such as eye movement to accompany recall. Exactly how EMDR works, though, is unclear. The psychologist Chris Brewin speculates that a simple procedure like tapping or eye movement impinges directly on the senses and gives the traumatic memory a new and distinctive encoding. The specific movement acts as a cue and, because it is associated with the safety of the therapy, it counteracts the distress of the trauma memory. Whatever the mechanism may be, what is particularly interesting about EMDR is the therapist's focus on the body, using body movement in a deliberate way to help reduce emotional distress. This is something that the body-based psychotherapies have taken further.

Levine's somatic experiencing and Ogden's sensorimotor psychotherapy

I asked Bonnie to recall a recent encounter with a colleague . . . and then we both noted her bodily reactions. Bonnie described a sinking sensation in her belly. I noticed that her shoulders were hunched over and brought that to her attention. When asked to describe how she felt in that position, she replied, 'It makes me hate myself.' Bonnie was taken aback by this outburst of self-loathing. Rather than analyzing *why* she felt that way, I guided Bonnie back to the sensations in her body. After a pause she reported that her 'heart and mind were racing a million miles an hour.'

She then became disturbed by what she described as a 'sweaty, smelly, hot sensation' on her back, which left her feeling nauseated. Bonnie now seemed more agitated – her face turned pale, and she felt an urge to get up and leave the room. After reassurance, Bonnie chose to remain and continued tracking her discomfort. Following this ebb and flow, Bonnie became aware of another sensation – a tension in the back of her right arm and shoulder. When she focused her attention on this, she started to feel an urge to thrust her elbow backward. I offered a hand as a support and as a resistance so that Bonnie could safely feel the power in her arm as she pushed it slowly backward. After pushing for several seconds, her body began to shake and tremble as she broke out into a profuse sweat. Her legs also began moving up and down as if they were on sewing machine treadles.

(From Peter A. Levine, *In an Unspoken Voice: How the Body Releases Trauma and Restores Goodness* (Berkeley North Atlantic Books, © 2010 by Peter A. Levine). Reprinted by permission of the publisher.)

This extract shows how Peter Levine, a leading exponent of a trauma therapy that he terms 'somatic experiencing', focuses on bodily reactions from the outset and how those reactions tell a story. Bonnie had volunteered in a class for a demonstration session saying that, in contact with colleagues, she would veer between submission and explosive rage and did not understand why this was happening to her. As the session with Levine continued, Bonnie was aware that her legs wanted to move. She got an image of a streetlight and then a memory returned of how eighteen months earlier, a stranger had pushed her into an alley, held a knife at her throat and tried to rape her. She had managed to get away unharmed, and afterwards her life seemed to go back to normal. But, as was clear from Levine's work with her in the session, although Bonnie had apparently forgotten the experience, her body retained the memory and was still responding. Her legs wanted to run away, her arm moved to push back the assailant, and all the while she felt sick and distressed. The body told the story.

Peter Levine is a psychologist who came to realize that treating trauma by purely verbal methods was not effective and at times could be counterproductive. From his extensive clinical experience he developed a way of working primarily with the body, as illustrated in the extract above, and, using this somatic approach, he was able to help trauma sufferers far more successfully. He has elaborated the theory and practice of somatic experiencing in two successful, popular books. Pat Ogden is another pioneer of the use of the body in trauma therapy, which she calls sensorimotor psychotherapy. Both Ogden and Levine have embedded their therapies in recent findings in neuroscience, in particular the failure of trauma memories to be fully processed and to remain trapped at a primitive level in the brain and the body (see Chapter 3). Bonnie's experience showed that nicely. Where they differ from therapies like reliving and EMDR is in their conviction that attention to the body is not an adjunct to therapy but the key to it.

Both Levine and Ogden believe that the problem for trauma sufferers lies not in the memory itself but the way the body reacts to the memory. Levine draws a parallel with the freezing response of animals under extreme stress. If the immobile animal eventually escapes, then there are rapid jerky movements, discharging the energy that had been held in stasis. With humans, that is usually not possible, leaving what he calls a 'frozen residue of energy'. What is needed is to complete the escape, physically to discharge the energy. Ogden focuses on how trauma sufferers have a phobic avoidance of the trauma memory because of the intense distress it causes. The body is geared to ensuring that nothing can trigger the memory, a state of tension that causes problems in itself. She uses the term 'the window of tolerance' to describe an individual's range of tolerance of bodily arousal. In trauma sufferers that window is pretty restricted and the idea is to learn to expand it in therapy ('stretch the window'). Both therapists suggest that the change needed is fundamentally restorative, that is, to return the body to a state of natural equilibrium, what Levine calls 'pendulation'. The movements used in therapy are designed to do just that. The approach is often called 'bottom up' because it starts with the body, in contrast to the 'top down' methods that begin in the mind. Changes in cognition and emotion follow the bodily changes. This is what happened to 'R' in Parnell's example of EMDR above, where a positive cognition (new meaning) followed the changes in 'R's body that EMDR brought about.

The body is an ally. This is a key part of the initial phase of therapy: learning to understand and trust one's own body. As with other trauma therapies, it is vital to establish a sense of safety, and this is achieved as a result of the sensitivity of the therapist, their care not to move too quickly, and their careful attunement to how the person physically reacts. I watched a DVD of Levine's initial session with a young, sceptical, traumatized US soldier, who had been blown up by two IEDs. It was impressive how gentle Levine was and how, by always drawing the man's attention to what was happening in his body, he ensured that the man remained in control.

This focus on the body and on the present experience is called mindfulness; instead of dwelling on worries about the future or the past, what might happen or what did happen, the attention is on right now and on the physical. 'What are you feeling in your body right now?' is a question the therapist might ask. Or they might note that the left hand has tightened up or that an arm showed a tiny jerk. This requires the therapist to be highly focused on the physical person in front of them and experienced in picking up often subtle movements. The therapist's own bodily reactions can mirror the client's and thereby confirm how the body is involved at times of emotional expression.

Levine describes the aim of therapy as 'softening the edge of the sensations' by attending to movement and releasing energy. The young soldier in the DVD was experiencing frequent tic-like jerks of the head to the side. Levine saw these as an attempted escape from the shock of the explosion, a natural reaction that had not been completed. Rather than seeking to eliminate the response, he encouraged its completion, albeit in a softer form. By the end of the session the soldier could soften the bodily movements and was astounded by the progress he made. In Ogden's terminology, this could be seen as 'stretching the window of tolerance' (she labels clients' successes as 'acts of triumph'). Therapist and client set up simple behavioural experiments to test what happens with certain movements and note the client's reactions and sensations. Behavioural experiments are done in CBT too, usually to challenge negative cognitions or to show that the reality is very different from the trauma memory (see Chapter 13). In any real-life experiment the body is active and the feedback provided is felt physically, which explains why this form of therapy is more immediate and powerful than talking about what might or should happen. The new experience is encoded in the body, challenging and replacing the trauma memory. Moreover, the client learns a different strategy, one of stepping back and observing their own body, being curious about what will happen, playing with different possibilities. This strategy, allied to the immediate feedback that comes from instant bodily changes, releases tension, whereas thinking about the trauma, recalling the experience, increases tension. Although methods like reliving and prolonged exposure aim to reduce tension over time, through repetition and new learning, the experience itself can be harrowing. In somatic experience and sensorimotor psychotherapy the approach is to build up tolerance slowly and to gain direct benefit from the physical movements.

The following is a brief description of somatic therapy in operation from Robin Shapiro's book.

> Your shoulders are tight? Can you exaggerate that tightness? That's right, pay attention to the sensation. What's happening in your arms? ... Right, they look clamped down to your sides. Notice the sensation in your arms and shoulders. Is there a movement that your arms want to do? Slowly, slowly, paying attention to the feelings in your arms, let them start the movement. [Client slowly brings both hands in front of face in a defensive posture.] What do you want to do now? Push? Before you start the pushing motion, could you sink into your legs? That's right. Bend your knees, feel the ground supporting you. How does that feel? More grounded? Great.

Therapist and client work together on the physical movements, trying things out, observing the client's reactions, then trying something else. There is no need to explore directly what's happening in the mind – images, fantasies or thoughts – except inasmuch as they are revealed by the body. This has one obvious benefit: it bypasses well-established mental defences and provides a different way of accessing the trauma. It is not focused on the trauma memory, but on what is happening to the body in the present moment. This does affect the memory and the somatic therapist will relate what is happening to events in the past, as Levine did with the tic-like jerks of the young soldier's head. The change, however, is in the present, and the outcome is in terms of releasing trapped energy, increasing tolerance of arousal, restoring natural equilibrium and allowing new sensations to be experienced. Out of this new physical state, cognitive and emotional changes arise. These are then brought into the therapy. Often there is revelatory feelings of positive change: 'This feels really good. I feel so much better.' How these new feelings can be integrated into the person's life, into their identity, their relationships with others, and their work, is the subject of the final phase of therapy, which is similar to that of other trauma therapies. In fact, Herman's tripartite template fits neatly on the somatic therapies. The first phase is about feeling safe, learning about the body, developing a good attachment to the therapist. The second phase is the body work. The final phase is about reintegration into normal life. I have never used the somatic way of working myself. As I learn about it, however, I am impressed not only by the speedy results it gets but also by the holistic nature of the approach, how it combines body and mind. With its particular attention on the body, it seems to enable often highly traumatized people to find an escape route, and do so quickly. This is also true of two newer and more controversial therapies, emotional freedom techniques (EFT) and energy psychology.

EFT and Energy psychology

'Tell me, Sarah, about a time when you used EFT.'

'It was in the hospital. I don't know if you remember we were all in the waiting room when the doctor came in to tell us about Rob.'

'I remember it well.'

'He told us very bluntly that Rob had a serious head injury and could die at any moment.'

'It was a terrible moment.'

'It was awful. Well, I was really troubled by the doctor's eyes when he told us. They sort of burned into me. It became like a hotspot. Afterward, I used EFT on that. And I used it again when Rob was in ITU.'

'What did you actually do?'

'First, I tapped on the front and side of the hand and said to myself, "Even though I have been traumatized I accept myself completely." Then I went round the different meridian points on the body, each time tapping.'

'And were you thinking about the doctor staring at you?'

'Yes. I'd go through tapping on each meridian point several times until I'd gone through the whole sequence.'

'And what did that do?'

'It was really helpful. It reduced the distress.'

'Completely?'

'Not totally, not at that point. But to a low level, like 1 on the SUDS [subjective units of distress scale]. What it did was help me manage my distress. I also used it much later a couple of years after the accident. I'd get the image of Rob lying on the road and that would set my heart racing, really highly aroused, a lot of anxiety in my chest. I thought I haven't really got over this. So I went through the EFT protocol and it got better. I reduced the anxiety to zero. I can still think about it like I'm doing now. I don't *like* it, of course, but I don't have that high arousal reaction. That's completely gone.'

Sarah is my daughter and she is recounting the awful event that I described in Chapter 1, when her partner, Rob, sustained a serious head injury and was admitted to a specialist unit. Like Sarah I recall the doctor vividly. His youth and his royal-blue scrubs stand out in my memory rather than his eyes. He had no choice but to tell us the facts and, however he had done it, it was bound to be upsetting. At the time I felt it physically, like a hammer blow, as did Sarah. She had trained in emotional freedom techniques (EFT) and her account shows how, later, she was able to use the approach to reduce her distress. There is a superficial similarity between EFT and EMDR. The client chooses a specific target problem (a trauma memory) to focus on while being taught to do something physical (bilateral tapping in EMDR, meridian-based tapping in EFT). The distress caused by the problems declines or disappears as a result. The effect is often achieved rapidly, especially for single-event traumas. In EFT, the major difference is the focus on acupuncture points rather than on bilateral stimulation, the following of defined sequences of tapping on different parts of the body and the links with traditional

Chinese medicine (TCM). EFT therapists may dispense with the specific trauma memory and reliving components; they suggest that tapping can be done to a general phrase like 'The Trauma' without the individual concerned having to say what the trauma is or to recall any of the details of the event. EFT is not the only therapy to use tapping. Roger Callahan developed an earlier therapy that he called thought-field therapy (TFT). This involved tapping meridian points in a precise sequence in order to relieve negative energy or *qi*. Tapas Fleming, an acupuncturist, developed her own version, which she calls the Tapas acupressor technique (TAT).

As Sarah's example indicates, EFT follows a clear protocol. First, the problem is identified and given a title. The client is asked to rate the degree of distress the problem causes on a 10-point SUDS scale (from 0 for no distress to 10 for extreme distress). The next stage is the *set-up*, in which the client taps on the side of his or her hand at the same time as saying a self-acceptance phrase, such as 'Even though I feel anxious I deeply and completely love myself anyway'. Then the *tapping sequence* starts. This involves tapping seven times on the end of each meridian point while thinking about the target problem. (I will come on to explain what meridian points are.) This is followed by the *gamut procedure*, in which the client taps on the back of the hand and performs a number of eye movements and simple actions like humming. The client re-rates the degree of distress and repeats the procedure until distress is eliminated completely or reduced to an acceptable level. As with other somatic therapies, the claim is that EFT reduces traumatic distress quickly and without the need to recall the trauma memory in detail or at all. With EFT, people learn to use the therapy on themselves, as Sarah did, and so have the benefit of having a simple and effective procedure that can be used whenever it is needed.

EFT's link to acupuncture and the meridian system can provoke scepticism. Although acupuncture has been used in the West for decades, it remains controversial; there is disagreement about the evidence for its effectiveness and, as yet, only preliminary suggestions that it may help trauma-related problems. The notion of 'meridians' is equally controversial. In TCM, the meridian is a path through which the life-energy known as *qi* is believed to flow. There are twenty meridians, including the 'twelve regular channels', with each meridian corresponding to each bodily organ. This notion goes beyond western science; it challenges established beliefs and, for many, it is a step too far. One does not need to embrace the theory, however, to appreciate the value of the methods. If EFT helps traumatized people to recover swiftly and effectively, then it is on a par with EMDR, somatic experiencing and sensorimotor psychotherapy, each of which is subject to some theoretical uncertainty and disagreement. It is possible to see EFT purely in terms of western science, for example, as a way of directly accessing the amygdala and allowing trauma memories to be processed, though some EFT practitioners see this as unnecessarily reductionist.

Energy psychology (EP)

EFT is an example of energy psychology in operation. Energy psychology (EP) has been around for over thirty years, although its influence on mainstream psychology has been limited. The fundamental assumption in EP is that physical-and-mental-health problems are related to disturbances in the body's electrical energy or its energy field. EP seeks to activate these electrical signals directly, and produce shifts in energy fields resulting in changes to emotions and thoughts, reducing distress and changing beliefs. Some practitioners use a procedure known as applied kinesiology to detect possible imbalances in the energy fields. The muscle-pressure test can be used, in which the practitioner applies force to a large muscle group (commonly in the arm), asking the client to resist. If the arm gives way, it is a 'weak' response and indicates some disturbance. It was muscle testing that led Roger Callahan to develop TFT, in which particular sequences of meridian points were tested in ways that related to particular problems and helped

to reverse or eliminate the distress triggered by thinking about a
problem. In EFT the kinesiology element was dropped in favour
of simple tapping, which seemed to work just as well and had the
additional advantage of being used by the clients on themselves.
The psychologist Phil Mollon has pioneered the application of EP
in psychoanalytic psychotherapy (which he calls PEP or psychoanalytic energy psychotherapy) and argues that attention to bio-
energy enables therapists to work more sensitively and quickly with
their clients' problems than the traditional psychoanalytic methods,
as he explains in his book, *Psychoanalytical Energy Psychology*.

> A basic principle is that all the traumas and psychodynamic
> conflicts of the psyche are encoded as information in the
> energy system at the interface of body and mind. Eschewing
> rigid protocols of technique, we can flow with the client's
> emerging thoughts and emotions, listening and responding
> to psyche, energy, and body, in a way that creates a powerful
> therapeutic synergy. Such work can be rapid and very deep.

One of the strengths of muscle testing is that the practitioner rapidly knows from immediate feedback whether an intervention has
worked or not. If an intervention fails to produce an effect then
other interventions are tried until a solution is found. What 'energy'
means is not totally clear. But Mollon argues that the procedures
appear to work with remarkable speed and that, at present, we
should be open-minded about the underlying theory, rather than
being put off by it. Like EMDR and other somatic methods, people who use EFT or other forms of EP, or see it being used by
therapists, as I have done, are singularly impressed by how well
often highly sceptical clients respond to it. Something important is
going on. The various somatic therapies are making a startling and
significant contribution to the psychological treatment of trauma.
I believe that psychologists and psychotherapists should be much
more body-aware, and that this will both benefit clients and improve
the understanding of how trauma affects the mind and the body.

Part 4:
Aftershocks

Chapter 15: Resilience

Susanna's story

On 3 April 2007, Susanna Graham-Jones was driving from Petersfield back to Oxford, having attended the funeral of a friend. The phone rang. She pulled up in a busy lay-by and, as lorries hurtled past, she was told that her son Tom, then twenty-two years old, had had an accident while snowboarding in Bulgaria, where he was on holiday with his girlfriend, Ellen. Susanna was given the name of a Foreign Office contact and Ellen's mobile number and by the time she had set off again, she knew that Tom had suffered an extremely serious injury. At that stage she did not know the full details, but very soon she heard that it was a spinal injury and she realized that, should he survive, he was very likely to be paralysed. Susanna is a GP. She was used to medical emergencies. But this was different. It was her son and he was 1,200 miles away. This is how she took up the account when I interviewed her in Oxford in January 2010.

'It was a completely surreal journey back. I kept driving and thinking of things that must be done and then thinking of somebody who could do them, and then stopping the car again and making that phone call. So by the time I got back to Oxford two and a half hours later, I'd got an appointment to talk to the hospital doctor in Bulgaria and I'd got a friend to look up flights for Bulgaria; I'd contacted David in New York [Tom's father] to give him the Foreign Office number and the hospital number.'

'Did you have any inkling at the time of how serious this was?'

'Well, at some stage on the journey, or once back here, I knew it was a high-neck fracture. I didn't know what Ellen must have known by then; that Tom had had a cardiac arrest on the way into the hospital in Sofia . . . Driving was extraordinary. I was busily saying to myself that what I had to do now was get home, not to think too much about it, not go into catastrophe mode. I had an awful lot to do. I'd got to be there for him as soon as I physically could. I had a job to do.'

Susanna's journey to Bulgaria was a nightmare. Tom's younger brother, Oliver, who was a student at Warwick University, accompanied her. But when they got to Heathrow, they discovered his passport was out of date. It meant missing the flight and going into central London to the passport office. They went to the wrong place first of all; and then Oliver had to have his photo retaken, as he was making a determined effort to smile normally. The passport office said the smile on his face invalidated the photograph for passport purposes. Then there was the long wait for the passport.

'We went and sat in Starbucks in Victoria Station, twiddling our thumbs and reading the papers and talking to each other and not texting other people, just sort of hoping we could get on a plane. Then we got that passport – within two hours. I had been told it was not possible to get a passport in anything less than four hours. So we seized the passport very gratefully and rushed back to Heathrow and were put on a plane . . . I mean, all this was just my "go, go, go" bit. It was the right mode to be in but it was extremely stressful having these setbacks, and I broke down and wept all over Oliver on the second leg of our journey. We flew to Munich from Heathrow and then from Munich to Sofia and by then it was sinking in that Thomas was paralysed – the surgeon must have told me that, after the operation, he would not walk again . . . and what I was saying to Oliver in my distress was that it was a waste about Thomas's physical prowess, about the waste of the life, I couldn't bear it and so on. Oliver just sort of held me, and he was very good. But what he made of it I do not know. It was terrible to impose that upon him. So the poor boy had a dry-eyed mother in "go, go, go" mode and then a collapsed mother weeping all over him on the plane.'

'Up to that time, when you were in the "go, go, go" mode, your feeling was one of trying to solve the problems that were put in front of you. Is that what was happening? You focused your energy on that.'

'That was very much my style. That is absolutely what I did over the break-up of our long, twenty-one-year relation-ship [with David]. I absolutely recognize myself in that.'

This chapter is about resilience, the capacity that some people have to bounce back from tragedy. Nietzsche's aphorism, 'that which does not kill us makes us stronger', captures the way adversity can be transformative, even as it is dealing us horrific and life-changing blows. For a parent there can be very little worse than hearing that your child has suffered a horrendous accident from which he might not recover and which, if he does recover, might leave him severely and permanently incapacitated. In the immedi-ate aftermath of Tom's accident, he had two cardiac arrests. He underwent a lengthy operation to stabilize his neck. He was fortu-nate in being treated in a highly specialized neurosurgery unit, one of the best in Eastern Europe, according to his mother. But it was in a foreign country with all the attendant difficulties that brings. Then, after it was clear that Tom would survive, his life was com-pletely changed. The location of the spinal injury was such that he was left tetraplegic, paralysed from the neck down, without vol-untary movement in any of his four limbs. He would need fifteen months of inpatient specialist treatment and then many months of rehabilitation. He would require a wheelchair and full-time care. For a twenty-two-year-old man who had been very active, a keen footballer, dancer, snowboarder and party-goer, who had been about to graduate from university and take a job as an electronics engineer, who was at the cusp of a new and independent life, all was suddenly changed.

For Susanna, her relationship with her son was all-consuming in the days after the accident. Being a doctor, she knew something about the care of spinal injuries, but she had never worked in that area. She needed to get up to speed. She knew it was vital that she arrange for his NHS care in England to be in place as soon as possible, which she did in the first twenty-four hours. She had work to do and she threw herself into it. The grief she had experienced on the plane with Oliver was shunted right away, and all her efforts went into helping her son. People cope with grief in different ways. Some break down, so distraught that they can do nothing but weep. Despair can descend like a dark, heavy blanket muffling the world outside. Some are galvanized into action, determined that, however disastrous the trauma, they will ensure that everything possible has been done. Throwing herself into a whirlwind of activity was Susanna's characteristic response. It was a manic defence against the grief, she admitted to me, a way of staving off the horror of what had happened. It also embodied a tremendous resilience, the capacity that some have for transforming a dreadful situation into something positive.

'I was glad to have had my weep, my catastrophizing moment when nothing was ever going to be worthwhile ever again because my eldest son, who was such a wonderful, fit young man, was never going to be wonderful and fit again. I think I just parked that and then revelled in the fact that he was not brain damaged, that he was being well looked after and that he was not dead. The moment when I looked into his eyes in the intensive care unit in Bulgaria and saw that he recognized us was actually wonderful. And so was the way his eyes lit up every time Ellen came into view.'

'So you focused on the positives?'

'Yes; a "come on, all is not lost" sort of attitude. In Bulgaria we all kept our acts up. Tom's sister, Polly, arrived, and also Ellen's mother – and the five of us spent the next few days sight-seeing: we went to the cathedral and lit candles on Good Friday, we shopped, ate, played cards, determinedly keeping going – Oliver was specially good about this – until it was time for two of us at a time to pop into the hospital for those precious ten-minute visits.'

Then one day, in the midst of this frenzied activity, she had a brilliant idea.

I remember I came bouncing down to the supper table one day because, in the bathroom brushing my teeth before the meal, I suddenly had a vision of the future that would work. And it has worked. It's been realized.

Susanna's father, Michael, has a house in Standlake on a completely flat area of land. He had got planning permission to build an extension to his house, and also a music room in the garden. The extension was envisaged as a living space for a musician friend, with the music room doubling as a venue for the charity concerts that Michael and the family hosted every summer. However, the friend had not been able to move, and the plans were shelved.

Susanna knew, somehow, that the planning permission would remain in force for five years. In her 'eureka moment' before supper in the hotel in Sofia, she realized that the single-storey extension could be built to house Tom, and the free-standing music pavilion, accessed by a walkway across the garden, could be a studio for him, where he might work or see friends. The whole village is flat and manageable in a wheelchair, with pubs, village hall, village shop and all – a total contrast to Susanna's own utterly vertical house in the city.

The family were initially 'gobsmacked', as Susanna put it, by the idea. But it worked.

All the planning permission had to be rejigged to make it all wheelchair-friendly. We eventually found a really good project manager, who built the extension first – and while that was under way, David set up a website and everyone we knew contributed to the fundraising for the Pavilion Trust. Tom moved into Michael's house once he was discharged from Stoke Mandeville National Spinal Injuries Centre, camping in a hospital bed in one room with very Heath Robinson arrangements. Two months later the extension was ready, and it was an amazing moment when he rolled right in and down his own spacious corridor.

And now Ellen and Tom cohabit there. She has stuck with him all the way through. So they live at Standlake. We still have concerts in the Pavilion, which they kindly come to, although it's not really their kind of music. One of Tom's carers lives in a spare room in Michael's part of the house, and Ellen has a little studio there too. And as it happens, it's my father who is now the focus of my care, so I drop in and look after him, and sort of wave at Tom in a very casual kind of way.

Susanna's remarkable resilience exemplifies one way of coping with adversity. After she had broken down the one time, over-whelmed by the realization of the loss, she picked herself up and got on with tackling the problems that needed to be dealt with. She would not dwell on her feelings after that: there was too much to do. She explained her behaviour in terms of her character, an existing mental toughness that had taken her through other dif-ficult life events. It exemplifies a particular attitude of mind that some people have. As the psychoanalyst Boris Cyrulnik put it, 'Misfortunes are never wonderful. A misfortune is like black, fro-zen mud or a painful bedsore. It forces us to choose: we can either give in to it or overcome it. Resilience defines the spirit of those who, having suffered a blow, have been able to get over it.'

Tom's story

I visited Tom Nabarro at his home in Standlake, where he had agreed to be interviewed. His home was as Susanna had envisaged it, a large, purpose-built space that allowed him to move easily from one room to another in his powered wheelchair. It was here that he lived with Ellen and his grandfather. As I waited for Tom to get ready for the interview, I felt apprehensive. I had no experience of interviewing people who are paralysed and no grasp of what might be acceptable to say or not to say. At the same time I berated myself for failing to see Tom as a person rather than a man in a wheelchair. Could I not treat him as I treated all the other interviewees for my book? My apprehension speaks volumes about how difficult it must be for those who are paralysed, having to deal on a daily basis with the prejudices, uncertainties and misconceptions of others. In the end, there was nothing difficult about interviewing Tom, apart from his getting a bit tired towards the end. Like his mother he was extremely candid about the trauma he had experienced and its effects on him and his family and, like his mother, he too showed remarkable resilience in adversity.

Tom told me what he recalled of the events leading up to the accident. He had travelled up into the mountains on his own, while his girlfriend Ellen stayed at college in Sofia, where she was working on her Erasmus project. He knows that he spent two to three hours snowboarding, though he has no actual memory of it. The accident had resulted in retrograde amnesia, the loss of any memory of the events immediately preceding the trauma.

'The last thing I remember was taking a photograph of a radar dome at the top of the mountain. I was intrigued by all the military warnings, "Don't proceed otherwise you'll be shot". And then I remember lying on my back looking at the sky with a feeling of fluid in the back of my throat, which was probably blood and probably fluid from the lungs, and not being able to move, knowing it was pretty serious. At that point I remember having the reflection of a feeling when I was in the air and knowing something wrong was happening.'

'So you had a very strong sensation that something was wrong?'

'It was a flashback to the time of being in the air from the jump and knowing that I wasn't going to land straight and thinking something bad was going to happen. That was a flashback while I was lying on my back. I remember looking at the clouds and feeling quite peaceful. It sort of faded off and then I had a sensation of floating above my body and looking down and seeing paramedics working on me. I remember floating in a circular motion, rotating around, and the view from the sky; that was quite a profound feeling. And then there was darkness and a tunnel sensation and it was as though I was at a bottom of a well and I couldn't get out. Then there was a series of hallucinogenic dreams which involved stories of being kidnapped in Bulgaria and some drug baron taking me away and locking me up in a cell; lots of very strange stories.'

'You thought they were actually happening at the time?'

'Yeah, they were 100 per cent real. They were very vivid, very horrible, really. They went on for about three weeks, while I was on morphine and other drugs.'

I asked Tom if, during his treatment in Sofia, he had been aware of what had happened to him.

'I was pretty well aware because I was paralysed within the dreams. I had damaged lungs. I knew that my neck was broken. I was aware of what was going on probably due to Mum and Dad and Ellen being very vocal about what was going on and having discussions about the surgery with me during the time.'

'Was that important?'

'Absolutely. Very important. I think the more you know about what's going on, the more you can understand about what's going to happen in the future, and the more you can prepare yourself for the changes in life which are going to have to take place.'

Susanna remembered deliberately telling Tom every day about his accident, injury and paralysis, when he was barely conscious in the intensive care unit. There was no way she could know what he was able to take in and remember while he was on the ventilator. But she wanted him to see his situation as something that he could work on himself, as soon as possible. I asked Tom if it was distressing him to remember what he'd been through.

Not particularly. It was a life-changing event and the whole process was part of the event, including the dreams, the time in Bulgaria, which wasn't nice, including the suffering of relatives, which was all very real. These are all things that have improved now, which we've learned and progressed from. They are all important parts of your life and therefore I don't find it too distressing thinking about it. They're learning points and challenges which, once you've overcome them, make you stronger. In that sense, it's not too much of a regrettable thought, thinking about them. It's only a reflection of how hard the times were then.

I asked him to tell me more about the learning points and he told me about two distinct periods, the first when he had to deal with the immediate consequences, the pain and the suffering, and then later when he had to come to terms with what had happened to him, how his life was irrevocably changed. He was on a ventilator at first, unable to move, unable to speak, unable to sleep, just staring at the ceiling.

'When you first experience the lack of mobility, it's quite challenging because you're used to being in complete control. Dealing with the lack of control was the first learning point, really, that and the pain, just being able to suffer them without going into a complete mental panic.'

'Where was the pain?'

'Everywhere really. Obviously as I was paralysed from the neck down, there was not much sensation below the neck. But the acute loss of sensation was almost like a pain. Not being able to feel was a huge void and the contrast from being able to feel everything to not being able to feel anything was very acute at the beginning stages. But the actual pain was in the head and neck, recovering from the surgery . . . And the waiting was very difficult. I ended up relying on visits from relatives, which weren't very frequent at the beginning because it was a military hospital and the visiting times were very stringent. And that was hard, me being there on my own.'

'When you said you were learning to cope with the pain, what did you learn and how did you manage that? Was it some mental activity, something that you thought?'

'I was trying to distract myself, trying to think of more pleasant experiences. I would try to imagine something which would distract me in a constant way, something that involved activity. I imagined the activity of snowboarding, the activity of running, and the way you envisage doing those activities is actually a constant process. So that's a good way to distract yourself. Typically the pain goes in waves. You get an acute pain sensation and that sensation will last a few minutes, up to ten minutes or so, and then ease off a little bit. It's in those initial periods of really acute pain where you've got to try and distract yourself otherwise you end up getting in a panic. I was trying to create diversions which would constantly distract my brain for short periods.'

In a state where he had no control over his body, in which he was suffering physical and mental pain, Tom used his mind to exercise a degree of control. In this way he learned to keep panic at bay. Having something positive to do is a key part of resilience. It was what galvanized Susanna as she planned the changes to her father's house that would eventually enable Tom and Ellen to live there. Tom could not physically do anything on his own. But he could use his mind. Even focusing on breathing was useful, as that too was an activity that demanded constant attention. The transition from being on a ventilator to re-learning how to breathe naturally (the unconscious reflex having been destroyed) was hugely challenging and demanded considerable conscious attention and hard work. When Tom was transferred to Stoke Mandeville hospital and entered a period of rehabilitation, there were the medical and other procedures to attend to. Then Tom experienced the second learning point, that of adjusting to the loss of his previous active self. There was no disguising that it was a huge loss.

'I was an avid clubber, a person who enjoyed dancing a lot, and a person who enjoyed sport a lot. Those are two very big parts of my life and coming to the idea that those are no longer going to be possible was very difficult. A lot of time was spent in emotional distress with family members, talking about it and just trying to get over that fact.'

'Was there anything that was particularly helpful for you, something that you thought or something that people said?'

'I think those [losses] have been the hardest things to deal with and I don't think anything really did help. I think those will never go away . . . They are still very difficult to deal with. I miss my sport and I miss my dancing and those things are never going to come back. Although most things have been helped by talking to people, those things haven't really.'

I was struck by Tom's realistic appraisal of what had happened and what it meant to him. Being resilient does not mean pretending that the loss is not real and painful. That would simply be deluding oneself. Any significant change also entails a significant loss. This is true of non-traumatic changes as well as traumatic ones. Getting married, for example, entails a loss of independence, just as getting divorced means the loss of an attachment and the loss of previously valued ideals and hopes. In Tom's case he mourned the loss of his physically active self, a reality that no amount of talking would take away or compensate for. In his new physical state there were new things to learn, some of which he learned in Stoke Mandeville while others he had to work out for himself. Personal care, for example, had to be carried out by employed personal assistants (PAs) and Tom had to learn how to instruct them in his needs.

'Personal care is still probably one of the most challenging aspects of life at the moment. Typically it takes about a month or two to adjust to dealing with a new PA and to be able to get them to understand my routines and the way I like things to be done and the tact that I require in their behaviour. Once that's learned, it's a huge investment and typically in the care industry the job expectancy is around three to six months before they move on . . . Continuity is a huge challenge and also another huge challenge is patience, not losing my temper, and irritability. Obviously, everyone gets moods. Typically the frustration is when people don't understand you and you're in a bad mood, and that can quite often lead to a loss of temper.'

'It sounds like you've got quite a lot of understanding of yourself and of other people. But it is also an understanding of how to control, if that's the right word, your emotions. Most of us don't think about that very much. Sometimes we don't control our emotions at all whereas you're having to think about that almost constantly.'

'Absolutely. Because I don't have the ability to be alone a lot of the time. Typically people's coping strategy with anger is to vent it when they're alone, to be able to relax on their own and do things which can dissipate their anger. I can't always do that. I can do that for short periods of time but there are always going to be things I need and a need to have someone close by in case of an emergency. So I don't have those extended periods of alone time where I can dissipate my anger. I need to find other ways of dealing with it.'

'What other ways do you have?'

'Music and also work. Mental processes. My work is problem solving in program-based work and that involves a lot of logical-based thinking. I find if I can focus on a logical problem for a period of time, that can offset some anger or some pent up feelings.'

'Is that a distraction or is it . . .?'

'I'd say that's more of a mental process, working things out. I also enjoy massage to reduce some tension and even small periods of meditation, just with my eyes closed, just focusing on breathing. That tends to dissipate anger.'

'Are these things that you have found for yourself or has someone else told you about them?'

'They are mostly things I have found for myself since the accident. I spend a lot of time when I am not actively involved in what's happening with me. This is why it's important to have good PAs because they can do things without my involvement, like dressing or washing. Once they know my routine well, I don't need to instruct them. Then I can focus on mental activity and typically I spend a lot of time relaxing. It sounds slightly strange. You're physically being moved around and having actions performed on you; but I use those times to close my eyes, relax, focus on breathing, or think through problems or plan the day. These are really important periods because for the rest of the day I am constantly active, focusing on what I'm doing, whether I'm instructing people or whether it's using voice activation on the computer. So those periods in the day when I can think about other things and relax.'

'And the relaxation happens, does it?'

'Yes. It's because I'm not focusing on time-limited activities. I am just doing hang-out periods.'

'Is that a way of separating your mind from your body, so to speak?'

'That's it exactly. You're completely detached because you are not having to interact with the outside world at those times.'

Tom and I talked about other aspects of his changed life, his relationship with Ellen, his work as an electronics engineer, his recent return to the ski slopes to watch others skiing and snowboarding. Towards the end of the interview I asked him how he viewed the future.

I tend to be preoccupied with immediate concerns a lot but I am always thinking of ways to improve my systems, the way I deal with care, the way I deal with employment and the way I deal with self-management. There is always going to be room for improvement and at present it's very evident because the systems aren't working as well as I would like. I am always thinking about future events; for example, if I get married, if I have children, if I change jobs, potential things that could happen sooner or later. In fact, carers are the more immediate thing [as] carers obviously affect everything to do with my life in the foreseeable future. Making sure the best and the most suitable care systems are in place is really important. The dominant factor is flexibility . . . The more flexibility you can have with your care arrangement, the more flexibility you can have with your day-to-day living. And flexibility is typically the first thing that is lost when you are physically disabled.

Conclusion

Tom's life had dramatically changed. He could no longer be the active person he had been. His loss of mobility forced him to think more, to plan ahead. He has had to rely on others for care. His life is radically different from what it was or from what it might have been. With determination he has applied himself to working out how to make the most of his situation. He continues to do that. Susanna told me that his determination to do that was a beautiful thing and how proud she was to have helped him to do that.

I hope the housing solution at Standlake lasts for as long as it can. It won't last forever. I am sure they will get impatient and want something else. But for the moment it's a good solution. So I think that is what I get by on, a vision that I have helped with and seen. Seeing that it has a life of its own, the thing that you've planted, the seed, the child. The idea grows and has a life of its own and that is infinitely satisfying really.

Boris Cyrulnik worked with very traumatized and damaged children, including survivors of torture and concentration camps. He points out that resilient people are those who can create a new narrative for themselves, one in which the self that has been split apart by trauma can be reconciled into a new, positive identity. A key factor lies in regaining the feeling of control. Major traumas like Tom's accident and its consequences take away the normal sense of control. It is psychologically important to get that back. Gill Hicks, who lost both legs in the 2005 London bombings, wrote movingly about how she learned to live what she called 'Life Two', which she promised to herself would be celebrated at every opportunity. The difficulties should not be underestimated and each person meets trauma in their own way. Character, that quality that constitutes the unique individuality of a person, plays a part, along with the capacity to adapt and change. In the next chapter I will discuss how the experience of trauma can release unexpected creative faculties in some people, and how this can lead to positive changes in themselves and their lives, a change that has become known as 'post-traumatic growth'.

Chapter 16: Post-traumatic growth

'I had never heard of Teenage Cancer Trust until a couple of weeks before Laurie died. Because of the way cancer works . . . we had a long period to think about how we would cope with this, I suppose three months from the day we got the news that the cancer had returned until the day he died. And we felt we wanted to do something . . . Somehow the name of Teenage Cancer Trust flitted into our consciousness and I rang their chief fund-raiser, a man called Richard Shaw, who was immensely sympathetic and responsive. So we began raising money for this notional idea of a teenage cancer unit at the Children's Hospital in Birmingham . . .'

'Looking back on it now, what do you think the psychological significance of this was for you and your wife and family?'

'It's giving yourself a purpose at that moment of maximum trauma, and what it also does – and I don't know how much of this we knew at the time – is enable your friends to give themselves a purpose . . . The fund-raising provided an opportunity and some people who were the most helpless when Laurie was ill became the most brilliant fund-raisers subsequently. It was a way of giving us a purpose and trying to achieve something for ourselves and also for Laurie. It has given his life a validation that it would otherwise not have had and, in a sense, given his death a validation. That unit would never have been there if Laurie had never been ill. There would have been no teenage cancer unit at the Children's Hospital in Birmingham . . . It happened because of Laurie and that's a source of immense pride and satisfaction.'

'Can you say whether it enabled you to cope better with
the grief and the sadness and the awfulness of his death?'
'Without any question.'

This is an extract from my interview with the *Financial Times*
journalist Matthew Engel, whose son, Laurie, died in September
2005 at the age of thirteen, from rhabomyosarcoma alveolar, a rare
and aggressive form of cancer. In December 2005 Matthew wrote
a moving piece in the *Guardian* about Laurie in which he mentioned the formation of the Laurie Engel Fund and the aim to build
a teenage cancer unit in Birmingham. Just over four years later a
huge amount of money had been raised and the teenage cancer
unit built and opened. It is a great achievement and, as Matthew
said, it would not have happened had Laurie not had cancer and
died. It is something good that came out of the horror of his illness
and death. This chapter is about how trauma can lead to positive
and unexpected changes in people and in people's lives. The death
of a child is a blow so grievous that parents never recover from
it. Yet the immense pain and terrible sadness it brings can lead
to something joyous and fulfilling. The video of the opening of
the teenage cancer unit shows a modern, cleverly designed and
attractive space attached to a 1970s wing of the Victorian building. It is abundantly clear how beneficial this will be to both the
patients and their families and to the staff working there. It will
enrich people's lives at a time when they most need it.

In the course of researching this book I met other trauma sufferers who had gone on to do something different with their lives
as a result of the traumas they had been through. In Chapter 11,
for example, I wrote about Tim Knatchbull, who survived the IRA
bomb that blew up the boat that he and his family were on. Tim's
eventual return to the west coast of Ireland, which he revisited
many times over the course of a year, proved to be a significant
project in his life. It enabled him to come to terms with the tragedy and resulted in his writing a successful book. In the same
chapter I gave an account of the film director, Mark Henderson,

who produced a remarkable film about his capture by Colombian guerrillas, including an interview with 'Antonio', one of his kidnappers. Mark is a film-maker by profession and he harnessed his existing talents to good purpose. Raj, who lost his good friend Benedetta in the 2005 London bombings, had no experience of film-making. Yet he was the inspiration for the making of a beautiful film about his friend's life and death, something that gave him immense pride and satisfaction. Trauma can lead to something creative whether it is a new building, a book, a film or something else altogether. It can also lead to changes in the traumatized person themselves, a discovery of talents and attributes that had lain dormant or they never knew they had. This happened to two survivors of the 2005 London bombings, Tim and Elaine (see Chapter 7). Tim took early retirement from his lecturing job and now spends a large part of his life in his pottery studio making pots. Elaine left her busy job in the St John Ambulance service and now runs shops that specialize in burlesque costumes, something she really loves doing. Going through a major trauma can be a terrible experience. But it can also be a force for change and that change can sometimes result in positive and enriching experiences, all the more valued because of the trauma that led to them.

Post-traumatic growth (PTG)

A major trauma destabilizes and disrupts a person's world. It can lead to feelings of vulnerability and uncertainty, undermining the illusion that life proceeds in an orderly, rational and friendly way. It can provoke powerful emotions on the one hand and a sense of detachment and numbing on the other. It challenges core beliefs, in the fairness of the world, for example. It undermines our sense of control, showing how fragile that control really is. It is out of these experiences that PTSD and other emotional problems can arise. But equally they are fertile ground for post-traumatic growth (PTG). Just as new shoots will grow from the blackened devastation left by a forest fire, so the very destructiveness of the trauma opens up the possibility of something positive. As the term 'growth' implies, it is not just the case that people recover from trauma, returning to a form of normality, but also that something *new* develops. This is an old idea. The ancient myth of the phoenix rising from the ashes of its old self is a familiar metaphor of renewal through destruction. The thirteenth-century Persian poet, Rumi, wrote of treating pains as messengers and of the value of listening to the message that the pains convey. The psychotherapist Viktor Frankl found spiritual transcendence in the midst of the horrors of Theresienstadt concentration camp, which changed his way of understanding himself and the world. In literature and film, it is a common theme for the hero to emerge from a traumatic ordeal to become a changed and better person.

However, for the forty or so years that I worked as a clinical psychologist, the focus of psychological work has been more on post-traumatic stress than post-traumatic growth, on documenting the pathological effects of trauma, and on helping individuals to recover from recognized mental conditions or illnesses. As is obvious from the preceding chapters in this book, there is no doubt that major traumas can wreak havoc on individuals and families, and the 'illness' model, if properly understood, can help sufferers understand both what their experiences mean and what they can do to help themselves. But the focus on illness can too readily be interpreted as the belief that trauma inevitably leads to psychological damage, and that the damage is long-lasting or even permanent. At a talk in London in late 2010, I listened while a major figure in the trauma field, who had himself suffered from PTSD, stated that once you had PTSD you had it for life: it never went away. This bleak and, in my view, erroneous conclusion comes from a misperception of how major traumas affect people. As I have already shown, the majority of people are *not* severely affected by trauma, even a major one. While many will experience some acute-stress symptoms in the trauma's immediate aftermath, those symptoms generally decline over time. Only a minority develop PTSD or other problems. Most of those who do so will recover, sometimes with professional help, sometimes on their own initiative, sometimes simply with the passage of time. The experience of trauma is not a life sentence of emotional distress; nor is it right to assume that the experience is wholly or largely negative. Anyone who has suffered the loss of someone they love knows about the pain of grieving and the emptiness that remains. At the same time the loss can be liberating as the survivor adapts to a new and changed world. The emptiness gets filled and, although the pain never goes away, it lessens and is transformed into something else. We are biological creatures, programmed to experience both pain and pleasure. The cliché 'life goes on' tells a truth: that even in the darkest moments, there are times of joy or simple pleasure.

Miriam and Esther Hyman

Miriam Hyman was thirty-two years old when she was killed in the 2005 London bombings. By a twist of fate she had been evacuated safely from the King's Cross underground. She phoned her father and agreed to have a coffee and await developments. But she must have changed her mind and boarded a number- 30 bus. This was the bus that the bomber, Hasib Hussain, blew up in Tavistock Square, killing himself and 13 others, including Miriam. In July 2009 I interviewed Miriam's only sibling, Esther, who is now a trustee of the Miriam Hyman Memorial Trust, set up to honour her sister's memory. Early on in our interview she told me that she realized that the pain of her sister's death did not blot out all positive feelings, and what that understanding meant for her. For Esther, finally hearing that her sister was dead was an intense and very physical experience. She described it to me as 'just raw pain, like someone has ripped your skin off and all your nerve endings are completely exposed'. She was in shock and consumed with grief. Yet at the same time the pain was not total. She recalled a crucial moment when she realized that she could feel pleasure at the same time. She called it her 'baked potato' moment.

'The night of the bombings we were getting very worried as Miriam hadn't made contact. I began to eat a delicious meal of baked potato, cheese and salad. And this is very important actually in the whole emotional process. As I took the first mouthful, it was delicious and I remember enjoying the pleasure of the flavour. Then a part of me said, "You can't experience pleasure; there is something really bad going on." And then another part of me said, "No. That bad thing is happening but I'm not going to feel guilty about enjoying the baked potato", and that has carried me through all my emotional reactions. I think that quite often we have an emotional reaction and then a reaction about how we are reacting. And it is quite often guilt, feeling guilty for feeling bad, feeling guilty for feeling happy.'

'And you experienced that right at the beginning?'

'Right from that moment. I let go of [controlling] any feelings. I allowed myself to feel whatever it is that I was feeling. So if I am feeling a bit low and depressed for any period, rather than thinking, "Oh I shouldn't be feeling like this", and putting pressure on myself to feel better when it really isn't coming from inside, allowing myself to go through that, knowing that's it temporary, knowing that I'll come through it. Or allowing myself to grieve, allowing myself to cry in public or with other people in private, and not feeling any sense of trying to repress or suppress those feelings, I've allowed them to surface.'

The truth is that feelings happen whether we want them to or not. Trauma shows us this all too well. This is true of pleasure as well as grief. Esther instinctively recognized this and made a conscious decision not to denigrate herself for feeling pleasure, however awful the situation was. At times, grief can be all consuming and it may feel as though nothing else can take its place. But the intensity lessens and other experiences press for attention. When these are simple pleasures, the mere fact of their experience can lead to guilt. Freud wrote about this is in his classic monograph *Mourning and Melancholia*, analyzing how, for some, the loss of loved ones can lead to guilt and severe depression (melancholia). In such cases, the loss of the actual person is inextricably bound up with the loss of a part of the self, and the person's inability properly to detach the real loss from the psychic one. Anger is felt at the person's untimely departure but it is directed at the self rather than the person. This leads to a spiral of depressive anger, guilt and further depression. Nothing else seems to matter and so simple pleasures can no longer give any satisfaction. All feeling is negative; intense grief becomes narcissistic and, literally, self-defeating. Esther's recognition that pleasure and pain can coincide protected her against intense depression. It also enabled her to do something positive in her sister's memory and thereby enabled her to grow as a person. She helped to set up the Miriam Hyman Memorial Trust in memory of her sister. The purpose of the Trust was to do something constructive and worthwhile, in direct contrast to the destructiveness that had led to Miriam's death. Miriam valued eye-care services, having discovered in her teens that she was short-sighted. A fund was created within the sight-saving charity ORBIS UK, and in 2008 the Miriam Hyman Memorial Trust (MHMT) became a registered charity and went into partnership with the L. V. Prasad Eye Institute in India. In May 2008, the MHMT equipped the Miriam Hyman Children's Eye Care Centre, based at the L. V. Prasad Eye Institute in Bhubaneswar, and the trust continues to support its expansion into a Child Sight Institute. I asked Esther about what that meant to her.

'For us it is a lasting and fitting and living memorial that does my sister's memory justice. It's brought us a lot of comfort as a family and it has given us a different perspective on the whole set of circumstances because we've made something positive come out of it. I think if we can do that, at least we haven't wasted the opportunity to make

something good come out of it. Quite apart from the fact
it's a huge focus for our time and energy.'

'Which is important, isn't it?'

'Absolutely . . . I feel that if I had gone into some sort of
long-term decline then the terrorists would have won. They
would have succeeded in terrorizing me. They would have
beaten me into submission. But by refusing to accept a
victim's mindset, by the determination to establish a legacy
for Miriam that reflects the way she lived, I feel [while]
they've taken her life, they haven't beaten any of us.'

Before her sister was killed, Esther had been drifting, unsure about
what to do with her life. She was working as a medical secretary.
Before that she had been a primary-school teacher. Now her role
within the MHMT means that she makes a vital contribution to
others who are less fortunate than herself. She summed up the
benefits of this change for her.

'It's given me a new sense of direction, a new raison d'être.
And it's put me in what I feel is a privileged position. [I
can see] the bigger picture. The aim of the World Health
Organization initiative "Vision 2020: The Right to Sight",
which the Miriam Hyman Children's Eye Care Centre is
part of, is to eradicate avoidable blindness globally by the
year 2020. By way of the paediatric ocular oncology facil-
ity at the Centre we have even gone into the realm of saving
lives. I feel that these events have indirectly given me the
opportunity to participate in that.'

'That's something that you might not have done at all?'

'There is no doubt that I wouldn't have done this.
Whether I would have come round to working for a charity in the long run? Perhaps. But the Children's Centre
is named after Miriam. One door closes and another one
opens. If you can get past the fact that it's a very painful
scenario, then it's one that can be used constructively. I feel

> that I would be doing Miriam an injustice and myself an
> injustice and my place in the world an injustice if I didn't
> fulfil that destiny to the best of my ability. Give it every-
> thing I've got to make it happen.'

There are other more public examples where a tragic event leads to people finding a new and different role in the world. Doreen Lawrence, the mother of teenager Stephen Lawrence who was stabbed to death on 20 April 1993, became a prominent human-rights campaigner, dedicated to securing justice for the victims of racially motivated crime and police misconduct. She founded the Stephen Lawrence Charitable Trust, a national educational charity committed to the advancement of social justice, the alleviation of poverty and the development of individual and community citizenship. Sara Payne, whose child, Sarah, was murdered by a known paedophile became a campaigner for parents to be given the right to know whether a convicted paedophile lived in their community. She wrote a memoir about her experiences and became an advisor to the government on changes to the law. She was awarded an MBE in 2008. A huge and tragic loss can galvan-ize an individual into a way of life that she or he would never otherwise have considered.

The link between trauma and creativity is something that the academic David Aberbach has explored. His contention is that unresolved grief has spurred artists and writers on to greater heights of creativity, citing, for example, Thomas Hardy's poems for his dead wife Emma, and Tennyson's 'In Memoriam', written after the death of his friend Arthur Hallam. The churning emotions become channelled into intense bursts of creative activity. But not everyone makes radical changes to their life after trauma and it would be misleading to suggest that somehow this is always to be expected or even required. Just as people grieve in different ways, so people develop in different ways. But the potential for doing something creative is there, enabled by the same processes that provoke grief and emotional disruption. There is considerable psychological value in carrying out a creative project. As Matthew Engel pointed out, it provides a much-needed focus for positive activity at a time of helplessness and grief. It restores a sense of control to the individual, when control has been wrenched away by the trauma and its consequences. While the trauma itself cannot be mastered, something else important can. Moreover, that something else can be hugely valuable as a public memorial to the person who has been lost. Hence the names live on: the Laurie Engel Fund, the Miriam Hyman Memorial Trust, Sarah's Law, the Stephen Lawrence Charitable Trust. Through creative projects, those who have been affected directly or indirectly by a trauma discover qualities within themselves whose existence was previously unknown to them.

Personal transformation

'Although there is nothing I wouldn't give for it not to have happened, I feel I wouldn't want to be the person I was on 19 April 2004, the day before Laurie was diagnosed. I wouldn't want to be that person again. It doesn't mean I'm particularly proud of the person I am now. But I feel that I have learned things about life, about what matters, about the sadness of the world, and the goodness of the world, that I did not know and might not have learned any other way. Maybe it's the nobility of suffering. I feel that because we have suffered as a family, because Laurie suffered terribly – he suffered the most dreadful pain. I don't know whether that response to pain is a sort a selfless emotion or a selfish one; perhaps the definition of love is that you can't tell the difference . . . I feel nonetheless that we have been through the worst. I feel I have acquired something that gives me a connection to the way the vast majority of human beings, past and present, have lived their lives.'

'It's as though the experience of this tragedy has pierced illusions we all have, that everything . . .' that life

is something that was always going to get better, which it
previously had done. But that's not how it works. It's not
a journey towards happiness. It's a journey towards understanding. And I feel that this has helped me on that journey
in a way that nothing else could have done.'

Matthew Engel revealed how the tragedy of Laurie's death had
changed him to the extent that he would not want to be the person
he was before Laurie's illness. A transformation had taken place
inside him, a greater awareness of suffering in the world, a loss
of the innocent belief that life would always get better, a deeper
sense of the world as it is. Georgie, the young woman who was
raped in her Paris apartment (see Chapter 8), said something similar when I interviewed her.

You know, I would never have wanted it to happen and I
would never say I wanted it to happen to anyone else. Of
course it happened. But I couldn't go back now. I wouldn't
want to go back and erase the last two years of my life and
start again. Because it's made me who I am. I definitely
didn't value other people. I mean I valued people before
but I don't judge any more. I learned that from Janice [her
psychologist] and from things in general.

Georgie had fallen into a state of depression after the rape, blaming herself for allowing the men to get into her apartment. She
felt she was being judged by everyone, by the French police, by
her parents, by society, and as a result she judged herself even
more harshly. She thought her psychologist would judge her, too,
but Janice did not judge her in any way. Instead, Georgie was
given the chance to talk and explore her feelings and beliefs. She
realized that it was the rapists who were at fault, not her. In the
warmth of the therapeutic relationship she discovered a better and
less judgemental sense of herself. Later, when she returned to
university, she spoke about the rape to her flatmates and to one of

her lecturers. She found they respected her and saw her as a strong person who had come through a terrible ordeal. She realized she was indeed much stronger than she had been, 'strong enough to be vulnerable', as she put it to me. She began reading about rape and about the way, even in western society, women are still exploited by men. She took an interest in the world in the way she had not done before her trauma. She registered for a course in psychology. These changes in her came about because of what she had been through. The trauma had changed her as a person.

The positive changes that people report after trauma include a greater appreciation of what life has to offer, setting new priorities, making significant changes to one's work or way of life in general, taking on a creative task or project, a resurgent feeling of personal strength and renewed vitality, greater closeness to loved ones, and an enhanced spiritual or religious awareness. Matthew Engel wrote of feeling liberated from his fear of illness and death.

> The worst has happened so what more can life throw at me? And my own mortality does seem somewhat trivial in comparison when you have lost a child at thirteen. The fact you can collapse in a heap at sixty is not going to be a bad result. I will have done all right.

But he was also more determined to live life to the full, celebrating his sixtieth birthday and seeking new goals as a writer.

> There are things that I want to achieve as a writer, [things] that I have become more focused on because of Laurie, who was a writer and was very likely to have followed in my footsteps or probably surpassed them. Perhaps on some level I feel I have to achieve what he can't now do.

The psychologist John P. Wilson delineated twelve principles of positive change in trauma survivors. Amongst these are the capacity to confront death with greater equanimity, an acceptance of pain and suffering, a more balanced, grounded way of life, increased empathy and compassion for others, loving and being loved by others, a renewed sense of purpose and meaning, and a greater spiritual awareness. As he put it, 'there is a reinvented self, one that is more grounded, centred and connected to ultimate values, higher states of consciousness, and Being-in-the-world'. Although the message of positive transformation after trauma is on the whole constructive and helpful, there is a risk of overegging the pudding, making people believe either that they *must* change or that any change that occurs after trauma is necessarily positive. There is also the question of timing. Positive transformation rarely occurs in the immediate aftermath of trauma and may not do so for some months or even years afterwards. For some it may not occur at all. In Judith Herman's model of trauma recovery, it is at stage three, the stage of reintegration into society, that these positive changes are most likely to take place. This is when Georgie began to experience a change in herself. Although the emphasis on positive transformation has arisen to counteract the excessive focus of psychopathology and PTSD, this does not mean it is an 'either/or' matter, either one is ill or one is transformed as a person. In fact, the huge disruption caused by major trauma commonly results in *both* negative and positive changes. This makes good psychological sense, for we are complex creatures, capable of both being overwhelmed by distress and seeing the world and ourselves differently.

Spiritual and religious experience

As I researched the effects of trauma I came across both individuals who had experienced a spiritual transformation after a major trauma, and those for whom religion provided a consolation and a sense of larger meaning in the wake of trauma. One of the most striking examples was one I read about in a newspaper. A young woman was kidnapped and beaten up by her ex-boyfriend, who then left her to die in the boot of a car in an isolated car park.

Very near to death she was discovered by chance after almost a week's incarceration. On recovery she said that she bore her ex-boyfriend no ill-will and, in accordance with her religious beliefs, she forgave him for his callous and awful act. A very strong religious belief can carry people though terrible traumas. It provides a larger explanation (God's will, or similar) and, if strong enough, can transcend the horror. This is what Viktor Frankl discovered in Theresienstadt concentration camp. For him it was a deep sense of love and the ability to find a larger meaning even in terrible circumstances. This is clearly not a rational process. God-fearing people see the survival of a single person under the rubble of an earthquake as a miracle. But the loss of tens of thousands in the same earthquake is not seen as a reason for abandoning God. Not everyone is protected by religious belief, however, and for some the pain of losing someone dear turns them away from religion. Charles Darwin, for example, reputably lost his faith after the death of his beloved daughter, Annie. His wife, however, remained a Christian despite her daughter's death. For religious belief to protect against trauma it must be firmly held. In Darwin's case he was already questioning the value of an omnipotent deity and a religious understanding of the natural world.

If we think about trauma as the shattering of illusions, we might imagine that one such illusion is religious belief. Yet religion has always offered meaning and consolation beyond normal experience. A belief in the afterlife provides succour for those who have lost a loved one; there is the prospect of being reunited at some point in the future. The belief that there is a larger meaning to life than is found in the purely natural order of birth, life and death can help us to accept the blows of outrageous fortune, for it suggests that there is an overarching purpose, even when matters seem entirely senseless. It is impossible to convince oneself of this by reasoned argument; it has to come from the heart. I asked Matthew Engel whether Laurie's death had led to any form of spiritual or religious feeling in him. He thought long and hard about this. No, he said. In the process of writing a book about England, he told me, he had visited every county, and in the course of those visits, he lit a candle in every cathedral in Laurie's name. But he felt that this was more about having a purpose than a faith, and of course a way of honouring Laurie's memory. You cannot convince yourself into a religious belief, but it can come about through experience.

I have no religious faith. I was brought up by parents who were non-believers, my father a secular Jew and my mother an agnostic. I have always regarded religion as a human construction, designed to help explain the world when better explanations were lacking, and a means of justifying the established political and economic order (*the rich man in his castle, the poor man at his gate*). My wife, Mary, is also an atheist, also the product of non-believing parents, and so our household has never had a religious influence of any sort. It has come as a surprise to us, therefore, to discover that our younger daughter, Sarah, has developed a strong spiritual side to her life. This followed a long and debilitating illness for which medical help was at best inconclusive, at worst hopeless. In a telephone conversation I asked her first what being spiritual meant to her.

'It means having an existential path in life, a meaning of why you are here, being connected to something larger than yourself, transcendence in that your path is bigger than your own individual needs, than your biology.'

'What do you mean by "transcendence"?'

'It's about a higher meaning to things, rising above your everyday needs and feelings to find a sense of purpose. Sometimes about experiences that can transcend the ordinary as well.'

'Can we talk about how it all happened?'

'First of all I had a very serious illness that took me out of everything that was important in my life, my job, my career, my friends. So my life became very barren and poor really. I didn't become spiritual then. I was just really miserable for a couple of years. Then accidentally I began having energy work. I went to see a massage therapist and she wanted to start doing kinesiology with me, which is a form of energy therapy. At first I was very suspicious but I let her do it for me and I started to find it very helpful. Over the course of about six months I started to experience the shift that comes with energy work and that opened me up to new experiences. And then I began to become more open, thinking that if this can work, perhaps other things can work. I stopped being so closed-minded to new things. Throughout the course of various energy approaches I have done, I started to have more experiences which don't fit with the classic, western scientific view of the world, which doesn't allow for the energy systems.'

'So your route into this was having had a serious illness and having had some kinesiology treatment which opened you up to the idea of energy and energy changes?'

'Yes. Then, as you work through things, spiritual things become more apparent to you. You become more open to those types of experiences. Many people who work in that realm – not everybody, mind you – become more spiritual. It's a relatively common route to a world view that is more spiritual.'

'Would it have happened anyway or is it only because of the trauma of your illness?'

'I don't think it would have happened anyway because I am very stubborn. I was very stuck in my way of thinking. My feeling is that sometimes when people are very resistant to other viewpoints, it can be a way of being in control, like "I understand everything and there isn't anything else." It can be frightening that there can be other ways of doing things. I think I would have stayed in that role had my life not been interrupted like that. I had to seek new ways of seeing things, of being.'

'That is something I have read about. A traumatic

experience opens up the possibilities of change. Something came in and you were more receptive to it.'

'For me, it didn't really open it up. I was still very resistant. It just forced me into it, for there was no other way I was going to get better. I tried all western medicine. It helped to a certain extent but it couldn't help me completely. My back was against the wall. My defences came down from sheer desperation rather than receptive openness.'

'And it was when you worked through the resistance that you began to feel some benefit. And it was physically that you first felt it?'

'Yes. First of all, I felt physically better and that was very interesting to me, for I didn't understand how that would work. And then I began to work much more on the emotional level and that helped too. But in my view it was energy psychology that got me better from that serious illness. So it had a very clear physical effect on me as well as helping me emotionally and helping me think more about existential issues too.'

'Now that you are better, how important is it to you? How does it help you in your life now?'

'The most important thing in my life is my spirituality. I would put it as my top priority and I would arrange my life around it. It's a complete change in my life that way. I feel much happier knowing my purpose in life. I am much more supported by it and by the whole idea of a higher power. I feel much less lost. I still can be very emotional and have ups and downs as I used to. But overall I have a sense of where I am going and that's a hugely positive thing in my life.'

'So life has more of a meaning for you?'

'Life has *a* meaning as opposed to not having a meaning. I would go so far as to say an overarching meaning, more than just to work, to get money or to have children. And you can always go back to it if you get confused or lost. It's helpful on a day-to-day basis, on how to live in a smaller way. Am I going in the right direction? Am I living the purpose I'm supposed to live by? Even small decisions it can be really helpful with, not just big ones.'

I envy Sarah's spiritual certainty. It has made a huge difference to her life. She is so much happier than she was. The precursor was the trauma of a long, frightening and debilitating illness. But it was also something physical, the recovery that she experienced through energy psychology (see Chapter 14) and the way it opened her up to new ideas about health and wellbeing. It suggests to me that the spiritual sense needs to be a *felt* sense, something confirmed in the body's core. This is why it is not possible simply to persuade yourself of its value, to become spiritual because it seems like a good idea. Just as a major trauma is felt physically in the body and the brain, so the recovery from trauma is also in the body and, for some, the way the body reacts opens up a spiritual dimension.

Chapter 17: In harm's way

'Two days ago I had the news that a colleague of mine stepped on a mine in Afghanistan. He's lost both his legs. And I just thought that I don't ever want to go back on patrol or something like that again. I think there is something in the fact that all of us journalists would see that stuff, witness it, and go through it, and then repeatedly go back. I think that must be part of the trauma too because it's not normal.'

'You would repeatedly go back to situations where you were in danger. You'd see people who are killed or maimed, and families that are bereft, and houses that are destroyed.'

'Or even worse. Ethnic cleansing, rape or torture. Repeated on a very [large scale]. I think if you go through one or two of those experiences, that's enough. For me it was a steady repetition of it. [It was] constant.'

'You are saying that there is something in you that impelled you to do that.'

'Yes. I do believe a big part of it is my innate sense of injustice because my parents, especially my father, had this huge sense of compassion. I got that from him. And also the fact that this stuff is really dark and it needs to be exposed. But another side of it was addiction. I am sure now, looking back, that it had to be addiction. And the fact that, in those places, you don't need to worry about the real world. You are not thinking about bills or the fact that I was in my thirties and didn't have a child yet . . .'

'There were more pressing, immediate concerns that took over your whole life once you were there.'

'You are living very much in the moment. There was no future, there was no past.'

This is an extract from a conversation I had with the acclaimed journalist and writer Janine di Giovanni in a café in Notting Hill Gate in October 2010. She was in the process of finishing her memoir, *Ghosts by Daylight: A Memoir of War and Love*, a candid exploration of her life as a war correspondent, mother and lover. I wanted to know more about why Janine chose to put herself into highly dangerous situations time and again and what effect it had had on her. Media coverage of major wars is part of our normal life; every day we hear reports, read articles or watch broadcasts from journalists in dangerous parts of the world. The risks they run are real. In the past couple of decades, increasing numbers of journalists have been killed and wounded in the course of their work. In 2010 alone, forty-four journalists were killed worldwide. Of these, six were killed in combat and eleven on dangerous assignments. Many more have been wounded or narrowly escaped death. This includes the BBC correspondent John Simpson, who was injured in a so-called 'friendly fire' incident in northern Iraq in 2003. Why do people work in a job where they will be exposed to major, life-threatening traumas? In this chapter I will attempt to answer this question, not just in relation to war correspondents but others whose work exposes them to danger, such as members of the armed forces who risk their lives fighting wars and engaging in peace-keeping duties in Iraq, Afghanistan and other conflict-ridden parts of the world.

There are professions where the risk of death is slight but the work entails exposure to some nasty and potentially traumatizing experiences. I spent ten years working for the Thames Valley Police Authority as their psychologist responsible for staff welfare. I saw firsthand police officers who had become traumatized by a particular event or series of events. Before I worked for the police I had only the haziest idea of what their work consisted of. I soon discovered that it is largely routine, and not dissimilar to the work that happens in any large organization. In fact, research has shown that police officers are most stressed not so much by exposure to traumas but by the day-to-day strains within the organization itself: by difficult managers, by budget cuts, by poor communication and by shift work. Yet there are groups within the police whose work brings them regularly into contact with major traumas. Roads policing, for example, involves attending serious road accidents, where the officers encounter gruesome sights of the dead and mutilated. Domestic-violence officers are frequently exposed to the trauma of actual or threatened violence by ex-partners and spouses. This can occasionally spill over into tragic events, such as the murder of the estranged partner and other family members. Police officers and other staff working in the area of child sexual abuse see highly disturbing videos and photos, as well as having direct contact with young victims and their abusers. Police and other emergency-service personnel are called in when major incidents occur, such as explosions, bombings, riots and major accidents. I recall debriefing the body-recovery teams after the Ufton Nervert train crash in 2004, in which a stationary car on a level crossing derailed a high-speed train. The job of members of the team was to meticulously scour the site of the accident, picking up, bagging and logging parts of dead bodies, something they had trained for but had never done before. These are experiences that few of us would deliberately seek, yet some professionals choose this sort of work and take pride in it.

Another question I will consider in this chapter is whether people whose work brings them into contact with trauma are likely to suffer psychologically as a result. In the last five to ten years there has been a particular interest in the welfare of soldiers and other military personnel returning from combat or after they leave the service. Soldiering has got more dangerous, as is evident from the increasing numbers wounded and killed in Iraq and Afghanistan. Although the armed forces have long acknowledged that the experience of combat can lead to psychological breakdown, going right back to 'soldier's heart' in the American Civil War and 'shell-shock' in the First World War, the military's understanding and treatment of psychological breakdown has been inconsistent and not always psychologically sensitive. How are soldiers and others exposed to life-threatening or highly disturbing traumas affected? What is the best way of helping them? Is there anything that might be done to make their experience easier to bear?

The attractions of the work

> What I got out of wars was a buzz. You don't ever feel more alive. You know the shelling is going on and you are exposed to this intense experience and at the time it seems like the most important thing in the world. It's just so addictive. So addictive.

This is a quote from the BBC journalist Fergal Keane. For him the danger and the intensity of covering conflict created a high, a buzz, that ordinary life cannot replicate. In the remarks that opened this chapter Janine di Giovanni expressed a similar sentiment. This is not to be equated with the behaviour of a few rogue journalists who deliberately court danger for the sake of it ('adrenaline junkies', as they are sometimes known), and who are generally looked down on by the journalist community as a danger to themselves and others. Responsible journalists seek to minimize the risks while at the same time recognizing that risk goes with the territory. But as Fergal Keane, Janine di Giovanni and other experienced journalists know, there is something distinctly attractive about the buzz of war and all that goes with it. This needs to be acknowledged and properly understood. But is it right to call it an addiction?

That many journalists reject the term 'addiction' is unsurprising; it is redolent with negative meanings (drug addiction, alcohol addiction), and carries the implication that addicts are self-centred hedonists, governed by their need for more and more sensational experiences rather than anything else. But that is not necessarily what addiction means. A valuable discussion of this issue can be found in Anthony Feinstein's book *Journalists Under Fire*. To explain the attraction of trauma, Feinstein drew upon the work of the psychologist Marvin Zuckerman and his colleagues who, in the 1960s, developed a measure of sensation-seeking behaviour. It has four components: thrill and adventure seeking, experience seeking, disinhibition, and boredom-susceptibility. Those who score highly on the scale like to pursue adventure and seek out new experiences, are readily disinhibited and easily bored. Young men in particular are strongly represented at the high end of the scale. Most war correspondents are young – the mean age of the sample Feinstein studied was in the late thirties – and most are men. There are of course several factors that could explain this. Feinstein believes that there is a genetic predisposition that draws certain people to this work; that, in effect, war correspondents are 'genetically primed' to respond positively to the thrill and danger that the work entails. In one sense this is simply stating the obvious: that certain types of people enjoy certain types of work because of the people they are, and this is a result of the combination of genes and environment. It is like saying someone very good at numeracy is drawn to a career in mathematics. In another sense, however, it suggests that an attraction to the buzz of war has a neurophysiological basis and, as such, may be hard for some people to resist. In other words, it works like any other addiction: once you have experienced it, your body wants more and more of it. There is a close link between fear and excitement. Both entail the release of stress hormones like adrenaline. Both result in similar physiological reactions such as increases in heart rate, breathing rate and sweating.

Captain Kevin Ivison was a bomb-disposal officer (known in the service as an ammunition technical officer or ATO) who worked in Iraq, doing one of the most dangerous jobs in the world. In his memoir, he describes his first experience of combat training under live fire.

> I had learned something from the exercise: I liked it. I loved the mayhem and confusion of battle and managed to keep a clear head when others seemed to buckle. My secret, as yet unspoken to my platoon commander or even close friends,

was that I wanted to find that kind of action. I wanted to find war.

Ivison was turned on by the sheer excitement of battle. Moreover, he realized that he could remain calm and clear-headed even under great stress. This was to serve him well when he worked as an ATO in Iraq. It enabled him to do his job well, saving many lives. However, it did not prevent him from suffering psychologically afterwards. After successfully defusing a device where he estimated his chances of survival were less than 5 per cent, he broke down and was forced to give up active work as an ATO.

What draws someone into a job is not necessarily the same as what keeps them there. The British army, the infantry in particular, has long recruited young men from problematic backgrounds with few or no qualifications, many of whom have problems with literacy. In effect, they are seeking a secure job in a market where few options exist for those without skills or experience. Many find the realities of army life, combat in particular, too difficult to take and leave. For others, the intensity seems to have the same attraction as it does to war correspondents. If Feinstein is right, those soldiers who remain and enjoy the work may have a genetic predisposition towards sensation-seeking. But making a genetic attribution risks oversimplifying human behaviour. People's motivations are complex; even those obviously addicted to drugs or alcohol are not driven solely by biological needs. There are other reasons for enjoying working as a soldier, a police officer or a war correspondent. For some it is an escape from a conventional and dull way of life. For others there is a sense of vocation, pride in doing something for the public good. In my police work I encountered many officers who were proud of their choice of career because it felt worthwhile to them and their families. Many journalists who cover conflicts throughout the world do so because it feels morally right to do so. Janine di Giovanni identified her strong sense of injustice and her desire to expose the wrongdoings of others as the reason she got into journalism in the first place.

Martin Bell's account of his experiences as a BBC reporter during the Bosnian conflict illustrates how important journalists can be in helping uncover horrific crimes. It was good journalism allied to television coverage that revealed the horrors suffered during the siege of Sarajevo (Janine di Giovanni experienced this firsthand and wrote powerfully about it). Journalists act as impartial witnesses to atrocities such as the massacre at Srebenica, in which thousands of Muslim boys and men were summarily executed. There is a need to expose such matters to the world so that justice can be done and such atrocities made less likely to happen in the future. For many war reporters this is an important motivation for taking the risks that such work entails.

Another psychological factor in working in difficult and dangerous situations is the close camaraderie that comes from team work and from sharing dangers and hardships. In February 2009 I interviewed Keith, a Thames Valley police officer who had worked for many years in the force. One of his earliest experiences was dealing with inner-city violence, something that was alien to him, as he had had a sheltered, largely rural upbringing. He told me how important the shift team was to him.

> That I got through that without any problems I attribute to the very close camaraderie and network of colleagues I had around me at the time. The shift was a very tight shift. You would go on, you would finish your night shift, and quite often you would drive down to Heathrow for breakfast because it was the thing to do. Or on a day off, the shift – the whole shift, wives, kids, the whole lot – would go down to a beach at Littlehampton or Bournemouth and spend the day there. The shift was very, very close.

Even war correspondents, who like to see themselves as hardened, self-sufficient individuals – and indeed are in direct competition with each other – develop close friendships. Only those who were actually *there* know what it was really like – unlike the rest of us. That creates a unique emotional bond. Soldiers not only share the experience of being exposed to life-threatening dangers, but their survival often depends on the actions of their comrades. In Iraq, ATO Kevin Ivison's life was literally in the hands of his fellow soldiers, in particular the 'bleep', the man who blocked out incoming radio-attack signals that could explode the bomb he was seeking to make safe. Kevin's small, close-knit team was hugely important to him. As he put it, 'They performed the most dangerous job in one of the most dangerous towns in the world, always putting other soldiers' lives before their own and I loved them for it.' Intense and dangerous experiences unite people in adversity, creating a bond that is unlike any other.

In summary, those people who choose to work in professions that expose them to dangerous and traumatic events do so for a variety of reasons: pride in the work, a sense of duty, a feeling of doing something for the public good, the desire to escape from a humdrum job, few other career choices, the appeal of something exotic, dangerous and risky. Whether, once experienced, the dangers and risks exert a pull equivalent to a physical addiction is an open question. It is not hard to understand that ordinary life can pale into insignificance compared to the heightened intensity of being in a war zone dodging incoming fire. As I have mentioned, there is a close link between excitement and fear. There are good psychological reasons for feeling the pull of danger and wishing to return to it. As Janine di Giovanni pointed out, you need not be concerned about paying your electricity bills. You are focused on what is happening right now, and that can be highly reinforcing.

The psychological cost

The first time I saw a child in extreme agony was in Central Bosnia in 1992. This kid had been hit by a mortar shell and his intestines were hanging out. There were no painkillers. Apparently intestinal wounds are the worst. I went outside and threw up. There were other journalists there. It was horrible but they got into their cars and drove back and filed their stories. I just didn't take it like that. It was such a visceral feeling that I literally threw up. Somehow I was able to cope with it until Luca was born and it then sort of all unravelled . . .

When my son was born, the birth was very traumatic. I'd had four miscarriages before that and so I was convinced he was going to die or wasn't going to be born normal. The first thing I said to the doctor when he handed him to me was, 'Is he dead?' And the doctor said, 'Of course he's not dead.' From that moment on I had this intense inability to separate myself from him . . . I was so freaked out that I thought I was going to have some kind of psychotic breakdown and throw him out of the window. I was afraid I was going to harm him in some way, unintentionally. I'd be holding him and I'd drop him. Or he'd choke and I wouldn't know what to do and I'd panic. Or I wouldn't be able to feed him or I would starve him and all these irrational fears. They were pretty extreme . . .

One of the things that I started doing was hoarding water and medicine and toilet paper. We were living in Paris. Bruno, my husband, kept saying to me, 'There is not going to be a siege in Paris,' and I'd say, 'How do you know that? People said that in Sarajevo and look what happened.' From one day to the next they went to banks and they couldn't get their money out. So I don't think I was acting completely irrationally. Things can happen and it was post 9/11 too. I had all these exit plans about how to get out of the city and I wanted to keep cash at home so that we had access to cash. It was a pretty extreme reaction I think. And then I started slowly realizing I was traumatized.

In our interview in the Notting Hill Gate café, the journalist Janine di Giovanni, was explaining to me how it was only after her son, Luca, was born that she suffered a psychological breakdown.

Before that, even though she saw some awful things including living through the siege of Sarajevo, she had coped. But the birth of her son triggered something in her and all the fears that she had held at bay for many years forced their way into her conscious mind. Before her son was born, it was not as though there were no psychological repercussions from what she had been through. She told me how, one day in Paris as she exited the Metro, every one of the people coming towards her in the street appeared as an amputee. She had come back from Sierra Leone where deliberate amputations were common; those sights had been transposed to Paris in a brief and vivid flashback. She suffered from emotionally harrowing nightmares in which she felt intense feelings of fear, guilt and shame. She was seeing a psychotherapist but when he asked her if she wanted to talk about her experiences on assignment she would say no. She believed she did not need to. But when Luca was born, the floodgates were opened and she began to talk about how she was truly feeling.

Janine's experience illustrates a particular psychological phenomenon. Those whose work brings them into regular contact with horrific, gruesome experiences are not immune from normal physical and emotional reactions, but they find ways of keeping a lid on them. They have a job to do and that takes precedence. The journalists go back to file their reports. The body-recovery team pick up parts of dead bodies, making a systematic recording of what they have picked up and its exact location. The bomb-disposal operator carefully goes through the appropriate safety procedures to defuse the bomb. The horrors do not go unregistered but they are subject to strong psychological defences, splitting, in which different aspects of the self are kept entirely apart, and denial, in particular. These defences continue long after the experience is over. In Janine's case she simply did not want to talk about it, not even to her therapist. Not talking is a way of keeping it out of the conscious mind which is also what Elaine did after the 2005 London bombings (Chapter 7). Soldiers coming back from conflict often do not want to talk to their families about what they have been through, as to do so would expose them to remembering the horrors. Sometimes, well-intentioned people suggest that talking it through will be helpful. But that need not be the case. The defences are there for a purpose and the ability to let them down without being overwhelmed is a matter of timing.

Other ways of defending against overwhelming emotions include black humour. When Keith was working as a senior accident-investigation officer in the Thames Valley Police, he recalled attending a major accident in the fog on the M4 motorway, where several cars and the people in them had gone up in flames. The forensic examiner was called to the scene and began certifying the deaths of people there one after the other.

> . . . and he came to one and he certified 'death at [the scene]'. My colleague was standing next to him said 'Are you sure?' And it turned out it wasn't a human being. It was an Alsatian. It had a paw. So of course everybody came to it and said why not throw a ball for it just to check. That sort of humour. If you were to say that in the cold light of day in my village pub, people at the bar would be absolutely horrified. But if you're faced with that situation, well actually, that was a way to cope. You've got to find mechanisms to get through things that are particularly unpleasant.

Black humour reinforces the camaraderie that exists between people sharing traumatic experiences. In the police I used to run psychological debriefings for groups of officers shortly after they had experienced a major event. Together with a welfare officer I would bring together the shift or the specialist unit that had been involved for a one-to-two-hour group session in which we would go through what had happened, how they felt at the time, how they were feeling now and what the future might hold. I was struck by how important the group itself was, how being able to share experiences with people who had actually been there was beneficial. This is very different from talking about it to your spouse or partner or a counsellor; however sympathetic or knowledgeable those people might be, they did not have first-hand experience of the trauma. The group acted as a bolster against being overwhelmed by feelings; if others shared those feelings, it made them a bit easier to bear.

Although many professionals in dangerous occupations successfully get on with the job, for some there can be a price to pay afterwards. The psychiatrist Anthony Feinstein compared a sample of war journalists with a sample of domestic journalists, whose job did not put them at significant risk. He found that over the course of their careers 29 per cent of the war journalists met the diagnostic criteria for PTSD, whereas none of the domestic journalists did so. He also found elevated levels of depression, alcohol and drug abuse amongst the war journalists. Elevated rates of PTSD have been found in soldiers returning from combat. Twenty-three per cent of around 100,000 US soldiers returning from the conflicts in Iraq and Afghanistan were diagnosed with PTSD; 16 per cent received a diagnosis of depression. Studies of police officers show rates of PTSD of between 7 and 13 per cent; similar figures have been found in firefighters and ambulance drivers. Although these figures provide statistical evidence of the psychological cost of working in certain professions, they need to be treated with some caution. Firstly, as more and more studies are published, the picture gets more complex. For example, in studies of US soldiers, the incidence of PTSD is higher in those deployed into combat than those not deployed. This makes sense, as it is assumed that the experience of being in combat creates an acute stress reaction that, in a number of soldiers, will lead to full-blown PTSD. Yet equivalent studies of UK regular soldiers found no difference in PTSD between those deployed into combat and those not. But then again, different PTSD rates emerged when those UK soldiers who were deployed into combat were subdivided into those experiencing combat directly and those who were in combat service or support roles (e.g. medical, logistics, aircrew signals). Here those in direct combat did show higher rates of PTSD.

A second reason for being cautious about the statistics is the way certain psychological disorders attract most attention and therefore more research. This is clearly true of PTSD which, for good or ill, has emerged as the most prominent psychiatric condition after major trauma. It can be hard sometimes to think in terms of other problems. Yet recent research on the UK military indicates that alcohol abuse and depression are more likely to be experienced than PTSD. A study of reservists who had served in Iraq showed that they 'were twice as likely to have symptoms suggestive of common mental-health problems (depression, stress, anxiety and so on) than fellow reservists who had not been to Iraq, and six times as likely to have symptoms suggestive of PTSD.' These are striking findings, although the actual rate of PTSD was low (6 per cent). Moreover, the categorization that researchers need to employ in order to make sense of their research tends to gloss over the fact that people experience several categories of problems at the same time: co-morbidity, as it is called. The reality is that those who work in dangerous professions are individuals with particular temperaments, backgrounds, relationships, levels of experience, desires and expectations, all of which will influence how they respond to the traumas they experience. For example, in Feinstein's study of war journalists, the average weekly limit of alcohol consumption was higher than the general average, though not that much higher (15 units a week). Further analysis revealed a skewed distribution, with 14 per cent of the sample drinking double the average and a few individuals drinking prodigiously. In other words, there was significant individual variation that would be masked by the simple average.

Despite the caution that is needed in interpreting research findings, research is necessary in order to go beyond anecdotal accounts so that general conclusions can be made and contested by further research. There is little doubt that, for a minority, there is a psychological cost to working in dangerous occupations, whether expressed in higher rates of PTSD, depression, alcohol and drug abuse or in other ways. This itself is not surprising. What is perhaps surprising is that many more people are not affected or, perhaps more accurately, are not observed to be affected.

Personalization of tragedy

It is of interest to think what happens when someone who has managed well for years does eventually break down. Why does this happen? One factor is that the trauma becomes directly personalized. Janine di Giovanni's defences against psychological breakdown no longer worked after her son was born. It is possible that hormonal changes made her more emotionally sensitive, but it may simply be that motherhood had changed her and her way of life. I think that the intense bond between mother and child made it hard for Janine to distance herself any more from the horrors and dangers of her work. This is because all the death, injury and heartache that are happening to others can be emotionally transposed to oneself and one's child. These emotions can no longer be contained, compartmentalized and locked away. They are no longer just to do with oneself. Another person is involved.

Keith experienced something similar after he had left front-line roads policing to work on a series of projects that linked him in with American enforcement agencies. In 2002 he was in attendance for a 9/11 memorial ceremony at the National Law Enforcement Officers' Memorial in Washington DC. This is how he described what happened.

'In Justice Square in DC there is a memorial where all the names of police officers that have died in the line of duty are put on it. It's a beautiful memorial and it's something that the Americans do very well. It's a very overt showing of grief and loss of colleagues . . . When I was over there, all of a sudden [it came to me], the continual loss of life throughout my service. It started to hit me hard.'

'Is that the first time it hit you hard?'

'That was the first time. It was the first time I had actually taken stock of the continual loss of life that I had seen
throughout my service. I think it was probably going to
the hole in the ground that was Twin Towers that really
brought it home . . . While I was there at the memorial
there was a little lad dressed in an Arizona State Trooper's
uniform. He would have been about the same age as my
son George, and he was a real cute lad with blond hair. He
saw me in my uniform and he asked his mummy who I
was. I went down to him and he started telling me how his
daddy had responded as a SWAT team officer in Arizona
to an organized motorcycle gang and how his body armour
hadn't been up to the mark and he got killed. And he was
there, not as all the 9/11 officers who died that year, but
as someone else and I just couldn't stop crying. This guy
gave me the most wonderful hug and he was the same age
as my son.'

Being at the site where there had been the massive loss of life
and talking to the little boy in his father's uniform, which had
been specially cut down to fit him, Keith's defences crumbled.
He saw vividly the personal nature of all the tragedies that he had
witnessed as a police officer.

'I put myself in that boy's father's situation and equating
that boy's hopes with my son's, and actually what if that
had been me, what if that had been my son . . .'

'It brought an awareness of the possibility . . .'

'Yes, of my mortality perhaps, and the fact that I wasn't
invincible. Here was a SWAT team officer, highly trained,
properly equipped, but actually the bottom line was he
was put into a situation where his armour plating wasn't
good enough. And there was I going through life with my
own invisible armour plating that I put up and it probably
wasn't good enough.'

The strongest defences can crack and once they do, emotions long held in check are released. Traumatic memories can return in the form of flashbacks or nightmares, still raw and unprocessed for reasons I have already discussed. Life can suddenly seem fragile and uncertain. It is at this point that psychological help can be most useful. When he returned to England, Keith was able to get counselling through one of the welfare officers whom he valued and trusted. It enabled him to work though his memories and gain a perspective on both the work and himself. He could let go of the idea that he was invincible and realize that being affected by the horrors he had seen was just part of the human condition. It made him more aware of the need to look after colleagues who might also be struggling.

In conclusion, it can be seen that those whose work brings them into harm's way can build up strong defences against being emotionally affected by the experiences they go through. These defences are necessary in order to carry on with the job. It would be wrong to suggest that there is always an emotional cost, since only a minority of professionals break down and seek help. Yet it is hard to imagine that constant exposure to life-threatening or horrific events does not have some effect on a person's well-being, unless that person tends to be unusually insensitive or lacking in empathy. The cost is offset by many positive aspects of the work, as I have shown. Professionals may become adept at titrating the amount of exposure they experience, and so protecting themselves, though, in many professions, that is not always easy. Some organizations, like the army and police, have put procedures in place to identify and help those who are psychologically affected. These procedures vary considerably. The system I was part of in the Thames Valley Police included occupational-health doctors, welfare officers, a psychiatrist and a clinical psychologist, and police were able to access counsellors and specialist psychological therapists if needed. It worked very well, especially in terms of identifying people who might be at risk and getting them help early, something that I believe is particularly important.

But the assistance available in other police forces was nothing like as sophisticated and, sadly, these services are particularly vulnerable to budget cuts. One significant development has been that more and more professionals are acknowledging that their work can affect them psychologically and are prepared to ask for and find appropriate help. This, together with greater awareness in society as a whole of the potential for psychological damage from exposure to traumatic events, should lead to better understanding of and help for those whose work puts them in harm's way.

Chapter 18: Trauma revisited

On the one hand, my world was completely turned upside down and totally abnormal in any sense of what normal ever meant before. But equally I think I very consciously and automatically realized that the only way I could cope with it was to treat *this* as my normality. I remember very consciously thinking of it in terms of this being my job. My job was to recover and to rehabilitate. It was a full-time occupation in that it had replaced [my actual job]. I suppose it was a frame of reference that I could understand. Because, otherwise, I felt there was nothing that I could hold on to in any of it. It felt like the sort of structure I could relate to.

There was a lot of uncertainty. I was told quite early on that my left leg was extremely badly damaged. I'd severed the main femoral nerve and for a long time I had no movement or feeling in that leg. There was a huge amount of uncertainty, first of all whether I would even retain the leg, whether it would eventually be amputated, and subsequently, even if they managed to keep it, whether I would ever be able to use it or walk on it again. I was told that I had to have realistic expectations. There was a very high chance that I would be wheelchair-bound. Strangely my reaction to that was . . . well, I don't think I ever really took it on board. I just refused to believe it and I don't really know why . . .

Obviously I was incredibly lucky and very determined and, with that combination, I was able to recover to the extent I did . . . I do think that one of the reasons that I recovered as well as I did was in some part due to that kind of refusal to accept the possibility [of not recovering fully].

I had this fighting spirit. It was a bit of a bolshie attitude:
'I'm going to show you. I'm going to walk out of here and
prove you wrong.' That was definitely part of it.

This is an extract from my interview with Jo, a young woman
who had been severely injured in a car accident. While on her way
home from work one day, a man driving a white van, overtaking
another car on a blind bend, smashed head-on into Jo's car. All
four of her limbs were broken and she endured many long and
painful operations over a period of six years. I first met Jo in my
professional practice when I was invited by the courts to carry out
a medico-legal assessment on her. I was struck then by her incredible positive attitude. She had been in her mid-twenties at the time
of the accident, with a successful career and an active social life.
In that one moment on the road, all changed and for the next six
years she faced an uphill struggle to regain her physical health and
to put her life together again. That she did this successfully was
in no small part due to Jo's psychological make-up, her determination and her single-minded focus on recovery. It was meeting her
that gave me the first glimmer of the idea of writing this book. A
year or so later I met another young woman who had also been
injured in a car accident that was not her fault, leaving her in pain
and with some physical disability. Mired in the injustices of her
injuries, Danielle could not shake off her anger at the perpetrator
and found it difficult to face up to her new reality. Despite my best
efforts, I was unable to help her psychologically.

Two similar stories but with different outcomes. Both Jo and
Danielle had been given a diagnosis of PTSD. Both had been
through the courts in compensation cases. Both had suffered physically as well as psychologically. Both had lost their jobs and both
had had their personal lives turned upside down by the trauma and
its consequences. Yet how different they were, and how deeply
their individual stories reflected their personal make-up. In all the
professional paraphernalia that surrounds trauma – the psychiatric
diagnoses, the psychological theories, the different psychological

treatments, and the claims for what psychological trauma is and what will help people recover – the individual's personal story is relegated to a minor role. In this book I have sought to correct that, and put people's personal stories centre stage.

In this final chapter I will revisit the topic of trauma, keeping in mind what I have learned from my own reading and experience and from the stories people have told me. I do not pretend to put forward a definitive answer to the psychology of trauma. But I will clarify what seem to me to be important themes, ranging from how trauma is defined to how best to treat those who have suffered distressing trauma reactions.

Trauma defined

In Chapter 1, I referred to a distinction that psychologists make between Type I and Type II traumas. The former are single events that hit us out of the blue; the latter tend to be continuous traumas going on over months or years, such as wars or abusive childhoods, which shape people gradually, in a way that a single event does not. The single-incident trauma is what I have focused on in this book. But in listening to the stories of the people I interviewed, it was obvious that no single-incident trauma is alike and that both the context and the person influence how people react to ostensibly the same event. The differing experiences of Elaine and Tim in the 2005 London bombings illustrate this nicely. Some traumas are intensely personal. Georgie's experience of rape was certainly so, whereas the freak accident that brought a Harrier Jump Jet down next to Steve's car was not. Whether the deliberate violation of another person's body is worse than being injured as a result of an accident or natural disaster is an open question, one that cannot be answered here. But the difference is surely important.

North American surveys tell us the most common reported single-incident traumas (see Table 1.1). While this list has some value, simple descriptors like 'rape', 'combat' or 'physical attack' miss out both the context and the personal reaction. *The*

Cambridge Dictionary of Psychology definition of trauma as 'any event which inflicts physical damage to the body or severe shock to the mind or both' brings in the person's reaction, although a term like 'severe shock to the mind' is vague. Yet it focuses attention on the experience and suggests that something extraordinary has been perceived, a shock that the mind finds difficult to accommodate to. Certainly, many people featured in this book experienced extraordinary events and were shocked by them. How that affected them is a large part of what this book is about, and I will return to that shortly. The context is also important. Those who fight in wars or work in dangerous professions expect to meet life-threatening events and are to some extent prepared for them. Here the context is one in which threat is to be expected, and that shapes how people react. It does not entirely prevent people from being affected by trauma, as the accounts of the police officer, Keith, and the journalist, Janine di Giovanni, testify (Chapter 17). But there is a degree of preparedness. The sudden disruption of an ordinary life, however, is different. Steve did not expect a Harrier Jump Jet to crash by his car. George did not expect a bomb to go off in his tube carriage as he went to work. Susanna did not expect her son, Tom, to become paralysed as a result of a snowboarding move that went wrong. Richard did not expect the train carriage he was in to be derailed and plunge down an embankment. The suddenness and unexpectedness, combined with the sheer magnitude of the threat, throw us off course. The context here is the illusion that normal life will always be serene, that it is ordered, predictable and under our control. Experiencing a sudden-onset major trauma shows us in no uncertain terms that this assumption is a precarious one.

It's the biology, stupid!

The context and the character of the person must be set alongside one of the most important lessons that sudden-onset trauma teaches us: everyone's initial reaction is, at heart, biologically driven. In Chapter 2 I described how those in the 2005 London bombings reacted to the explosions and the immediate consequences. Theirs were *physical* experiences, powerful, visceral reactions to an unprecedented and, for many, inexplicable event. The body takes over and archaic survival responses are automatically triggered, causing reactions that the individual is not consciously making or controlling. This is the fear response. In Chapter 3 I showed how this worked, using the simple example of Karen, the teacher, threatened by a youth in the street. I used the term 'innate fear reaction' to describe the body's automatic response to threat; this includes the activation of the autonomic nervous system, the shutting down of peripheral activities, the mobilization of the body's defences and its preparing to activate the fight-or-flight response. For good reasons these biological reactions do not depend on deliberation; they happen whether we like it or not, and they happen instantaneously. In the animal world where, as Tennyson put it, 'Nature [is] red in tooth and claw', the fight-or-flight reaction is common. In our world, the western world in particular, we have eliminated most tangible threats to our existence. Life is no longer a continual battle for survival. But when, unexpectedly, there is a real threat, the body takes over. For many, this experience is unprecedented and that can present problems both at the time and later on.

Understanding that our first reaction to trauma is biologically driven gives us a framework for understanding what is happening. It is about survival, and if we behave in ways that seem to us strange or shameful, then we should forgive ourselves, since it is the body that is reacting in order to ensure our survival. The separation of mind and body is an artifice, a product of our desire to see ourselves as intentional human beings. One of the lessons that trauma teaches us is how important the body is, the brain in particular, and that our behaviour is determined as much by our animal heritage as by our thinking selves. The sense of being in control of our lives is something we take for granted, yet it is in part an illusion. Under severe threat, the illusion disappears like a mirage in the desert, as the body makes its presence known.

Primary appraisal

The innate fear reaction is part of what I have called *primary appraisal*. Our senses are alert, seeking to understand what the threat is and what to do about it. We take in the outside world and, in doing that, the basic biological reaction becomes psychological. As a teacher, Karen knew something about the bravado of youth, as well as being experienced in handling aggression, and she appraised the threat as something she could handle. This happened instantaneously and without conscious forethought. It reflected her personality and her experience. In her Paris apartment, Georgie told me she acted *logically* once the men came on to her. Her primary appraisal was that, despite the friendly conversations she had had with them, they were intent on raping her. She needed to get out of the situation without serious injury, and so she had little choice but to comply and hope it would soon be over. In darkness in the underground, with debris filling in the air, Elaine's primary appraisal was that two trains had crashed into one another. She was terrified that she would die in a fire – she thought the debris was smoke – or that another train would crash into her stalled train. In primary appraisal the event takes on meaning. What the meaning is, and what we do as a result, is a product of our history, personality and understanding. This is why people react differently. Years before she found herself on the underground on 7 July 2005, Rachel North had experienced a life-threatening trauma, that of being raped and physically battered in her own home. By chance, she was reading an article about that experience just as she got onto the train, and so her mind and body were already attuned to threat. She believes this explained her calm reaction in horrifying circumstances.

Secondary appraisal

In a sudden-onset trauma, like a bombing, an earthquake, a fire or a physical attack, the unprecedented nature of the event overwhelms primary appraisal, causing terror, confusion and uncertainty. We may struggle to understand what is happening. This is the beginning of *secondary appraisal*, the term I introduced in Chapter 3; it is how we evaluate and put into context both what is happening and what we are doing. If the event is over quickly, as it was with Karen, secondary appraisal may be about what has just happened: Karen's 'Bloody hell, what was I doing?' But many traumas are not over quickly and a sequence of events is played out over some time. In many such situations, the person caught up in it has no control over the events taking place. In addition, because the body reacts automatically, it feels like we are not in control of ourselves either. This happened to Elaine on the underground and her response was to retreat into herself and wait for help. The numbness and dissociation she experienced as she exited the tube station put her at one remove from what was happening around her; it added to her sense of passivity and helplessness. Secondary appraisal takes the form of evaluating not only the nature of the trauma but also one's own reactions. How that happens depends on two fundamental factors, cognition and personality.

Cognition

By 'cognition' I mean the way the event is processed in our mind. As I showed in Chapter 9 this can be broken down into three components, the stream of consciousness (what we are thinking at any moment), perception (how we view ourselves and the world) and beliefs (fundamental assumptions that we hold important). The experience of a major trauma can disrupt any or all of these. Distressing flashbacks can intrude into the stream of consciousness, we can become hyper-sensitive to possible dangers, distorting our normal perception, and we may come to believe that the world is no longer such a safe place. Like an earthquake that shatters the earth's landscape, changing it totally, so a trauma shatters the mind's landscape, forcing a transformation that we have not wished for or expected. This is the 'severe shock to the mind' mentioned in *The Cambridge Dictionary of Psychology*. Psychoanalysts see the shock as a breakthrough in the mind's normal defences, flooding it with anxiety, reactivating primitive fears of infancy and early childhood, fears of death and dying. There is a loss of trust, not just in the external world but in the person's own internal capacity to withstand threats. The boundaries between the external and internal worlds are eroded in a flood of stimulation, expressed in flashbacks, nightmares and constant anxiety. Feelings of insecurity and vulnerability abound. In different language, but making a similar point, the psychologist, Janoff-Bulman, wrote about the shattering of basic assumptions after major trauma, namely the belief that we are invulnerable, that the world is meaningful and our life is generally a positive one. These fundamental assumptions are embedded in the felt sense of who we are in the world, what we call 'identity'. This is why many feel changed after trauma, as though they are, in some ways, a different person. The foundations on which our sense of self is built have been shattered. The person no longer feels safe. This insecurity can be specific – Steve's fear that planes might fall out of the sky, or Richard's anxiety about another train derailment. It can also be pervasive, affecting every area of our lives. After the horror of the rape, Georgie felt depressed and vulnerable, shutting herself away in her bedroom for months. After the London bombings, Tim Coulson could not face meeting people, choosing to go on long, solitary walks. Following the shooting in Milton Keynes, Janine shut herself in her home, refusing to see friends and colleagues whom she thought might put her into a madhouse. Put simply, after trauma, people do not feel themselves, or at least the self they were familiar with. Regaining trust in oneself and the world is the central task for those recovering from trauma.

Personality

The sort of person we are and our personal history will influence how we respond during trauma and how we recover later. The differing stories of Jo and Danielle illustrate this. Jo's determination carried her through difficult times, whereas Danielle could not relinquish her past. In Chapter 15 I described the remarkable resilience shown by Susanna, whose son, Tom, had been paralysed in a snowboarding accident. Her strength of character enabled her to overcome her sorrow and apply herself to finding a solution that would enable her son to be as independent as possible. I found something of the same resilience in Tom's thoughtful adjustment to a very different way of life. Is resilience a useful term? There is a risk of seeing those people who do well after trauma as 'resilient' simply *because* they do well. There needs to be more to it than that. Psychologically, there are two aspects that are significant in resilient people. First is their willingness to deal with what is in front of them, together with the capacity to leave behind their previous life. Grief and sorrow, while present, do not overwhelm their ability to move on. There is a process of adjustment and an immersion in action, in sorting out practicalities, as Susanna did for her son. Having things to do orientates the person outwards, becomes 'the job', as it did in Jo's case. Second is the weaving of a new narrative of one's life, one that takes into account the changes that have happened, and integrates them into a new and positive framework. Going through a major trauma shatters the sense of trust in oneself and in the world. The old narrative with which we described our life has been fatally undermined. Finding a new narrative, one with which we can shape our new life, enables us to move forward and regain trust in ourselves and the world.

There are other personality characteristics that influence the way people respond to trauma. George's phlegmatic nature, for example, enabled him to return to travelling by tube in the week after the London bombings, because he knew he needed to do so for his work. Kathryn recounted how, after the South African church massacre, she visited her injured friend in hospital every day for several months, revealing a strong sense of responsibility and concern for others. Richard's resourcefulness helped him in his long recovery from the physical and psychological effects of the Grayrigg rail crash. Personality is a general term, a summation of a variety of personal characteristics and experiences that make up an individual. It is little mentioned in psychological theories about trauma reactions. This is because theorists seek to create explanations that apply to all those who have been through trauma, leaving individual differences aside.

PTSD

The psychiatric diagnosis of PTSD has become the diagnosis of choice in summarizing the distress that a major trauma can cause. Yet it makes no reference to personality; the diagnosis is arrived at by ticking off key symptoms from a list, as though the person is just a passive recipient and his or her personality unimportant. It creates the impression that PTSD is an illness like mumps or measles that can strike irrespective of who you are. But it is psychologically unsophisticated to exclude people's personality and personal history when describing how trauma has affected them. This should be obvious from the various stories in this book. Janine Luck's experience showed this nicely (Chapter 4). While she had all the symptoms that were diagnostic of PTSD, her strong sense of right and wrong infused her with intense feelings of anger. This anger was, she recognized later, the driving force behind the persistence of her post-traumatic symptoms, and something that she needed to address in order to recover. This is not to discount the diagnosis of PTSD. It is helpful to know that one's experiences are recognized and have a name. Being given a diagnosis offers the promise of help and recovery. The downside of being given a label is that everything untoward may be subsumed under it, as though the diagnosis alone is a sufficient explanation of what someone is going through. But who we are and our personal history shape how we respond after trauma. Something as simple as the experience of a previous trauma can markedly affect a person's response. The example of the man who was beaten up a gang of youths in Chapter 1 illustrated this. Psychologically, it is not surprising that going through one trauma can evoke memories of a past one, or that personality and context will shape the way people respond. All good psychotherapists know this and take it into account when providing help.

Why trauma reactions persist

To trauma survivors, the persistence of distressing reminders of the trauma weeks, months or occasionally years after the event is both puzzling and disturbing. Why does this happen? Firstly, being reminded of the trauma is not in itself abnormal or unusual. Everyone who has been through the sorts of events described in this book will be affected emotionally at first, and be subject to occasional, unwanted memories afterwards. Only in a minority will these be in the form of intense flashbacks. As the psychologist Nick Grey puts it, after trauma, for everyone there is 'a continuum of nowness', ranging from the realization that the event is in the past, to the feeling that it is actually happening again. Over time, the memories fade and become less disturbing. For a few people, this does not happen. They continue to be assailed by flashbacks with all the distress they lead to. One explanation of this lies in the specific nature of trauma memories.

Trauma memories

Fear, particularly the intense terror that is experienced in major trauma, activates the older parts of the brain that are concerned with basic survival. The result is the innate fear reaction, the body's automatic response. Once the event is over, we would expect it to be processed in the brain into verbal memory, becoming part of our autobiographical memory like other memories, and for most people this is what happens. Even for those who find themselves subject to distressing flashbacks, a large part of the traumatic experience will have been processed in exactly this way. What remain are raw spikes of unconsolidated memory, reactivations of the brain's alarm system, even though the event is over. While these flashbacks appear to come out of the blue, they are in fact triggered by particular stimuli, most commonly sensory stimuli, or by the reoccurrence of intense feelings that are very like those experienced in the midst of the trauma (hotspots). When Andy suddenly found himself vomiting as he passed a butcher's shop in Witney, it was because the smell of the meat had triggered a reaction to the smell of the decaying body he had uncovered days before in the bedsitter (see Chapter 6), a connection he was unaware of. Similarly, Elaine's agitation in a therapy session arose in response to the smoke from a bonfire as she arrived at the hospital, unconsciously triggering memories of the 'smoke' (actually debris in the air) she had experienced in the tube (see Chapter 13). The psychologist Chris Brewin suggests that trauma memories persist because they function differently from verbal memories (this is known as the dual-processing theory). Trauma memories are primarily sensory, activated in the amygdala, the brain's alarm system, and generated without volition. Because of the distress they cause, people resist attending to them or try to suppress them and so conspire to prevent the memories from shifting into verbal memory. Only when these sensory memories are properly processed do they begin to lose their influence. Understanding this process can be helpful in itself; flashbacks can be seen in a different light and their power to evoke distress reduced. Therapies that focus specifically on recalling traumatic memories, such as prolonged exposure, reliving and EMDR, help facilitate emotional processing.

Energy discharge

Another theory for the persistence of trauma reactions suggests that the inability to take action at the time is the key. The energy marshalled to cope with threat has no outlet; it remains undischarged and emerges later in muscle tension, tics and other physical manifestations. The body remembers, and it is argued that it is through the body that improvement is best made (Chapter 14). A parallel is drawn with animals that freeze into immobility when under extreme duress. If they escape, then, typically, they leap around in rapid, jerky movements discharging pent-up energy. It is a nice analogy and rightly draws attention to the physical aspects of both our response to trauma and how we might best recover. Peter Levine, one of the major proponents of this theory, bases his therapeutic approach on attending to bodily signs, with some dramatic results.

I believe that psychologists and others working in the trauma field should pay more attention to the body's response in both understanding the effects of trauma and treating people suffering afterwards. But *energy* is a woolly term and humans are more than animals reacting instinctively. In the 2005 London bombings, Tim Coulson smashed his way out of the carriage he was in and went into a bombed-out carriage, attending to the wounded and dying. He took action and in doing so, he could be said to have discharged pent-up energy. Yet Tim was emotionally affected by what he saw that day, and had to take early retirement (Chapter 7). The interaction between body and mind is what determines the human response. Humans are burdened with a consciousness of ourselves in the world; we seek to make sense of what is happening around us (secondary appraisal). There is always a part of the self that monitors what we are doing or not doing, evaluating and judging our performance. Regardless of how the body is responding, that plays a significant part in the trauma response.

Professional help

Whenever a major trauma is announced on the news I now expect to hear the phrase 'trained trauma counsellors have been called in to help the survivors'. It is part of the professionalization of trauma, what some disparagingly call 'the trauma industry', and carries the implication that professional help after trauma is not just desirable but necessary. The truth is that, left to their own devices, most people will recover after a major trauma; only a minority need professional help and very few will need that help right away. In my work with Thames Valley Police I understood that what people most needed in the immediate aftermath of a major trauma was what the Red Cross used to call 'tea and sympathy'. People in shock need time and support. They do not need to talk to trained counsellors about what has happened. The support of colleagues, friends and family is far more important. This is most obvious when that support is absent. I recall being asked to see two young WPCs a few days after they had been trapped for several hours in a building in which a man had brandished a firearm. One of them was angry at the police for, in her view, abandoning her and, in particular, for failing to ask her how she was feeling or whether there was someone at home to look after her (there was not). In the shock of recovering from a major trauma it is not specialist help that people need but care and sympathy.

Psychological debriefing

For many years the emergency services provided (and still, to some degree, do provide) psychological or critical-incident debriefing for their personnel who have been involved in a major trauma. This consists of a group meeting of all those involved within a period of three days or, at most, a week after the event, facilitated by a trained counsellor or psychologist. In the meeting, everyone is asked in turn to talk about the event and encouraged to describe what happened and their own reactions in some detail. There is no obligation to talk, but the idea is that it could be helpful to do so. Information about the possible psychological consequences of the event is given out. Along with a welfare officer, I ran a number of these groups for the police. In the last few years, however, psychological debriefing has been criticized. Research studies appear to have shown that not only is no discernible benefit derived from debriefing, but there is also some suggestion that some people are made worse by it. The recommendation is that they should be abandoned. This is a pity, since the research on which this conclusion was largely based consisted of two studies that did not involve groups but individuals, one study done after road accidents and the other after burns injuries. Being in a group is a very different experience from talking to a single counsellor. One of the strengths of the group is that it brings together the people who were involved and allows them to exchange their stories and support each other. The understanding and support of people who have actually been there can be immensely valuable.

There is a misunderstanding about psychological debriefing, namely that it requires everyone to talk about their feelings and that this will be beneficial. People do not need to talk if they do not wish to. As I have argued elsewhere in this book, talking about one's feelings after trauma should be a matter of personal choice and, crucially, of timing. When Richard's GP first asked him if he wanted to see a psychologist, he knew he was not ready to do this. Later, he was. For some, being required to unburden themselves could make matters worse, especially if the person is left with uncontained and distressing emotions. This may be why research has shown that some people get worse after debriefing.

Psychological therapies

There are now many more psychological therapists around than there were forty years ago, when I first embarked on training as a clinical psychologist. They come in all shapes and sizes and armed with a confusing plethora of qualifications and experiences. In Chapters 13 and 14 I reviewed two main therapeutic approaches (reliving, and somato-sensory therapies), and in Chapter 12 I looked at the general benefits of seeing a psychotherapist. In the interviews I have done for this book, people have told me of their experiences in therapy, and for many of them it was enormously helpful. There is a value in talking to a stranger, if he or she is experienced in trauma and skilled in the art of psychotherapy. Certain matters are difficult, if not impossible, to talk to friends or family about. As I have said, it is not always necessary to see a therapist. For most people, there is a natural recovery process after trauma and nothing more is required than to let that happen. But for a few, the difficulties caused by trauma threaten to overwhelm them. Seeing a therapist can help a person take stock and begin to gain a different perspective on themselves and the world. There are specific psychological techniques that can help unlock trauma memories and others that enable the body to release the tension that such memories give rise to. If the timing is right and the person ready for it, then seeing a psychotherapist can be beneficial.

I was a psychotherapist and you might think I would be likely to say that psychotherapy can be helpful. But I am not uncritical of psychotherapy, and I am aware that much depends on the skill and personality of the therapist. I have been sceptical of the idea that scientifically proven forms of therapy exist for trauma or for any other problem, or that therapy works like a course of medication, making people better irrespective of their personality or personal history. Psychotherapy can be useful but it also can be useless or worse. As I have mentioned, anyone seeking therapy for trauma-related problems would do well to be informed about what a particular therapy consists of, what the therapist will set out to do, how long it will take and, if not on the NHS, how much it will cost. (For more on seeking psychological help, see Appendix A.)

One of the major changes that occurs after trauma is the rupturing of the narrative of one's life, of that which gives us our sense of identity and our place in the world. As was often true of the people in this book, there is no preparation and the shock of the event reverberates through mind and body, causing ripples that persist long after the event. Weaving a new narrative, one that takes these changes into account, is the overarching task for the trauma sufferer; not just recovering from the distress but being able to incorporate the experience and move on. The personal stories in this book show how certain people have sought to do this, many of them successfully. It is my hope that these stories will help others to make a similar adjustment.

Appendix A

Psychological treatment of trauma-related problems

Introduction

This book includes three chapters about the treatment of trauma-related problems (Chapters, 12, 13 and 14). This brief addition is by way of personal advice to anyone who may be seeking a therapist or has a friend or family member who needs help. Before electing for therapy there are three questions you can ask yourself:

- Do I need professional help now?

- What sort of help am I looking for?

- How do I hope to be different after therapy?

Do I need professional help now?

The period immediately following a trauma is not always the best time to seek therapy from a professional. Body and mind need to recover from the shock, and for many the natural process of recovery is all that is needed. Support and succour from friends and family is often the best medicine. In other words, do not rush into therapy simply because you have been emotionally affected. Allow some time to pass. The exception is if you feel dramatically worse, overcome by a confusion of anxiety and fear, unable to sleep, or unable to work or even to talk to others. This could be an acute stress reaction, for which some simple medication and advice can help. Consult your GP and if he or she is not helpful, change GPs. Not all GPs understand the effects of trauma.

Psychotherapy is most helpful later, when you feel ready to work on your persistent problems. *Later* means any time from a month to several years. By *ready* I mean that you are in a position to give the space and time to do the psychological work required. This is something intangible and it comes as a feeling that it is the right time for you. Sometimes a particular experience makes you realize you are not coping so well on your own, and therefore need professional help. A persistent flashback memory, avoiding a person or activity, an explosive outburst, a problem at work – anything that is not really 'you', or at least the 'you' who existed before the trauma. Any of these might be a trigger for seeking help.

What sort of help am I looking for?

Psychotherapy has two important features: helping with specific problems (like flashbacks, high arousal or feelings of guilt) and providing a space to explore and understand what is happening to you. Ideally, both should be part of any therapy but therapies can emphasize one over the other.

Therapies that focus on specific problems will draw on established techniques (see, for example, Chapters 13 and 14). The therapist will explain what the techniques are and what the benefits are likely to be. These problem-solving therapies are usually of short duration (weeks rather than months). Sometimes there can be an immediate benefit, but that is not always the case. Usually, you will be asked to carry out homework assignments between sessions. Sometimes the therapist will accompany you on agreed tasks, such as revisiting the place where the trauma happened. The value of these specific methods is that you can directly see if you are improving or not, and the therapy can be adjusted accordingly. A possible drawback is that it is possible to move too quickly to using specific techniques, before enough time has elapsed to explore the full meaning of the trauma.

Psychotherapy can be valuable in helping you understand what your feelings and problems are about. This is sometimes called 'counselling', but the differences between psychotherapy and counselling are not clear-cut. Some counselling can be practical and focused on problem-solving, for example. Therapy in which you are encouraged to talk and explore your feelings, rather than going through specific techniques, is sometimes called 'non-directive' or 'person-centred'. The personal space that therapy provides and the therapeutic relationship are what matter. This may seem vague compared to using techniques, but many people find it enormously helpful simply to talk to someone neutral who is experienced and understanding, without necessarily being required to do something specific. Your goal is to understand yourself better and, from that understanding, improve and change your life. Unlike in the problem-solving therapies, where the therapist is active and directive, here the therapist will sit back and allow you to talk. This does not mean the therapist says nothing, but he or she will say less, and what is said is designed to foster understanding, rather than being part of a specific treatment technique. The advantage of this approach is that you have the time to explore yourself and your problems. A possible drawback is that this may not lead to the resolution of specific problems as quickly as other methods.

Because there are differences in the way therapists work, it is important to ask the therapist which approach they adopt, what their qualifications are, roughly how long they expect therapy to last, and, if it is private therapy, what it will cost. This could be done before or during the first session. No therapist should evade answering these questions and, if they do, my advice is not to proceed. It is also important that you feel the therapist is someone you can get on with, that their personality and yours gel, something you can usually tell in the first session.

How do I hope to be different after therapy?

An obvious answer to this question is that you want to feel better. But what might 'better' mean for you? Do you want to get rid of unwanted symptoms such as flashbacks or high arousal? Do you want to make sense of difficult feelings like guilt or shame? Do you hope to get back to the way you were before the trauma? Are you looking to move on and change your life in some way? You may not know exactly what you want, and in therapy there should be an opportunity to explore your possible goals. These can become clearer after you spend some time talking to a therapist. But it is useful to think ahead, as it will affect your choice of therapy.

Therapy is no panacea and those who enter it thinking it will solve all their problems are likely to be disappointed. Trauma changes us, so no therapy will be able to take you back to exactly how you were before the trauma. As I discussed in Chapter 16, going through a trauma can sometimes lead to positive changes, and therapy may help you to move on to something new. It is never possible to predict exactly what will happen when you undergo therapy. Therapy, like life, changes as you experience it, and you are also changing as a person over time. There is a value in entering therapy with an open mind and a willingness to experiment.

Conclusion

Professional assistance from a psychotherapist can be helpful. It is not a sign of weakness to seek such help. In fact, seeing a therapist can be hard work. Each person is different, including therapists of course, and if a first attempt at therapy does not work out, finding a different therapist may be the answer. A list of accredited UK therapy organizations and their websites appears in Appendix B.

Appendix B

UK psychotherapy and counselling organizations

The UK Council for Psychotherapy (UKCP)

http://www.psychotherapy.org.uk

The UKCP is a membership organization, with over seventy-five training and listing organizations and over 7,000 individual practitioners. It holds the national register of psychotherapists and psychotherapeutic counsellors, listing those practitioner members who meet exacting standards and training requirements.

The British Association for Counselling and Psychotherapy (BACP)

http://www.bacp.co.uk

The BACP is a membership organization and a registered charity that sets standards for therapeutic practice and provides information for therapists, clients of therapy, and the general public. As the largest professional body representing counselling and psychotherapy in the UK, the BACP aims to increase public understanding of the benefits of counselling and psychotherapy, raise awareness of what can be expected from the process of therapy and promote education and/or training for counsellors and psychotherapists.

The British Psychological Society (BPS)

http://www.bps.org.uk

The BPS is the representative body for psychology and psychologists in the UK, responsible for the development, promotion and application of psychology for the public good. It has a directory of chartered psychologists, with their professional qualifications and what services they offer to the public. It also has a register of psychologists specializing in psychotherapy.

The British Psychoanalytic Council (BPC)

http://www.psychoanalytic-council.org
The BPC is a professional association, representing the profession of psychoanalytic and psychodynamic psychotherapy. The organization is itself made up of twelve member institutions, which are training institutions, professional associations in their own right and accrediting bodies. Individual psychoanalytic and psychodynamic psychotherapists are members of these organizations and are 'registrants' of the BPC. There are around 1,450 registrants of the BPC, working across the public, voluntary and private-practice sectors.

Appendix C

Self-help and other useful books

A visit to Amazon or another Internet bookseller reveals a growing number of self-help books on trauma, stress, anxiety and PTSD. The sheer number can be overwhelming. I have selected a few books that I can recommend. Good, accurate information is valuable and working through a self-help book can be useful if the methods are well-chosen. But bear in mind that it is not always easy to undertake treatment on one's own. There is an additional benefit in working with someone who understands traumatic stress and can act as a guide and supporter.

Self-help books

Claudia Herbert and Ann Wetmore, *Overcoming Traumatic Stress: A self-help guide using Cognitive Behavioral Techniques* (London: Robinson, 2008). One of the better self-help books, clear and easy to follow. Very much the CBT/reliving approach.

Gillian Butler and Tony Hope, *Manage Your Mind: The Mental Fitness Guide* (2nd edition, Oxford: Oxford University Press, 2007).This is, deservedly, a classic CBT self-help book. The chapter on trauma is admirably clear and concise.

Roger Baker, *Understanding Trauma: How to Overcome Traumatic Stress* (Oxford: Lion Publishing, 2010). This is an account of the emotional-processing approach to treating trauma-related problems, and benefits from Dr Baker's clinical knowledge and sensitivity.

Babette Rothschild, *8 Keys to Safe Trauma Recovery: Take-Charge Strategies to Empower Your Healing* (New York: Norton, 2010). Ms Rothschild describes an approach to recovery that does not require the individual to remember the original trauma. Instead she focuses on mindfulness and self-acceptance. This book contains some useful exercises and the focus on the self is in contrast to the focus on PTSD symptoms.

Other useful books

The books that I have selected here are ones that stand out in terms of the quality of the work and their usefulness to anyone seeking to understand more about trauma.

Chris R. Brewin, *Post-traumatic Stress Disorder: Malady or Myth?* (New Haven and London: Yale University Press, 2003). For those interested in understanding more about psychological theory and research, this is a masterly account of what we know and do not know about the psychological response to trauma.

Judith Herman, *Trauma and Recovery: The Aftermath of Violence – from Domestic Abuse to Political Terror* (New York: Basic Books: new edition, 1997). Rightly regarded as a classic book on trauma; the volume that introduced the Type I/Type II distinction.

Peter A. Levine, *In an Unspoken Voice: How the Body Releases Trauma and Restores Goodness* (Berkeley, California: North Atlantic Books, 2010). The culmination of Dr Levine's work with trauma sufferers, presenting his notion of energy discharge and illustrating how working directly with the body can be highly effective.

Stephen Regel and Stephen Joseph, *Post-traumatic Stress (The Facts)* (Oxford: Oxford University Press, 2010). Part of OUP's 'The Facts' series, this straightforward account of PTSD is up-to-date and exceptionally well presented.

Robin Shapiro, *The Trauma Treatment Handbook: Protocols across the Spectrum* (New York and London: Norton, 2010). Primarily written for therapists, this book is nevertheless informative and accessible for clients. It includes a useful list of the commonest techniques, and explanations of common acronyms such as EMDR and EFT.

Claudia Zayfert and Jason C. DeViva, *When someone you love suffers from posttraumatic stress: What to expect and what you can do* (New York: The Guilford Press, 2011). This American book fills a gap in the market, directed as it is at the family and friends of those who suffer from post-traumatic stress. A comprehensive account and nicely illustrated with case material.

Notes and references

Chapter 1: When lightning strikes

p. 11 David Matsumoto (ed.), *The Cambridge Dictionary of Psychology* (Cambridge: Cambridge University Press, 2009).

p. 12 For further discussion of the Type I/Type II distinction, see Judith Herman, *Trauma and Recovery: The Aftermath of Violence – from Domestic Abuse to Political Terror* (new edition, New York: Basic Books, 1997).

p. 13 Judith Herman proposed a new diagnostic category of 'Complex PTSD' to describe people who had suffered from many traumas over a period of time. However, she was not successful at getting a separate diagnosis into the 1994 *Diagnostic and Statistical Manual of Mental Disorders* (DSM-IV). Nevertheless, it makes psychological sense to distinguish complex from simple traumas. Herman argued that there are three particular psychological symptoms shown by people who have been through complex traumas, namely a tendency to express psychological states in the body (somatization), experiencing feelings of dissociation, and problems in regulating emotions. For more detail see Judith Herman's Foreword in Christine A. Courtois and Julian D. Ford (eds.), *Treating Complex Traumatic Stress Disorders: An Evidence-Based Guide* (New York: The Guilford Press, 2009).

p. 13 The vignette about the man beaten up outside a supermarket is taken from Felicity Zulueta, 'Post-Traumatic Stress Disorder and Dissociation: The Traumatic Stress Service in the Maudsley Hospital', in Valerie Sinason (ed.), *Attachment, Trauma and Multiplicity: Working with Dissociative Identity Disorder* (London: Brunner-Routledge, 2002).

p. 14 For a discussion of the prevalence of single-incident traumas see Patricia A. Resick, *Stress and Trauma* (Hove and New York: Psychology Press, 2001).

p. 14 M. B. Stein, J. R. Walker, A. L. Hazen and D. R. Forde, 'Full and partial post-traumatic stress disorder: findings from a community survey', *American Journal of Psychiatry*, 154 (1997), 1114–19.

Chapter 2: 7 July 2005

p. 19   The fact that people retain a vivid memory of iconic events does not mean that their memory is necessarily accurate. In fact, the emotional intensity of the event can make the memory *less* reliable, as studies have shown: see Eugene Winograd and Ulric Neisser (eds.), *Affect and Accuracy in Recall: Studies of 'Flashbulb' Memories* (Cambridge: Cambridge University Press, 1992). In an experiment following the 1986 Challenger disaster, when the space shuttle exploded soon after lift-off, a sample of students were asked within the first twenty-four hours of the event to fill in a questionnaire describing when they heard about the disaster, what they were doing at the time, and other such matters. When the students were re-assessed two-and-a-half years later, many provided contradictory accounts, which they believed were totally accurate, but were clearly not. Memory is a reconstructive process and when events are repeatedly rehearsed, they take on the conviction of truth, even when they are actually false.

p. 21   Aaron Debnam, *One Morning in July* (London: John Blake Publishing, 2007).

p. 24–5   Rachel North, *Out of the Tunnel: Before and after 7/7: One Woman's Extraordinary Story* (London: The Friday Project, 2007).

p. 25   Robert J. Lifton, *Death in Life: Survivors of Hiroshima* (London: Weidenfeld & Nicholson, 1967).

p. 27   Ronnie Janoff-Bulman, *Shattered Assumptions: Towards a New Psychology of Trauma* (New York: The Free Press,1992).

p. 28   Gill Hicks, *One Unknown.* (London: Pan Macmillan, 2008).

p. 31   The Channel 4 documentary film is called *The Miracle of Carriage 346:* see <http://www.channel4.com/programmes/7/7-the-miracle-of-carriage-346>. For the article, *The Angel of Edgware Road*, see <http://www.telegraph.co.uk/news/2254864/Tim-Coulson-The-angel-of-Edgware-Road.html>.

p. 33–4   The importance of discharging energy can be found in Peter A. Levine, *Waking the Tiger: Healing Trauma* (Berkeley: North Atlantic Books, 1997).

Chapter 3: The nature of fear

p. 45   John Marzillier, *The Gossamer Thread: My Life as a Psychotherapist* (London: Karnac, 2010), Chapter 3.

Chapter 4: Post-traumatic stress disorder (PTSD)

p. 52   There are two first-class books on the history of psychiatry
            in the military: Ben Shephard, *A War of Nerves: Soldiers and
            Psychiatrists, 1914–1994* (London: Pimlico, 2002) and Edgar
            Jones and Simon Wessely, *Shell Shock to PTSD: Military
            Psychiatry from 1900 to the Gulf War*, Maudsley Monographs,
            47 (Hove and New York: Psychology Press, 2005).

p. 53–5   See <http://www.psychiatryonline.com> for the full version
            of DSM-IV-TR. The American Psychiatric Association has
            published a DSM-IV Sourcebook, which documents the
            rationale and empirical support for the text and criteria sets
            presented in DSM-IV, see *DSM-IV Sourcebook: Volume 3*
            (Washington D.C.: American Psychiatric Association, 1997).
            The website where the proposed revisions to DSM-IV-TR can
            be found is <http://www.dsm5.org>. The proposed changes
            to the diagnosis of PTSD are listed there under 'G.05.
            Posttraumatic Stress Disorder'.

p. 56   The DSM-V revision lists four ways by which the individual
            may encounter trauma that may lead to PTSD: (1) experi-
            encing the event(s) him/herself, (2) witnessing, in person,
            the event(s) as they occurred to others, (3) learning that the
            event(s) occurred to a close relative or close friend, if the
            actual or threatened death had been violent or accidental, and
            (4) experiencing repeated or extreme exposure to aversive
            details of the event(s), e.g. police officers who are tasked
            with picking up body parts or repeatedly hearing details of
            child sexual abuse. This may lead to some tightening up of
            the diagnosis. But retaining the reference to *threat* of death or
            serious injury in the introduction to Criterion A could mean
            that a diagnosis of PTSD is still possible for relatively minor
            events.

p. 57   In the proposed revision, *avoidance* is given a separate cat-
            egory (Criterion C in DSM-V) and the symptoms previously
            placed together with *avoidance* are placed in a new category:
            'Negative alterations in cognitions and mood . . . associated
            with the traumatic event(s)' (Criterion D in DSM-V). This
            acknowledges that the lumping together of avoidance with
            emotional numbing and the inability to remember aspects of
            the event was not sensible, as these often occur independently.

p. 59   *Acute stress disorder* is retained in the proposed DSM-V revi-
            sion. Criterion A is the same as for the diagnosis of PTSD.
            For Criterion B, eight or more symptoms in four categories

(Intrusion, Dissociation, Avoidance, Arousal) need to be present that were not present prior to the trauma or have worsened since. Duration of the symptoms is from three days to one month after the event. (These proposals may change as the DSM-V system is firmed up.)

p. 61   Richard Bentall, *Doctoring the Mind: Why psychiatric treatments fail* (London: Penguin, 2010).

p. 61   There are some mental illnesses, the so-called personality disorders, that do not fit the picture I described of a relatively short-lived condition that is amenable to therapy. I have always believed that personality disorders are not illnesses. In fact, a disorder of personality is a misnomer, as personalities are not the sort of things that can be disordered in the medical sense. People may have chaotic and self-destructive personalities, but that is more to do with temperament and upbringing than illness. This does not mean that people diagnosed as having a personality disorder do not have serious problems, or that providing psychotherapy cannot be helpful.

p. 61   Gordon Turnbull, *Trauma: From Lockerbie to 7/7: How trauma affects our minds and how we fight back* (London: Bantam Press, 2011).

Chapter 5: Richard's story

p. 69   Energy psychology is a school of thought that believes that physical and mental health problems are related to disturbances in the body's electrical energy (its energy field). Practitioners work directly on the body in order to restore its natural equilibrium, sometimes using methods derived from eastern medicine (<http://energypsych.com/what-is-energy-psychology/>).For more discussion of the therapeutic value of energy psychology, see Chapter 14.

Chapter 6: Flashbacks

p. 85   A study of involuntary memories in a sample of students showed that they occurred, on average, 3–5 times daily, indicating that experiencing an involuntary memory is quite normal. Between 80 and 90 per cent of the memories were triggered by identifiable stimuli or cues. But only 10 per cent of these stimuli were sensory stimuli, in contrast to traumatic flashbacks, which tend to be triggered by sensory cues. For more on involuntary memories, see John H. Mace (ed.), *Involuntary Memory* (Oxford: Blackwell, 2007).

p. 86   The intrusions into my consciousness that occurred immediately after Smudge's death persisted over the next two or three days, getting less and less frequent and less distressing. Of course this was not a major trauma. But it had similar features, i.e. it was sudden, unexpected and distressing.

p. 87   George completely recovered from his sudden amnesia. He told me that in the four years since 7/7 he had had only one further episode.

p. 88–9   A. Ehlers, A. Hackmann, R. Steil, S. Clohessy, K. Wenninger, and H. Winter, 'The nature of intrusive memories after trauma: The warning signal hypothesis', *Behaviour Research & Therapy,* 40 (2002), 1021–8.

p. 88–9   For a good discussion of imagery and trauma, see Nick Grey, 'Imagery and psychological threat to the self in PTSD', in Luis Stopa (ed.), *Imagery and the Threatened Self* (London: Routledge, 2009).

p. 89   The relationship between intrusive imagery and memory is thoroughly explored in Chris R. Brewin, James D. Gregory, Michelle Lipton and Neil Burgess, 'Intrusive images and memories in psychological disorders', *Psychological Review,* 117 (2010), 210–32.

p. 89   Nick Grey, *Imagery and psychological threat to the self in PTSD*, op. cit.

p. 92   Chris R. Brewin, 'The nature and significance of memory disturbance in Posttraumatic Stress Disorder', *Annual Review of Clinical Psychology,* 7 (2011), 203–27.

p. 93   The example of the woman who imagined her clothes being burned is taken, with permission, from Nick Grey, *Imagery and psychological threat to the self in PTSD*, op. cit.

p. 94   Nick Grey and Emily Holmes, '"Hotspots" in trauma memories in the treatment of post-traumatic stress disorder', *Memory,* 16 (2008), 788–96.

p. 94   A. Hackmann, A. Ehlers, A. Speckens and D. Clark, 'Characteristic and content of intrusive memories in PTSD and their changes with treatment', *Journal of Traumatic Stress,* 17 (2004), 389–402.

Chapter 7: Avoidance

p. 99   In the proposed revision for DSM-V, avoidance has a category of its own, Criterion C:
          Persistent avoidance of stimuli associated with traumatic

event(s)(that began after the traumatic event(s)), as evidenced by efforts to avoid one or more of the following:

1. Avoids internal reminders (thoughts feelings, or physical sensations) that arouse recollections of the traumatic event(s)

2. Avoids external reminders (people, places, conversations, activities, objects, situations) that arouse recollections of the traumatic event(s).

Rightly, in my view, this underlines the importance of avoidance in PTSD as well as placing experiences like emotional numbing, dissociation and the inability to recall aspects of the trauma in more appropriate categories.

p. 104   Chris R. Brewin, *Post-traumatic Stress Disorder: Malady or Myth?* (New Haven and London: Yale University Press, 2003).

p. 105   C. A. Morgan, M. G. Hazlett, S. Wang, E. G. Richardson, P. Schnurr and S. M. Southwick, 'Symptoms of dissociation in humans experiencing acute, uncontrollable stress', *American Journal of Psychiatry*, 158 (2001), 1239–47.

p. 105   The correlation between dissociation and later PTSD does not mean everyone who experiences dissociation will go on to develop PTSD. It simply shows that those who experience dissociation are more likely to develop PTSD than those who do not, i.e. it is a risk factor. This has both clinical and theoretical implications. Clinically, it indicates that it is of value to pay particular attention to the experience of dissociation around the trauma, perhaps using a screening measure to highlight potentially vulnerable people. Theoretically, it suggests that a dissociative state could play a part in the way trauma memories are registered, perhaps in some way hindering emotional processing. For a good discussion, see Chris R. Brewin, *Post-traumatic Stress Disorder: Malady or Myth?* op. cit., Chapter 3, 44–62.

p. 106   The positive benefits of touching have been undervalued in psychological therapies, to the extent that some approaches frown upon any contact, as though the client and therapist need to inhabit separate bubbles. One reason for this is the worry about the potential for abuse. But this is a poor argument since other therapies such as massage and osteopathy involve touching, with measures in place to ensure that it is done appropriately. The somato-sensory psychotherapies (Chapter 14) reveal that attention to the body can be hugely beneficial in the treatment of trauma, see Peter A. Levine,

In an Unspoken Voice: How the Body Releases Trauma and Restores Goodness (Berkeley, California: North Atlantic Books, 2010).

Chapter 8: Guilt, shame and anger

p. 116   The Fawcett Society report, *Rape: The Facts* (The Fawcett Society, London, 2007).

p. 116   Joanna Bourke, *Rape: A History from 1860 to the Present* (London: Virago Press, 2007).

p. 116   It could be argued that Bourke's subjective definition of rape helps to empower rape victims, by taking on trust what they claim has happened. Apart from the problem that some people, albeit a small minority, make false claims, a definition is not about empowerment but about accuracy. In her book on the history of rape, Bourke stresses that she chose this way of defining sexual violence as a heuristic device suitable for her purpose and not as a normative measure. In the end an objective definition of rape is important in order to collect accurate data about sexual assaults.

p. 117   HM Crown Prosecution Service Inspectorate (HMPCS) and HM Inspectorate of Constabulary (HMIC), *Without consent: A report of the joint review of the investigation and prosecution of rape offences* (London: Central Office of Information, 2007), see <http://www.hmic.gov.uk/media/without-consent-20061231.pdf>.

p. 117   World Health Organisation, *Multi-Country Study on Women's Health and Domestic Violence against Women: Initial results on prevalence, health outcomes and women's responses* (Geneva: WHO, 2005), <http://whqlibdoc.who.int/publications/2005/9241593512_eng.pdf>.

p. 118   The Fawcett Society Report, *Rape: The Facts,* op. cit.

p. 118   See Table 1.1.

p. 118   A. W. Burgess and L. L. Holmstrom, 'Rape Trauma Syndrome', *American Journal of Psychiatry,* 131, (1974) 981–6.

p. 118   B. O. Rothbaum, E. B. Foa, D. S. Riggs, T. Murdock and W. Walsh, 'A prospective examination of PTSD in rape victims', *Journal of Traumatic Stress,* 5 (1992), 455–73.

p. 118   D. G. Kilpatrick, B. E. Saunders, L. J. Veronen, C. L. Best, J. Von, 'Criminal victimization: Lifetime prevalence reporting to police, and psychological impact', *Crime and Delinquency,* 33 (1987), 479–89.

p. 118   J. Petrak, 'The psychological impact of sexual assault', in

J. Petrak and B. Hedge (eds.), *The Trauma of Sexual Assault: Treatment, Prevention and Practice* (Chichester: Wiley, 2002).

p. 122   J. P. Tangney and R. L. Dearing, *Shame & Guilt* (New York: The Guilford Press, 2002). See also Boris Droždek, Silvana Turkovic and John P. Wilson, 'Posttraumatic shame and guilt: culture and the posttraumatic self', in John P. Wilson (ed.), *The Posttraumatic Self: Restoring meaning and wholeness to personality* (London: Routledge, 2006).

p. 124   Incident reported in Peter E. Hodgkinson and Michael Stewart, *Coping with Catastrophe: A Handbook of Post-Disaster Psychological Aftercare* (revised edition, London: Routledge, 1998), 4.

p. 126–7 Susan Brison, *Aftermath: Violence and the Remaking of a Self* (Princeton: Princeton University Press, 2002).
          Ibid. 13.

Chapter 9: Shattered Illusions

p. 135   A. Ehlers, and D. M. Clark, 'A cognitive model of posttraumatic stress disorder', *Behaviour Research & Therapy*, 38 (2000), 319–45.

p. 138   For a general account of cognitive therapy, see Judith S. Beck, *Cognitive Behavior Therapy. Basics and Beyond* (2nd edition, New York: The Guilford Press, 2011). For cognitive therapy in the treatment of PTSD and other psychological problems after trauma, see Nick Grey (ed.), *A Casebook of Cognitive Therapy for Traumatic Stress Reactions* (London: Routledge, 2009).

p. 142   R. Janoff-Bulman and I. H. Friese, 'A theoretical perspective for understanding reactions to victimization', *Journal of Social Issues*, 39 (1983), 1.

Chapter 10: The past and the present

p. 149   <http://www.sleepeval.com/hypnagogic_hallucinations.htm>

p. 149–50 M. R. Lansky and C. R. Bley, *Post-Traumatic Nightmares: Psychodynamic Explorations* (Hillsdale, NJ: Atlantic Press, 1995).

p. 153–4 Robert J. Lifton, *Death in Life: Survivors of Hiroshima*, op. cit.

p. 154   John Marzillier, *The Gossamer Thread: My Life as a Psychotherapist*, op. cit., Chapter 19.

p. 158–9 D. W. Winnicott, 'The Concept of the False Self', in *Home Is*

Where We Start From: Essays by a Psychoanalyst (London: Pelican Books, 1986).

p. 160   Robert Scaer, *The Trauma Spectrum: Hidden Wounds and Human Resiliency* (New York: Norton, 2005).

p. 160   Caroline Garland, *Understanding Trauma: A Psychoanalytical Approach* (2nd edition, London: Karnac, 1998).

Chapter 11: Revisiting

p. 163   Timothy Knatchbull, *From a Clear Blue Sky: Surviving the Mountbatten Bomb* (London: Hutchinson, 2009). It might seem to readers that the Mountbatten family is not a typical or average one. That is true. But it is one strength of this book that the family is described so lovingly, openly and honestly that the *people* – not their ranks or titles – stand out. In the latter part of the book, Tim's own personal journey is described, including what it was like to lose an identical twin brother and how he eventually came to terms with that loss when he revisited Ireland decades later.

p. 164   I discuss the therapies that incorporate revisiting the trauma site in Chapter 13.

p. 166   Timothy Knatchbull, *From a Clear Blue Sky*, op cit., 214.

p. 168   Timothy Knatchbull, *From a Clear Blue Sky*, op. cit., Chapter 26, 353–8.

p. 171   From Mark Henderson's account of his experiences in *The Forgiveness Project;* see <http://www.theforgivenessproject. com>.

p. 171–2 From Kate Horne, 'Face to face with his kidnapper', *Daily Telegraph* (8 Nov., 2010).

p. 172   Mark and his fellow director's film, *My Kidnapper*, was shown in selected cinemas on 11 February 2011, and on *More 4* on 22 February, 2011.

p. 176   <http://www.theforgivenessproject.com>.

Chapter 12: Psychotherapy

p. 179   An account of the range of trauma therapies can be found in Robin Shapiro, *The Trauma Treatment Handbook: Protocols across the Spectrum* (New York and London: Norton, 2010). Primarily written for therapists, it is nevertheless an informative and accessible guide for clients. It includes a useful list of the acronyms that seem to be particularly prevalent in this field.

p. 179 Research has shown that the quality of the therapeutic relationship is one of the strongest predictors of good outcome, see M. J. Lambert and D. E. Barley, *Psychotherapy*, 38 (2001), 357–61.

p. 180 John Marzillier, *The Gossamer Thread: My Life as a Psychotherapist*, op. cit. The gossamer thread of the title refers to the therapeutic relationship, something that runs through all therapies.

p. 180 'Non-specific factors' are only non-specific in the sense that they are contrasted with specific techniques. In another sense, they are quite specific features of therapy, e.g. working in a safe and neutral environment, being respectful and setting out a therapeutic contract.

p. 180–1 J. D. Frank and Julia Frank, *Persuasion and Healing: A Comparative Study of Psychotherapy* (*3rd edition*, Baltimore, Maryland: The Johns Hopkins University Press, 1993).

p. 181 The non-specific effect is like the placebo effect in pharmacology, where psychological variables account for improvement rather than the ingredients of the medication. In psychotherapy, the therapist's belief in the effectiveness of the techniques is vital for the effect to work, even if that belief is misplaced. This is why new therapies, enthusiastically heralded by their founders, tend to get greater success rates than older ones, and why that success rate declines over time as others in the field come to question the particular approach.

p. 182 Judith Herman, *Trauma and Recovery: The Aftermath of Violence from Domestic Abuse to Political Terror* (new edition, London, Rivers Oram Press: 1994).

p. 188 In opting for a particular therapy, it might be thought that the therapist, as the expert, should decide what the best treatment is. But because different therapies have different aims, the client needs to know exactly what is being offered, what the goal of the therapy is and what alternatives there are, in order to make an informed choice. I discuss this and other practical considerations on entering therapy in Appendix A.

p. 192 For a detailed account of the behavioural approach in the treatment of a woman with a phobia of dogs, see my memoir, John Marzillier, *The Gossamer Thread: My Life as a Psychotherapist*, op. cit., Chapter 3.

Chapter 13: Reliving

p. 195 Judith S. Beck, *Cognitive Behavior Therapy: Basics and Beyond* (2nd edition, New York: The Guilford Press, 2011).

p. 195–6   The National Institute for Health and Clinical Excellence
           (NICE) identifies cognitive therapy as the treatment of choice
           for many mental health problems. See <http://www.nice.org.
           uk/usingguidance/commissioningguides/cognitivebehav-
           iouraltherapyservice/summarycbtinterventions.jsp>.   This
           includes PTSD, for which the guidelines state that 'Trauma-
           focused CBT should be offered to people who present with
           PTSD within three months of a traumatic event.' But NICE
           guidelines are based upon the medical model, where all
           problems are seen as illnesses and experiences as symptoms.
           This is a simplistic view of psychology and mental health.
           Because cognitive therapy lends itself more readily to the
           medical model than other psychotherapies, it is easier to
           attract research funding and the research findings conform to
           what NICE expects of outcome research (evaluating specific
           techniques). This gives the impression that CBT methods are
           of greater effectiveness than any others simply because there
           is a larger body of studies to draw on. Assessing the value
           of the various psychotherapies is more complicated than
           simply focusing on symptoms, especially if the therapeutic
           relationship is given the prominence it deserves. For a dis-
           cussion, see John Marzillier, 'The Myth of Evidence-Based
           Psychotherapy', *The Psychologist*, 17 (2004), 392–5

p. 196   A good example of a self-help guide is Claudia Herbert and
           Ann Wetmore, *Overcoming Traumatic Stress: A self-help
           guide using Cognitive Behavioral Techniques* (London:
           Robinson, 2008).

p. 196   The computer programme *FearFighter* has been specifically
           designed to help sufferers overcome panic and phobic anx-
           iety, see <http://www.fearfighter.comv. For a general review,
           see P. Cuijpers et al, 'Computer-aided psychotherapy for anx-
           iety disorders: A meta-analytic review', *Cognitive Behaviour
           Therapy* 38 (2009), 66–82.

p. 196   Edna B. Foa, Terence M. Keane, Matthew J. Friedman and
           Judith A. Cohen (eds.), *Effective Treatments for PTSD* (New
           York: The Guilford Press, 2009). An interview with Edna Foa
           can be found at <http://www.psychotherapy.net/interview/
           edna-foa-exposure-therapy>.

p. 196   M. B. Powers, J. M. Halpern, M. P. Ferenschak, S. J. Gillihan,
           E. B. Foa, 'A meta-analytic review of prolonged exposure',
           Clinical Psychology Review, 30 (2010), 635–41.

p. 198   Helen Kennerley, *Overcoming Anxiety: A self-help guide
           using Cognitive Behavioral Techniques* (London: Robinson,
           2009).

p. 199 A. Ehlers and D. M. Clark, 'A cognitive model of post-traumatic stress disorder', *Behaviour Research & Therapy*, 38 (2000), 319–45.

p. 203–4 Robert Scaer, *The Trauma Spectrum: Hidden Wounds and Human Resiliency*, op. cit.

p. 204 See Christine A. Courtois and Julian D. Ford (eds.), *Treating Complex Traumatic Stress Disorders: An Evidence-Based Guide* (New York: The Guilford Press, 2009).

p. 205 Nick Grey (ed.), *A Casebook of Cognitive Therapy for Traumatic Stress Reactions*, op. cit.

p. 206 Rachel Handley, Paul Salkovskis, Ann Hackmann and Anke Ehlers, 'Travel, trauma and phobia: treating the survivors of transport-related problems', in Nick Grey (Ed.), *A Casebook of Cognitive Therapy for Traumatic Stress Reactions*, op cit., 31–48.

Chapter 14: The body remembers

p. 211–12 From Peter A. Levine, *In an Unspoken Voice: How the Body Releases Trauma and Restores Goodness*, op. cit., 24.

p. 212 See Pat Ogden, Kekuni Minton and Clare Pain, *Trauma and the Body: A Sensorimotor Approach to Psychotherapy* (New York: Norton, 2006) and Peter A. Levine, *In an Unspoken Voice: How the Body Releases Trauma and Restores Goodness*, op. cit.

p. 212 Gary Craig, *The EFT Manual* (2nd edition, Santa Rosa, CA: Energy Psychology Press, 2011). See also <http://www.energypsychologypress.com/> and <http://www.emofree.com/>.

p. 213 From Francine Shapiro and Margot Silk Forrest, *EMDR: The Breakthrough Therapy for Overcoming Anxiety, Stress, and Trauma* (updated edition, New York: Basic Books, 2004), 9.

p. 214 P. R. Davidson and K. C. Parker, 'Eye movement desensitization and reprocessing (EMDR): a meta-analysis', *Journal of Consulting and Clinical Psychology*, 69 (2001), 305–16.

p. 214–15 Laurel Parnell, *Transforming Trauma: EMDR* (New York: Norton, 1997).

p. 216 E. B. Foa, E. A. Hembree, S. P. Cahill, S. A. M. Rauch, D. S. Riggs, N. C. Feeny and E. Yadin, 'Randomized trial of prolonged exposure', *Journal of Consulting and Clinical Psychology*, 73 (2005), 953–64.

p. 216 Chris R. Brewin, *Post-traumatic Stress Disorder: Malady or Myth?*, op. cit., 202–3.

p. 216–17 Extract taken from Peter A. Levine, *In an Unspoken Voice:*

How the Body Releases Trauma and Restores Goodness (Berkeley, CA: North Atlantic Books, copyright 2010 by Peter A. Levine), 169–170. Reprinted by permission of the publisher.

p. 218   Peter A. Levine, *Walking the Tiger: Healing Trauma.* op. cit., and *In an Unspoken Voice: How the Body Releases Trauma and Restores Goodness*, op. cit.

p. 218   Pat Ogden, Kekuni Minton and Clare Pain, *Trauma and the Body: A Sensorimotor Approach*, op. cit. See also <www.sensorimotorpsychotherapy.org/index.html>.

p. 219   Peter A. Levine, *Resolving Trauma in Psychotherapy: A Somatic Approach*, DVD: <http:// www.psychotherapy.net/video/trauma-therapy-PTSD>.

p. 221   Extract taken from Robin Shapiro, *The Trauma Treatment Handbook: Protocols across the Spectrum* (New York and London: Norton, 2010), 101. Reprinted by permission of the publisher.

p. 224   Roger Callahan,with Richard Trubo, *The Healer Within: Using Thought Field Therapy to Instantly Conquer Your Fears, Anxieties, and Emotional* Distress, (New York: McGraw-Hill/Contemporary Books, 2001). See also <http://www.rogercallahan.com/>.

p. 224   Tapas Fleming, *How to Do TAT for a Stressful Event You Experienced* (<www.tatlife.com>, 2006).

p. 224–5   See <http://nccam.nih.gov/research/results/spotlight/092107.htm>.

p. 225   David Feinstein, 'Energy psychology: a review of the preliminary evidence', *Psychotherapy: Theory, Research, Practice, Training*, 45 (2008), 199–213.

p. 225   See <http://energypsych.com/what-is-energy-psychology/>.

p. 226   See <http://www.appliedkinesiology.com/>.

p. 226   See <http://www.philmollon.co.uk>.

p. 226   Phil Mollon, *Psychoanalytic Energy Psychology*, London: Karnac, 2008.

Chapter 15: Resilience

p. 234   Boris Cyrulnik, *Resilience: How your inner strength can set you free from the past* (London: Penguin, 2009).

p. 242   There is a full transcript of our interview on Tom Nabarro's website <www.tomnabarro.com>.

p. 243   Gill Hicks, *One Unknown:* op. cit.

Chapter 16: Post-traumatic growth

p. 245   Matthew Engel's 2005 *Guardian* article can be found at <http://www.guardian.co.uk/lifeandstyle/2005/dec/03/familyandrelationships.health?INTCMP=SRCH>.

p. 245   Matthew Engel published an update on the Laurie Engel fund in 'Making Sense of Laurie's life', the *Guardian*, (5 December 2009), 30–31.

p. 245   For a video of the Birmingham teenage cancer unit, see <http://www.ustream.tv/recorded/4813822>.

p. 246   Raj Babbra's film, *Life without Benedetta*, can be found at <http://www.lifewithloss.org/lwb/>.

p. 247   Rumi, *Selected Poems*, translated by Coleman Barks, with John Moyne, A. J. Arberry and Reynold Nicholson (London: Penguin, 2004).

p. 247   Viktor E. Frankl, *Man's Search for Meaning: The Classic Tribute to Hope from the Holocaust* (London: Ebury Publishing, 2004).

p. 250   Sigmund Freud, 'Mourning and Melancholia', in *The Standard Edition of the Complete Psychological Works Of Sigmund Freud*, volume xiv (1914–1916), 'On the History of the Psycho-Analytic Movement, Papers on Metapsychology, and Other Works' (London: Vintage, 2001).

p. 250   <http://www.miriam-hyman.com/index.html>.

p. 250   <http://www.miriam-hyman.com/mhcecc-partnership.html>.

p. 252   <http://www.stephenlawrence.org.uk/the-trust/>.

p. 252   Sara Payne and Anna Gekoski, *Sara Payne: A Mother's Story* (London: Hodder & Stoughton, 2004).

p. 252   David Aberbach, *Surviving Trauma: Loss, Literature and Psychoanalysis* (New Haven: Yale University Press, 1989).

p. 255   John P. Wilson (ed.), *The Posttraumatic Self: Restoring Meaning and Wholeness to Personality* (London: Routledge, 2006).

p. 256   The quote is from John P. Wilson (ed.), *The Posttraumatic Self: Restoring Meaning and Wholeness to Personality,* op. cit., 405.

p. 256   Judith Herman, *Trauma and Recovery: The Aftermath of Violence – from Domestic Abuse to Political Terror*, op. cit.

Chapter 17: In harm's way

p. 263   Janine di Giovanni, *Ghosts by Daylight: A Memoir of War and Love* (London: Bloomsbury, 2011).

p. 263   The DART Center for Journalism <http://dartcenter.org/>.

p. 263   <http://www.cpj.org/killed/2010/>.

p. 263   Jennifer A. Brown and Elizabeth A. Campbell, *Stress and Policing: Sources and Strategies* (Oxford: Wiley-Blackwell, 1993).

p. 264–5   Ben Shephard, *A War of Nerves: Soldiers and Psychiatrists, 1914–1994*, op. cit.

p. 265   Reprinted with permission, from Anthony Feinstein, *Journalists Under Fire: The Psychological Hazards of Covering War* (Baltimore: Johns Hopkins University Press, 2003, 2006), 47.

p. 266   Anthony Feinstein, ibid., 46–71.

p. 266   For a discussion of the underlying neurology, particularly the role of neurotransmitters, see Anthony Feinstein, *Journalists Under Fire: The Psychological Hazards of Covering War*, op. cit., 51–3.

p. 266–7   Reprinted with permission from Captain Kevin Ivison, GM, *Red One: A Bomb Disposal Expert on the Front Line* (London: Weidenfeld & Nicholson, 2010), 25.

p. 268   Martin Bell, *In Harm's Way: Reflections of a War-Zone Thug* (London: Penguin Books, 1996).

p. 269   Reprinted with permission from Captain Kevin Ivison, GM, *Red One: A Bomb Disposal Expert on the Front Line*, op. cit.

p. 273   From Anthony Feinstein, *Journalists Under Fire: The Psychological Hazards of Covering War*, op. cit. Other studies of journalists have found lower rates of PTSD, ranging from 6 per cent to 13 per cent. See the Dart Center for Journalists website <http://dartcenter.org/content/covering-trauma-impact-on-journalists>.

p. 273   Rates of PTSD in the military can be found at <http://www.armytimes.com/news/2009/01/military_veterans>.

p. 273   A study of those who worked at Ground Zero in the immediate aftermath of 9/11 found probable PTSD rates of 6.2 per cent for police officers, 12.2 per cent for firefighters, and 11.6 per cent for emergency workers, see M. A. Perrin, L. DiGrande, K. Wheeler, L. Thorpe, M. Farfel, R. Brackbill, 'Differences in PTSD prevalence and associated risk factors among World Trade Center disaster rescue and recovery workers', *American Journal of Psychiatry*, 164 (2007), 1385–94.

p. 273–4   The King's Centre for Military Health Research, *What has been achieved by fifteen years of research into the health of the UK Armed Forces?* (London: The King's Centre, 2010).

p. 274   The King's Centre for Military Health Research, ibid.

p. 274   Anthony Feinstein, *Journalists Under Fire: The Psychological Hazards of Covering War*, op. cit.

Chapter 18: Trauma revisited

p. 280   The name Danielle is a pseudonym.

p. 282   David Matsumoto (ed.), *The Cambridge Dictionary of Psychology*, op. cit.

p. 282   Adapted from the slogan of the Clinton Presidential election campaign, 'It's the economy, stupid!'.

p. 284   Rachel North, *Out of the Tunnel: Before and after 7/7: one woman's extraordinary story*, op. cit.

p. 286   Ronnie Janoff-Bulman, *Shattered Assumptions: Towards a New Psychology of Trauma*, op. cit.

p. 291   Peter A. Levine, *In an Unspoken Voice. How the Body Releases Trauma and Restores Goodness*, op. cit.

p. 292   S. Wessely and M. Deahl, 'Psychological debriefing is a waste of time', *British JournaL of Psychiatry,* 183 (2003), 12–14.

Index